Normativity

Normativity

Judith Jarvis Thomson

Open Court
Chicago and La Salle, Illinois

To order books from Open Court, call toll-free 1-800-815-2280 or visit www.opencourtbooks.com.

Open Court Publishing Company is a division of Carus Publishing Company.

Copyright ©2008 by Carus Publishing Company

First printing 2008

Library of Congress Cataloging-in-Publication Data

Thomson, Judith Jarvis.
    Normativity / Judith Jarvis Thomson.
        p. cm. — (The Paul Carus lecture series ; 22)
    Includes bibliographical references and index.
        Summary: "A work in metaethics that focuses on the two types of normative judgments, evaluative judgments and directive judgments; how the two interconnect; and what makes them true when they are true" — Provided by publisher.
    ISBN 978-0-8126-9658-5 (trade paper : alk. paper) 1. Normativity (Ethics) I. Title.
    BJ1458.3.T46 2008
    170'.42—dc22

                                               2008027129

For Peter, Nedra, Pam, and Alex

Contents

Preface

The following material is an expanded version of the Carus Lectures that I gave in April, 2003. I thank the American Philosophical Association's Board of Officers for inviting me to give those lectures that year.

I had originally intended that this material should form the first of two connected volumes on normativity, this one on metaethics, the second on moral theory. In light of the amount of time it took me to think through what seemed to me to be the most important issues in metaethics, I decided not to wait until the second volume is completed, and instead to submit what I have in hand to readers for consideration now.

Earlier versions of various parts of the material were presented at several seminars at the Massachusetts Institute of Technology, and at a seminar I gave at the University of California at Los Angeles in the winter of 2003. Versions of parts were also presented as the Shearman Lectures (2004) at University College, London, as the Howison Lecture (2005) at the University of California at Berkeley, and as a keynote address at the Second Annual Metaethics Workshop at Madison, Wisconsin (2005). I am very grateful for the participants' comments and criticism on all of those occasions.

I thank Richard Kraut for written comments on an early draft of parts of the material. I also thank Mahrad Almotahari, Selim Berker, Tom Dougherty, Adam Hosein, and Seth Yalcin for helpful discussion, and for suggestions for revision of parts of more recent drafts.

I

Goodness

1.

Our thinking is rich in what is often called normativity. We think that
A ought to be kind to his little brother, that B ought to move his
rook, and that C ought to get a hair cut. These are normative judgments. Intuitively, they differ starkly from such nonnormative judgments as that A kicked his little brother, that B is playing chess, and
that C has brown hair.

Moreover, we think that D is a good person, E is a good tennis
player, and F is a good toaster. These too are normative judgments.
Intuitively, they differ starkly from such nonnormative judgments as
that D is a human being, E is a tennis player, and F is a toaster.

Our aim will be to try to come to an understanding of what
makes our normative judgments true when they are.

As is plain, we make a great variety of normative judgments. Our
judgment that A ought to be kind to his little brother is presumably
a moral judgment; our judgments that B ought to move his rook and
that C ought to get a hair cut are presumably not moral judgments.
Our judgment that D is a good person is presumably a moral judgment; our judgments that E is a good tennis player and that F is a
good toaster are presumably not moral judgments. We can think of
normativity as the subject matter of ethics, but if we do, we need to
remember that moral philosophy is not the whole of ethics, but only
part of it. So the enterprise we will be engaged in is not restricted to
moral philosophy.

I suggest that we should focus on a different difference among
our normative judgments. I will call our judgments that A ought to
be kind to his little brother, that B ought to move his rook, and that

C ought to get a hair cut, *directives.* Intuitively, they differ from our judgments that D is a good person, that E is a good tennis player, and that F is a good toaster, which I will call *evaluatives.*[1]

We will want to attend to both kinds of normative judgment. I begin with the evaluatives.

2.

Which judgments are the evaluatives? I gave three examples; what have they got in common? One thing we can say straightway is that they are judgments to the effect that a certain thing is good in a certain respect. Let us have a closer look at such judgments.

Twentieth-century ethics opened with the appearance in 1903 of G. E. Moore's *Principia Ethica*, in which Moore made some claims that we do well to begin with.

Moore said at the outset of *Principia Ethica*:

> Ethics is undoubtedly concerned with the question what good conduct is; but, being concerned with this, it obviously does not start at the beginning, unless it is prepared to tell us what is good as well as what is conduct. For 'good conduct' is a complex notion: all conduct is not good; for some is certainly bad and some may be indifferent. And on the other hand, other things, beside conduct, may be good; and if they are so, then, 'good' denotes some property, that is common to them and conduct; and if we examine good conduct alone of all good things, then we shall be in danger of mistaking for this property, some property which is not shared by those other things: and thus we shall have made a mistake about Ethics even in this limited sense; for we shall not know what good conduct really is.[2]

A number of things seem to be suggested in this passage. One is perfectly clear: Moore claims that there is such a property as being good, or, as I will sometimes put it, goodness—it is the property that all good things have in common. I will call that the Goodness Thesis.

---

[1] That there is a difference between what I call directives and evaluatives is familiar enough. I borrow the names from David Wiggins, "Truth, Invention, and the Meaning of Life," *Needs, Values, Truth* (Oxford: Oxford University Press, 1998), 95, with an emendation: I substitute "evaluatives" for his "evaluations".

[2] G. E. Moore, *Principia Ethica*, rev. ed., ed. Thomas Baldwin (Cambridge: Cambridge University Press, 1993), 54.

But more seems to be suggested. One hypothesis is suggested by his example of 'good conduct'. Moore seems to be suggesting that for a thing to be an instance of good conduct is for it to have the following two properties: being good and being an instance of conduct. So one might take him to be suggesting, similarly, that for a thing to be a good person is for it to possess the properties being good and being a person, for a thing to be a good tennis player is for it to possess the properties being good and being a tennis player, and for a thing to be a good toaster is for it to possess the properties being good and being a toaster. More generally, for a thing to be good in a respect is for it to possess the properties being good and being of the relevant kind. I will call this thesis the Rationale.

My reason for giving the second thesis that name lies in its relation to the Goodness Thesis. Suppose we accept the Rationale. There *are* things that are good people, good tennis players, and good toasters. From the Rationale, it follows that there *are* things that possess the property goodness. So there is such a property—and the Goodness Thesis is true.

Did Moore really accept the thesis I am calling the Rationale? I suspect that he did. But whether or not he did, it won't do.

Many philosophers have drawn attention in recent years to the fact that it won't do.[3] Peter Geach said that the adjective "good" is not a *predicative* adjective: it is an *attributive* adjective. We can express what he had in mind as follows.

Let K_1 and K_2 be any pair of kinds of things, and let "adj" be any adjective. "Adj" is a predicative adjective just in case the conjunction of the propositions

---

[3] See Peter Geach, "Good and Evil," *Analysis* 17 (1956); Paul Ziff, *Semantic Analysis* (Ithaca: Cornell University Press, 1960); and G. H. von Wright, *The Varieties of Goodness* (London: Routledge & Kegan Paul, 1963). I take it that Philippa Foot's "Utilitarianism and the Virtues," *Mind* 94 (1985), can be interpreted as expressing the same objection. I have discussed these matters in a number of places in recent years, for example, in "The Right and the Good," *Journal of Philosophy* 94 (1997), and in "The Legacy of Principia," Spindell Conference 2002, *Southern Journal of Philosophy,* Supplement (2003).

J. L. Austin's discussion of the adjective "real" is worth drawing attention to in this connection. He said that "real" is "substantive-hungry": "whereas we can *just* say of something 'This is pink,' we can't *just* say of something 'This is real'. . . . An object looking rather like a duck may be a real decoy duck (not just a toy) but not a real duck." And he drew attention to the fact that "real" is in this respect like "good". See his *Sense and Sensibilia* (Oxford: Oxford University Press, 1962), 69–70.

A is an adj K_1

and

A is a K_2

entails the proposition

A is an adj K_2.

"Red", he said, is a predicative adjective, since the conjunction of

A is a red car

and

A is a Mercedes

entails

A is a red Mercedes.[4]

By contrast, "big" is an attributive adjective, since the conjunction of

(1) A is a big mouse

and

(2) A is an animal

does not entail

(3) A is a big animal.

"Good" is also an attributive adjective, since the conjunction of

(4) A is a good tennis player

---

[4] For more on "red" and other issues that I discuss in this chapter, see Addendum 1 on "Red" and "Good".

and

(5) A is a chess player

does not entail

(6) A is a good chess player.

Other attributive adjectives are "tall", "slow", and "heavy".

A consequence of the fact that "big" is an attributive adjective is this: we cannot say that for a thing to be a big K—mouse, animal, teapot, chair—is for it to have the following two properties: being big and being a K. For suppose that being a big K *was* having the following two properties: being big and being a K. Then (1) would be equivalent to

(1*) A is big and A is a mouse,

and (3) would be equivalent to

(3*) A is big and A is an animal.

It is plain, however, that the conjunction of (1*) and (2) entails (3*). So if it were the case that being a big K was being big and being a K, then the conjunction of (1) and (2) would entail (3). Which it doesn't.

Similarly for "good". We cannot say that for a thing to be a good K—tennis player, chess player, toaster—is for it to have the following two properties: being good and being a K. For suppose that being a good K *was* having the following two properties: being good and being a K. Then (4) would be equivalent to

(4*) A is good and A is a tennis player,

and (6) would be equivalent to

(6*) A is good and A is a chess player.

It is plain, however, that the conjunction of (4*) and (5) entails (6*). So if it were the case that being a good K was being good and being a K, then the conjunction of (4) and (5) would entail (6). Which it doesn't.

According to the Rationale, for a thing to be good in a respect is for it to possess the properties being good and being of the relevant kind. That is false, since being a good K isn't being good and being a K.

We should notice a second reason for rejecting the Rationale, which I'll express as follows: there isn't always such a thing as 'the relevant kind'. What I have in mind is this. I take it that a thing can be a big K for very many K—mouse, animal, teapot, chair, and so on. Similarly, a thing can be a good K for very many K—tennis player, chess player, toaster, and so on. But a thing can be good in a respect without there being any kind K such that for a thing to be good in that respect is for it to be a good K. As we may put it: "good" has a much broader range of occurrences than "big" does. For we may say, not only for very many K that a thing is a good K, we may also say, for example:

> A is good at doing crossword puzzles
> A is good for England
> A is good for use in making cheesecake
> A is good to use in teaching elementary logic
> A is good to look at
> A is good in *Hamlet*
> A is good as Ophelia in *Hamlet*
> A is good with children.[5]

To say any of these things is to say that A is good in a respect; but there are no kinds K such that to say these things is to say, for some K, that A is a good K.

So we must plainly reject the Rationale.

---

[5] Paul Ziff drew attention to still other uses of "good", as in saying "Good morning!" (I might say this to you even though I am well aware that it's a terrible morning, rainy and windy.) Again, consider the butler who replies "Very good, Sir," when his master has asked that dinner be served at eight. (The butler is not telling his master that serving dinner at eight is a very good idea.) See Ziff, *Semantic Analysis*, 207–10. I throughout ignore these nonsentential uses of "good", as they might be called.

3.

Perhaps we should have focused on something different in that passage I quoted from Moore, namely:

> . . . other things, beside conduct, may be good; and if they are so, then, 'good' denotes some property, that is common to them and conduct. . . .

We very often say sentences such as "A is a good tennis player," "A is a good toaster," and "A is good at doing crossword puzzles." But we also very often say the sentence "A is good." Perhaps what Moore had in mind was really this: when we say "A is good," we are ascribing to A the property goodness—and the property goodness just is the property had in common by all those things such that if you said the sentence "That is good" about them, you would be speaking truly. I will call this thesis the Alternate Rationale.

My reason for giving this idea that name lies in its supplying an alternate rationale for the Goodness Thesis. For suppose we accept the Alternate Rationale. There *are* things such that you would be speaking truly if you said "That is good" about them. From the Alternate Rationale, it follows that there *are* things that possess the property goodness. So there is such a property—and the Goodness Thesis is true.

Did Moore really accept the thesis I am calling the Alternate Rationale? I suspect that he did. But whether or not he did, it won't do.

It pays to notice first that anyone who opts for the Alternate Rationale has a job ahead of him. Suppose we were to grant that when we say "That is good" about a thing we are ascribing the property goodness to it. Now when we say "That is a good toaster" of a thing, we are presumably ascribing the property being a good toaster to it. But as we just saw, the property being a good toaster is not the conjunction of the two properties being good and being a toaster. So how does what we ascribe when we say "That is a good toaster" connect with what we ascribe when we say "That is good"? There ought to be *some* answer to that question. After all, it is one and the same word "good" that appears in both sentences. But it is not in the least clear how you are to answer it if you accept the Alternate Rationale while rejecting the Rationale.

Let us bypass that difficulty. *Is* it true that when we say "That is good" about a thing we are ascribing the property goodness to it?

And that the property goodness just is the property had in common by all those things such that if you said the sentence "That is good" about them, you would be speaking truly?

We very often say such sentences as "A is a big mouse," "A is a big animal," and "A is a big teapot." But we also very often say the sentence "A is big." Should we similarly say that when we say "A is big," we are ascribing to A the property bigness—and the property bigness just is the property had in common by all those things such that if you said the sentence "That is big" about them, you would be speaking truly?

It's a terrible idea! Suppose that on Wednesday, I show Smith my new pets: six mice. Five are small mice, one is a big mouse. "Remarkable," Smith says about my sixth, "That's big!" Does he speak truly? Suppose he does. Then the idea we are looking at yields that my sixth has the property bigness. On Thursday, Jones tells me about his trip to the Museum of Natural History, which currently has a display of animals that describes the sources of the immense variety in animal size. "That," he says, by way of example, pointing to my sixth, "is small." Does he speak truly? Suppose he does. If there is a property bigness, then there surely also is a property smallness, so the analogue of the idea we are looking at yields that my sixth has the property smallness. Did my sixth have bigness on Wednesday and smallness on Thursday? Well, it didn't shrink over night. So did it, throughout both days, have both bigness and smallness? If so, what on earth can those properties *be*?

We could, of course, insist that when Smith said on Wednesday "That's big," he didn't speak truly, that one doesn't speak truly if one says "That's big" of any mouse. That one doesn't speak truly when one says "That's big" unless the thing is as big as an elephant. Or better, as big as the Empire State Building. Or better, as big as our galaxy—though even that is dubious, for our galaxy is a small galaxy. To say this is to float free of reality. When people say, in amazement, "That's big" of a certain mouse or cat or tree or house, they may very well be speaking truly.

Similarly for goodness. When we were choosing tennis players for our tennis team, Smith said of Alfred "Choose him. He's good." When we were choosing chess players for our chess team, Jones said of Alfred "Don't choose him. He's bad." Did Smith and Jones both speak truly? If so, then Alfred had both the property goodness and the property badness; and if so, what on earth can those properties *be*? Or should we insist that Smith didn't speak truly? Even if Alfred really is a good tennis player? What's missing in Alfred that he would have to have or be if Smith was to have been speaking truly of him when he said "He's good"?

It's all a mistake. When people say "That is big" of a thing, they are not ascribing a property bigness to it: they are ascribing different properties to the things. One person may be ascribing the property 'being a big mouse'. Another may be ascribing the property 'being a big animal'. Yet another may be ascribing the property 'being a big teapot'. More generally, a person who says "That is big" is, for some kind K, ascribing the property 'being a big K'. The context in which a person says "That is big" tells us which kind K it is such that he is saying that the thing is a big K, for it tells us which kind is under discussion—thus perhaps mice, or animals, or teapots. Where a speaker can assume that his hearers know which kind is under discussion, he need not say "That is a big K"; he can say, more briefly, "That is big." But if we don't know which kind is under discussion when we overhear a person say "That is big," then we don't know what property the speaker is ascribing to the thing.

We should be clear that there is a difference between its being the case (i) that a person is, for some kind K, ascribing to a thing the property 'being a big K,' and its being the case (ii) that a person is ascribing to the thing the property 'being a big K for some kind K'. There is such a property as 'being a big K for some kind K', but it is a boring property, a property that just about every physical object has. (Perhaps it is lacked only by the smallest of the small strings that physicists tell us everything is composed of.) So I doubt that anybody ever ascribes that property to a thing in saying "That is big". What a person ascribes to a thing in saying that sentence is instead, for some K, the property of being a big K.

Similarly for people who say "That is good" of a thing. They are not ascribing a property goodness to it: they are ascribing different properties to the things. One person may be ascribing the property 'being a good tennis player'. Another may be ascribing the property 'being a good chess player'. Yet another may be ascribing the property 'being good at doing crossword puzzles'. More generally, a person who says "That is good" is, for some respect R, ascribing the property 'being good in respect R'. The context in which a person says "That is good" tells us which respect R it is such that he is saying that the thing is good in respect R, for it tells us which respect is relevant—thus perhaps tennis playing, chess playing, or doing crossword puzzles. Where a speaker can assume that his hearers know which respect is relevant, he need not say "That is good in respect R"; he can say, more briefly, "That is good." But if we don't know which respect is relevant when we overhear a person say "That is good," then we don't know what property the speaker is ascribing to the thing.

And again, we should be clear that there is a difference between its being the case (i) that a person is, for some respect R, ascribing to a thing the property 'being good in respect R', and its being the case (ii) that a person is ascribing to the thing the property 'being good in respect R for some respect R'. There is such a property as 'being good in respect R for some respect R', but it is a boring property, a property that just about everything has. Indeed, I should think that everything has it. If you think that you have fastened on a thing that is not good in any respect at all, then you should notice that it is good in at least this respect: it is good for use in a discussion of the question whether everything is good in at least some respect. So I doubt that anybody ever ascribes that property to a thing in saying "That is good." What a person ascribes to a thing in saying that sentence is instead, for some respect R, the property of being good in respect R.

I asked earlier: how does what we ascribe when we say "That is a good toaster" connect with what we ascribe when we say "That is good"? And I said that there ought to be *some* answer to that question—after all, it is one and the same word "good" that appears in both sentences. The answer to it is easy. When Smith says "That is good," the property he is ascribing to the thing may just *be* the property being a good toaster. Though of course it may instead be the property being good for use in burning secret messages from one's spies.

4.

Let us return to Moore. The Goodness Thesis says: there is such a property as being good, or, alternatively, goodness—it is the property that all good things have in common. I said that I suspect that he believed both the Rationale and the Alternate Rationale, and I suspect that that is why he believed the Goodness Thesis. Thus he simply overlooked the fact that "good" is like "big" in being an attributive adjective.

In that "good" is like "big" in being an attributive adjective, there is no such property as goodness just as there is no such property as bigness.

Moore was not the first philosopher to overlook the fact that "good" is an attributive adjective, but in light of the impact *Principia Ethica* had on twentieth-century moral philosophy, he made a major contribution to the two bad effects of that omission. Let us have a look at them.

First, the omission had a bad effect on twentieth-century metaethics. Suppose we think that there is such a property as goodness, and that it is the property that people ascribe to the things they refer to when they say "That is good," thus the property that all and only good things have in common. Then the property goodness that we are committed to is epistemologically dark. It is fairly easy to find out whether a thing is a good tennis player or a good ham sandwich; how is one to find out whether the thing is (simply) a good thing? The other side of this coin is that the property goodness that we are committed to is metaphysically dark. For what could it consist in? It is clear what it is for a thing to be a good tennis player or a good ham sandwich; what could it be thought to come to for a thing to be (simply) a good thing?

Moore himself concluded that goodness is a nonnatural property. And what is that? Moore's characterization of the notion 'nonnatural property' in *Principia* was grossly unsatisfactory, as he himself later recognized.[6]

Others resisted. They concluded (rightly) that there is no such thing as the property goodness, which a person who says "A is good" is ascribing to A. But they thought that the only available alternative was to say that a person who says "A is good" ascribes no

---

[6] Moore wrote: "Can we imagine 'good' as existing *by itself* in time, and not merely as a property of some natural object? For myself, I cannot so imagine it, whereas with the greater number of properties of objects—those which I call the natural properties—their existence does seem to me to be independent of the existence of those objects. They are, in fact, rather parts of which the object is made up than mere predicates which attach to it. If they were all taken away, no object would be left, not even a bare substance: for they are in themselves substantial and give to the object all the substance that it has. But this is not so with good" (*Principia*, 93).

I think it possible that what lay behind, and issued in, these dark words was Moore's having intuitively felt that "good" is an attributive adjective.

property at all to A. Then what does the speaker do? They said he merely displays a favorable attitude toward A. Those who chose this option came to be called Emotivists—in later years, they came to be called Expressivists—and twentieth-century metaethics was dominated by debate over whether they were right.

What was overlooked was the markedly better third alternative, namely that "good" is an attributive adjective. Opting for this alternative allows us to avoid the epistemological and metaphysical darkness consequent on taking it that there is such a thing as the property goodness which a person who says "A is good" is ascribing to A. (Compare the epistemological and metaphysical darkness that would be consequent on taking it that there is such a thing as the property bigness which a person who says "A is big" is ascribing to A. It is fairly easy to find out whether a thing is a big house or a big football player; how is one to find out whether the thing is [simply] a big thing? It is clear what it is for a thing to be a big house or a big football player; what could it be thought to come to for a thing to be [simply] a big thing?) And it also allows us to have that when a person says of a thing "That's good," he does ascribe a property to the thing, and that the assertion he makes about the thing is true or false, and that there is room for asking or wondering which it is, and for arguing with those who disagree.

I said that overlooking the fact that "good" is an attributive adjective had two bad effects. I have mentioned one, namely its effect on metaethics. The other was its effect on moral theory.

Consequentialism is the thesis that what we ought to do is (very roughly) to maximize the amount of goodness in the world. So if of all the courses of action open to you at a time you would produce most good by doing such and such, then, according to the Consequentialist, you ought to do the such and such. What is goodness? Well, following Moore, it is the property which a person who says "A is good" is ascribing to A, thus the property that all and only good things have in common. Then it is intuitively plausible to think that those who resist Consequentialism have the burden of proof—they are under pressure to explain how it could be perfectly all right for a person to choose to produce less of what has that property than he could produce. Twentieth-century moral theory was dominated by debate about efforts to carry that burden—a debate that issued from a mistake.

5.

How could Moore have overlooked the fact that "good" is an attributive adjective? Wasn't he, after all, the patron saint of what later came to be called Ordinary Language Philosophy? Well, his attention was fixed on philosophy, and not on ordinary language.

What I have been concerned with is our actual, ordinary, common or garden use of the word "good". You are standing in front of the array of melons at your grocer's, feeling helpless. Your grocer notices. He points to one in particular, and says, "That one's good." It is quite certain that he is not ascribing Moore's (putative) property goodness to the melon he points to; what he is ascribing to it is probably the property of being a good melon. It would be utterly astonishing if when you asked, "Do you mean that that's a good melon?" he replied, "Oh dear me no, I haven't the faintest idea whether it's a good melon, I meant only that it's a good thing."

It is worth stress that the fact that our actual, ordinary, common or garden use of the word "good" is such as to mark it as an attributive adjective is not itself a philosophically deep fact that calls for argument: it is an empirical fact about ordinary English usage.

However, there are places where one finds "good" used differently: many books by philosophers. W. D. Ross drew attention to the attributive use of "good", and allowed that in ordinary life it is much the most common. But he said that there is another use of "good", a philosopher's use, "as when it is said that knowledge is good or that pleasure is good." A philosopher who says "Knowledge is good" or "Pleasure is good" does not mean, for some respect R, that knowledge, or pleasure, is good in respect R. He means that knowledge, or pleasure, is (simply) *good.* And Ross said that it is this—its use to ascribe a property—that is the use of "good" that is most important for philosophy.[7]

It is certainly not impossible for an adjective to have two uses, only one of which is attributive. Here is an example: "famous". We might at first thought have taken it to be only an attributive adjective, for there are pairs of kinds of things K_1 and K_2 for which the conjunction of

---

[7] W. D. Ross, *The Right and the Good* (Oxford: Oxford University Press, 1930), 65.

A is a famous K_1

and

A is a K_2

does not entail

A is a famous K_2.

For example, the conjunction of the propositions that A is a famous novelist, and that A is a physicist, does not entail the proposition that A is a famous physicist. (A may be famous as a novelist, that is, well known as a novelist, but not well known as a physicist.) And a person who says "A is famous" meaning, for some K, that A is a famous K, is using "famous" as an attributive adjective.

But on second thought we remember that "famous" has a second use, for a person may say "A is famous," meaning to ascribe to A the property of being (simply) famous—that is, the property of being (simply) well known. So there is nothing in the mere fact of an adjective F's having an attributive use that prevents it from also having a use to ascribe the property F-ness.[8]

What assures us that "famous" does have this second use is that we know what the property of being (simply) famous *is*—it is the property of being (simply) well known. What is the property that Ross claims is ascribed to knowledge, or pleasure, by a philosopher who says "That is good" of it?

When philosophers ask, as many have done, "Is knowledge, or pleasure, good?" what exactly do they mean? Geach said there is no good reason to think they mean anything at all.

Geach was too hasty, I think. Here is a hypothesis. What those philosophers want to know is what people ought to do—for example, whether we ought to act in such a way as to conduce to or promote the existence of A, more briefly, whether

(1) We ought to promote A.

And when they ask whether

---

[8] I thank Matthew Hanser for "famous".

(2) A is good,

what they are asking is whether A has the property such that A's having it would make (1) true. Alternatively put, when such a philosopher asks whether (2) is true, what he is asking is whether A has the property that is 'conclusively ought-making'.

Now that hypothesis is over-simple, for most (all?) of the philosophers I have in mind accept that it is possible that we ought to promote A, but only where promoting A does not conflict with promoting B, which takes pride of place. (As Ross said, some philosophers say that knowledge is good; and some say both that knowledge is good and that pleasure is good, one taking pride of place.) When such a philosopher asks whether (2) is true, then, what he is asking is not whether A has the property such that A's having it would make (1) true, but instead whether A has the property such that A's having it would count in favor of (1)'s being true, and, if other things are or were equal, would make (1) true. Alternatively put, when such a philosopher asks whether (2) is true, what he is asking is whether A has the property that is 'prima facie ought-making' or (as some put it) 'pro tanto ought-making.'[9]

So if my hypothesis is right, then the philosophers we are concerned with do mean something when they ask, "Is pleasure good?" What they are asking is whether pleasure has the property that is prima facie ought-making.

Alas, we have to ask: what property is that? Three answers suggest themselves.

(i) The property they have in mind is just, simply, prima facie ought-makingness. Thus when they ask, "Is pleasure good?" what they are asking is just, simply, whether other things being equal, we ought to promote pleasure. But if that is what a philosopher means when he asks, "Is pleasure good?" we might well wonder why he asks his question in those words. Why does he help himself to the

---

[9] Shelly Kagan says: "on one level, to say that there is a pro tanto reason to promote the good is actually to make a trivial claim. Everyone has a standing reason to promote the objectively best outcome, because the existence of such a reason is in part just what it *is* for something to have objective value." *The Limits of Morality* (Oxford: Oxford University Press, 1989), 61. If we ignore that unexplained "in part," we can take him to think that for (2) to be true is for A to be prima facie (he calls it "pro tanto") ought-making. (See also his pp. 65–80.)

word "good"? Why doesn't he just, simply, ask whether other things being equal, we ought to promote pleasure?

We can surely suppose that it is not for nothing that he asks his question in those words. Yes, he does want to know whether other things being equal, we ought to promote pleasure; but he thinks that that is true only if pleasure has the property that would *make* it true—and it is because he takes "good" to stand for *that* property that he asks his question in the words "Is pleasure good?"

The property, then, is the property whose possession by pleasure would *make* it the case that other things being equal, we ought to promote pleasure, *that* being the property that he takes "good" to stand for.

But what property *is* it? He can't really take "good" to stand for (ii) the property being good in some respect or other. Everything is good in some respect, so whatever A may be—whether pleasure or anything else—the question "Is A good in some respect?" is all too easily answered yes.

At the bottom of the barrel is the remaining alternative, that the property he takes "good" to stand for is (iii), our old friend, the property goodness. Unfortunately there is no such property, so there is no room for thinking that A's possessing that property would make it the case that other things being equal, we ought to promote A.[10]

---

[10] I am sure that some readers will say that there is another, and better, alternative at the bottom of the barrel, namely that the property our philosopher takes "good" to stand for is (iv) intrinsic goodness. But what is that? We might well suppose it to be nonderivative goodness: that is, the goodness a thing has, but not because it stands in a suitable relation to (as, for example, being conducive to) something else that is good. This does seem to be what Moore had in mind when he used the term in *Principia*. So understood, however, there is no such property as intrinsic goodness if there is no such property as goodness.

In a later work, Moore pointed to the possibility of an account of intrinsic goodness according to which it consists in oughtmakingness, though he himself rejected it. See his "Reply to My Critics," *The Philosophy of G. E. Moore*, ed. P. A. Schilpp, 3rd ed. (La Salle: Open Court, 1968).

A recent oughtmakingness account of intrinsic goodness may be found in Michael J. Zimmerman, *The Nature of Intrinsic Value* (Oxford: Rowman & Littlefield, 2001): for A, B, C, and so on, to possess intrinsic goodness is for it to be the case that "*there is a moral requirement to favor them* (welcome them, admire them, take satisfaction in them, and so on) *for their own sakes*" (24, Zimmerman's own italics). (That "for their own sakes" is presumably intended to ensure that intrinsic goodness be nonderivatively ought-making.) This account of intrinsic goodness should remind

In the end, then, Geach was right: the philosopher who asks, "Is knowledge, or pleasure, good?" is not asking an intelligible question—it is no more intelligible than the question whether the melon your grocer points to is (not a good melon, but all simply) a good thing.

But only in the end. It is worth taking note of what it is (if my hypothesis is right) that motivates such philosophers, for there unquestionably is a link between a thing's being good in thus and such respects, and its being the case that other things being equal, we ought to promote it. Arguably, it is never the case that a person ought to do a thing unless his doing it would be good in certain respects; and arguably, there are respects in which a person's doing a thing would be good such that it follows that other things being equal, he ought to do it. What goes wrong in the literature I refer to is only the idea that there is something simple at work here—the idea that the link between "good" and "ought" is like that between a hook and an eye.

6.

I asked earlier: which judgments are the evaluatives? I gave three examples, namely that D is a good person, E is a good tennis player, and F is a good toaster. They are obviously judgments to the effect that a certain thing is good in a certain respect.

We also took note of the existence of such judgments as that G is good at doing crossword puzzles, H is good for England, and I is good for use in making cheesecake. These too are judgments to the effect that a certain thing is good in a certain respect.

We can surely say that all judgments to the effect that a certain thing is good in a certain respect are evaluative judgments. Let us look at a way of organizing them.

---

us of alternative (i) in the text above. And if offered as an account of what the philosophers I discuss in the text above have in mind, it would be subject to the same objection, namely that what they have in mind by "good" is not just, simply, being ought-making, but rather the property that *makes* its possessors be ought-making.

II

Goodness Properties

1.

Let us begin by asking: for which kinds K is there such a property as being a good K? I make two suggestions.

First, being a good K is being good *as*, or *for*, a K. Alternatively put: being a good K is being a model, exemplar, paradigm, or good specimen of a K. In brief,

(i) Being a good K is being good *qua* K.

For which kinds K is there such a property as being good *qua* K? Here are some examples. Being a toaster is being an artifact manufactured for use to toast toastables—bread, bagels, waffles, and so on. I'll say, for short, that being a toaster is being an artifact manufactured to toast. Then there is such a property as being good *qua* toaster: it consists in being a toaster that toasts well. Similarly for such other artifact kinds as lawnmower, food processor, and tennis racket.

The kind seeing eye dog is not an artifact kind since seeing eye dogs are not manufactured. All the same, being a seeing eye dog is being a dog trained to serve as eyes for the blind. Then there is such a property as being good *qua* seeing eye dog: it consists in being a seeing eye dog that serves well as eyes for the blind.

Tennis players are also not manufactured. All the same, being a tennis player is being a person who plays tennis. Then there is such a property as being good *qua* tennis player: it consists in being a tennis player who plays tennis well.

The kinds toaster, seeing eye dog, and tennis player are sometimes called function-kinds: to be a member of one of those kinds is
to have a certain function. A fortiori, to be good *qua* member of one
of those kinds is to be a member of one of those kinds that performs
the appropriate function well.

But there are other examples that are not function-kinds.
Beefsteak tomatoes have no function—there is nothing they do
about which it could be asked whether or not they do it well. But
being a beefsteak tomato is being a tomato of a kind whose members are bred to be large at maturity while nevertheless tasting good.
Then there is such a property as being good *qua* beefsteak tomato:
it consists in being a beefsteak tomato that is large at maturity while
nevertheless tasting good.

The kind tiger is also not a function-kind—there are things tigers
do about which it can be asked whether or not they do them well,
but there is nothing tigers do about which it can be said that doing
that is the function of a tiger. Still, being a tiger is being a member
of a certain biological species, and there therefore is such a property
as being good *qua* tiger: it consists in being a well-grown member
of the species 'tiger'.[1]

The kind human being is also not a function-kind. Being a
human being is also being a member of a certain biological species,
and there should therefore, here too, be such a property as being
good *qua* member of the species. But there is a complication here.
Being good *qua* tiger is being a well-grown tiger. That is, it is being
a physically fit tiger. There is such a property as being a physically
fit human being, but having that property is not sufficient for being
good *qua* human being: a villain is not good *qua* human being even
if he is physically fit. And having that property is not necessary for
being good *qua* human being: a person born blind, or blind due to
disease, may all the same be good *qua* human being.

Being good *qua* tiger is being a physically fit tiger; being good
qua human being is being a morally good human being. This difference is not due to the fact that we just happen to impose moral
considerations in our evaluating of people: it is due to the difference

---

[1] Since a species evolves, what counts as a well-grown member of the species
at one time might not so count at another time. Similarly, toasters and tennis players
have improved over the years. We will return to these cross-temporal considerations
in the following chapter.

between the capacities of members of the different species. Unlike tigers, human beings *can* act morally well or badly, and that is why their being good *qua* human beings consists in their acting morally well. We will be looking at this idea more closely later.

So we now have some examples of kinds K for which there is such a property as being good *qua* K—being a model, exemplar, paradigm, or good specimen of a K—namely the kinds toaster, seeing eye dog, tennis player, beefsteak tomato, tiger, and human being.

Those kinds have something in common: each of them is such that what being a K *is* itself sets the standards that a K has to meet if it is to be good *qua* K. Thus being a toaster is being an artifact manufactured to toast, and that itself sets the following standard for being good *qua* toaster: toasting well. Similarly for the kinds seeing eye dog, tennis player, beefsteak tomato, tiger, and human being. Let us call kinds that meet this condition *goodness-fixing kinds.* It is plain that there is such a property as being good *qua* K if K is a goodness-fixing kind.

I suggest that we can also say: there is such a property as being good *qua* K only if K is a goodness-fixing kind. That is, if what being a K is doesn't itself set the standards that a K has to meet if it is to be good *qua* K, then nothing sets them—thus there is no such property as being good *qua* K. Thus my second suggestion is:

>   (ii) There is such a property as being good *qua* K if and only if K is a goodness-fixing kind.

By way of reminder, my first suggestion was:

>   (i) Being a good K is being good *qua* K.

From the conjunction of (i) and (ii) we can draw the following strong conclusion:

>   (Strong Conclusion) There is such a property as being a good K if and only if K is a goodness-fixing kind.

2.

It *is* a strong conclusion, but isn't it plausible? Consider the kind pebble. What is a pebble? According to the *Oxford English Dictionary,* a pebble is "a small, smooth, rounded stone, worn by the action of water, ice, or sand." That, I should think, is as good a definition as any.

But given that that is what being a pebble is, the kind pebble is not a goodness-fixing kind, for what being a pebble is does not itself set the standards that a pebble has to meet if it is to be good *qua* pebble.

Suggestion (ii) therefore yields that there isn't any such property as being good *qua* pebble. And isn't that plausible? There is such a property as being a pebble that would be good for Smith to use to replace the pawn he just lost. There is such a property as being a pebble that would be good for Jones to use to fill the hole at the bottom of his flowerpot. But there is no such property as being good *as*, or *for*, a pebble—no such property as being a model, exemplar, paradigm, or good specimen of a pebble. There therefore is no such property as being good *qua* pebble.

Suggestion (i) therefore yields that there is no such property as being a good pebble. And isn't that plausible too? If I say to you, "Please find three good pebbles for me," then what do you do? You ask: "How d'you mean, good pebbles?" I help you not a bit if I reply, "I said 'good pebbles', and that's what I meant."

Similarly for the kind smudge: it too is not a goodness-fixing kind. No doubt there is such a property as being a smudge that would be good for use in a Rorschach test, but there is no such property as being (simply) a good smudge. Similarly for the kinds cloud, shade of gray, and piece of wood.

3.

There is room for an objection, however. What I have in mind is an objection to suggestion

(i) Being a good K is being good *qua* K

in particular. For it might be asked why we shouldn't allow that a K might be a good K, not in that it is good *qua* K—not in that it is good *as*, or *for*, a K, not in that it is a model, exemplar, paradigm, or good specimen of a K—but rather in that it answers to people's interest in Ks.

Suppose that people dearly love pink pebbles—they pay enormously high prices for pebbles that are all over bright pink.

(Compare tulip-mania in seventeenth-century Holland.) Perhaps we can therefore say that there *is* such a property as being a good pebble—a property that consists in being a pink pebble. Thus

(α) Being a good pebble is being a pink pebble.

Being a pink pebble isn't being good *qua* pebble. (Being a rare tulip isn't being good *qua* tulip.) So if (α) is true, then (i) is false.

Well, what if some time has now passed, and tastes have changed: people have come to be bored by pink pebbles. (Compare the sudden collapse of tulip-mania.) Indeed, they have come to dearly love blue pebbles instead. Would it be the case that, in light of the change, being a good pebble now consists in being a blue pebble? It can't be the case that being a good pebble was identical with being a pink one, and now is identical with being a blue one.

So a better alternative would have been to say that being a good pebble is being a pebble that answers to people's interest in pebbles, whatever those interests may be.[2] Thus

(β) Being a good pebble is being a pebble that answers to people's interest in pebbles.

Opting for (β) instead of (α) would allow us to say that there has been no change in what being a good pebble *consists in*: there has been a change only in which pebbles are in fact the good ones. Pink pebbles used to answer to interests, so they used to be the good ones; they don't now answer to interests, so they aren't now the good ones. Blue pebbles didn't answer to interests, so they weren't the good ones; they now do answer to interests, so they now are the good ones.

We should ask: why should time be thought to differ from space in this respect? Suppose that the following is and always has been the case: in the southern hemisphere, people dearly love pink pebbles, and in the northern hemisphere, they dearly love blue ones. Then are we to say that pink ones are good pebbles in the southern hemisphere, and blue ones in the northern hemisphere? And

---

[2] This claim is suggested by remarks by Ziff in *Semantic Analysis*. I say only "suggested by": I do not attribute the claim to him.

that if you carry a blue pebble from south to north, it becomes a good one when you cross the equator? There can be no objection to the idea that a blue pebble is worth more in the north than in the south—thus that it would pay you to bring it north if you are thinking of selling it; what is unacceptable is the idea that a blue pebble is a better pebble when it is in the north then when it is in the south.

Tastes are relatively trivial interests, of course, and they do vary widely. So let us bypass tastes. Suppose, instead, that we discover that pink (and only pink) pebbles are good for use to cure the common cold. (Grind them up into powder, mix in tomato juice, and drink on an empty stomach.) That is in everybody's interest, north and south both! Then have we discovered, not merely that pink pebbles are good for use to cure the common cold, but *therefore*, and thus also, that pink pebbles are good pebbles?

But suppose it is now 2051, and by energetic distribution of pink pebbles, the governments of the world eradicated the common cold by 2050. Then although the chemistry of pink pebbles remains unchanged, that chemistry is no longer of any use to us—pink pebbles no longer answer to any interest of ours. If it was the fact of their answering to our interests that made pink pebbles be good pebbles, then the fact that they no longer answer to our interests makes them have ceased to be good pebbles. *We* eradicated the common cold, and that made *them* cease to be good pebbles? It can't be right to think that they really were good pebbles if our eliminating the common cold would have to be taken to have made them cease to be.

Contrast toasters. If the peoples of the world came to dislike toast by 2050, then a toaster's ability to toast well is no longer of any use to us—toasters that toast well no longer answer to any interest of ours. (So of course nobody will any longer manufacture toasters.) But a toaster that toasts well remains a good toaster—no change in our interests alters *that*. This difference issues from the fact that 'toaster' is a goodness-fixing kind and 'pebble' is not.

I suggest, then, that we should agree that our having interests in Ks does not by itself fix that there is such a property as being a good K, much less what it is. And that we really should accept:

> (Strong Conclusion) There is such a property as being a good
> K if and only if K is a goodness-fixing kind.

4.

We should stop over some further kinds.

Moral philosophers often say that such and such a human act is a good one, or that such and such an event, or fact, or state of affairs, or possible world is a good one, and they then draw conclusions from its being a good one. Are these goodness-fixing kinds?

What are human acts?—"acts", as I will often say for short. I take it we can say, roughly anyway, that being an act is being an event that consists in some human being's causing something. Does what being an act *is* itself set the standards that an act has to meet if it is to be good *qua* act?—a model, exemplar, paradigm, or good specimen of an act? Isn't any event that consists in a human being's causing something as good a specimen of a human being's causing something as any other? No less so than any pebble or smudge is as good a specimen of a pebble or smudge as any other.

There are sub-kinds of the kind 'act' that are goodness-fixing kinds. Being a pronouncing of the word "clematis" is an example, for what being a member of that sub-kind is itself sets the standards that a member has to meet if it is to be good *qua* member—a pronouncing of the word is good *qua* pronouncing of the word just in case it is it is a correct pronouncing of the word. ("Cle′matis" not "clema′tis".) But nothing similar is available for the super-kind 'act' of which this is a sub-kind.

Similarly for the super-kind 'event'. An event is a happening. An occurrence. There is nothing in what being an event is that itself sets the standards that an event has to meet if it is to be good *qua* event.

Then the kinds 'act' and 'event' are not goodness-fixing kinds, and there therefore are no such properties as being (simply) a good act or event.

What are facts? On some views, being a fact is being a true proposition. If that is what facts are, then the kind 'fact' is plainly not a goodness-fixing kind—for there is nothing in what being a true proposition is that itself sets the standards that a true proposition has to meet if it is to be good *qua* true proposition.

On other views, facts are not true propositions, but instead things that make true propositions *be* true. Here again there is nothing in what being a fact is that itself sets the standards that a fact has to meet if it is to be good *qua* fact—thus if it is to be good *qua* thing-that-makes-some-true-proposition-be-true.

On some views, states of affairs are propositions, true or false. On other views, states of affairs are not themselves propositions (for they are not assertibles) but are instead correlated one-to-one with propositions. (Either way, a state of affairs obtains just in case the proposition it is, or is correlated with, is true.) Either way, there is nothing in what being a state of affairs is that sets the standards that a state of affairs has to meet if it is to be good *qua* state of affairs.

And what about possible worlds? Many people say that a possible world is, roughly, 'a way the world might be'. Or that it is a suitably large state of affairs—all possibilities 'filled in' yes or no. I know of no account of what a possible world is such that what being a possible world is itself sets the standards that a possible world has to meet if it is to be good *qua* possible world. Isn't anything that consists in being a way the world might be, or being a suitably large state of affairs, as good a specimen of that kind as any other? No less so than any pebble or smudge is as good a specimen of a pebble or smudge as any other.

I therefore invite the conclusion that there are no such properties as being (simply) a good act, event, fact, state of affairs, or possible world. That is of course compatible with there being such properties as

> being a morally good act,
> being an event, fact, or state of affairs that is good for Jones
> being a possible world in which all governments are good
>   governments,

just as there being no such properties as being (simply) a good pebble or smudge is compatible with there being such properties as being a pebble that would be good for Jones to use to replace the pawn he just lost, and being a smudge that would be good for use in a Rorschach test.

5.

We can express the point I have been making as follows: there is a property that is an instance of "being a good K" just in case it is an instance of

(I) being a good K_{gf}

where K$_{gf}$ is a goodness-fixing kind.

Every such property consists, for some respect R, in being good in respect R. But as we know, there are other properties each of which consists, for some respect R, in being good in respect R. Here are some examples that we met in the preceding chapter:

> being good at doing crossword puzzles
> being good for England
> being good for use in making cheesecake
> being good to use in teaching elementary logic
> being good to look at
> being good in *Hamlet*
> being good as Ophelia in *Hamlet*
> being good with children.

I hope it will be intuitively clear enough what I mean when I say that these properties are instances of

(II) being good-modified.

6.

Two more groups of properties are worth our attention.

Expressions of the form "being a K that is good-modified" are ambiguous: we might mean by such an expression being both a K and good-modified. Or we might mean by it being good-modified anyway for a K—being a K that is anyway good-modified as Ks go.

For example, consider the expression "being an athlete who is good at doing crossword puzzles". If Smith says, "Alfred is an athlete who is good at doing crossword puzzles," he is likely to be ascribing to Alfred the compound property of being both an athlete and good at doing crossword puzzles. But he might not be ascribing that compound property to Alfred. Smith might believe that no athletes are good at doing crossword puzzles, though some are better at it than others, and mean to be ascribing to Alfred only the property of being good at doing crossword puzzles for an athlete—that is, being, as athletes go (which isn't very far), good at doing crossword puzzles.

Again, if Jones says, "Alice is a six-year-old child who is good at doing crossword puzzles," he is likely to be ascribing to her the property of being good at doing crossword puzzles for a six-year-old child. But he might not be. He might say what he said in amazement. If Alice wins the crossword puzzle contest among New Yorkers, he might mean that she is (only!) a six-year-old child and (amazingly!) is also good at doing crossword puzzles. A child prodigy isn't just good, as children go, at (as it might be) playing the violin; the child prodigy is (simply) good at playing the violin.

All of the good-modifiers yield ambiguities in the same way. I might say of a shoe, "It's an orthopedic shoe that is good to look at," and I might mean either that it is an orthopedic shoe and good to look at (not likely to be true, given what orthopedic shoes look like), or that it is good to look at for an orthopedic shoe (which might just possibly be true).

So let us distinguish. For all kinds K, there is such a property as being a K. For all good-modifiers, there is such a property as being good-modified. If being F and being G are properties, then there is a compound property being both F and G. So for all kinds K, and all good-modifiers, there is a compound property

> being both a K and good-modified.

There isn't anything new for our purposes in those compound properties.

What is new for our purposes is that for all kinds K, and all good-modifiers, there is a property that is an instance of

> (III) being good-modified for a K—

that is, being, as Ks go (which may or may not be far), good-modified. These are not compound properties. Being good at doing crossword puzzles for an athlete is not identical with being both an athlete and good at doing crossword puzzles. For it might be the case, or anyway have been the case, that athletes aren't good at doing crossword puzzles; and if that is or were the case, then Alfred could be good at doing crossword puzzles for an athlete, while not being good at doing crossword puzzles.

7.

Is there really a property that is an instance of (III) for *all* kinds K, and *all* good-modifiers? That commits us to there being some very odd-looking properties. Thus, for example,

being good at doing crossword puzzles for a tablecloth
being good for England for a color
being good for use in making cheesecake for an adjective
being good to its mother for a shoelace
being good to eat raw for a prime number
being morally good for a toaster.

Should we allow that there are such properties? Well, why not?

"Nothing can possess them!" Nothing can be good at doing cross-word puzzles for a tablecloth—nothing can be, as tablecloths go, good at doing crossword puzzles. (Tablecloths don't *go* at all in that dimension. It isn't that they are all *bad* at doing crossword puzzles; they don't compete in that market.) Similarly for the others on the list. But that isn't a good reason for rejecting them. For there are such properties as being a tablecloth and being good at doing crossword puzzles. As I said in the preceding section, if being F and being G are properties, then there is a compound property being both F and G. So there is such a compound property as

being both a tablecloth and good at doing crossword puzzles.

Similarly, there are such compound properties as

being both a color and good for England
being both an adjective and good for use in making cheesecake
being both a shoelace and good to its mother
being both a prime number and good to eat raw
being both a toaster and morally good

despite the fact that nothing can possess any of these properties.

There really is no more reason to reject the noncompound properties on the first list than there is to reject the compound properties on the second, so we had better make room for both.

Odd-looking properties like those on the first list won't figure in what follows. I drew attention to them only because the careful reader will have noticed that accepting my claim—namely that for all kinds K, and all good-modifiers, there is a property that is an instance of

(III) being good-modified for a K—

commits us to them.

8.

Let us look, finally, at some properties that are first cousins of instances of (III). I have in mind such properties as

> being a good tennis player for a six-year-old child
> being a good cookbook for a cookbook for dieters
> being a good toaster for a ten-year-old toaster
> being a good typewriter for a typewriter made in 1900
> being a good computer for a computer made for sale for $100.

Just as a person can be good at doing crossword puzzles for an athlete without being good at doing crossword puzzles, a person can be a good tennis player for a six-year-old child without being a good tennis player. (There are lots of people who are good tennis players, but none of them is a six-year-old.)

These properties, I will say, are instances of

> (IV) being a good K_{gf} for a K

where K_{gf} is a goodness-fixing kind, and K is any kind. We will have occasion to look at these again in the following chapter.

9.

Every property that is an instance of one or another of

> (I) being a good K_{gf}
> (II) being good-modified,
> (III) being good-modified for a K

and

> (IV) being a good K_{gf} for a K

consists, for some respect R, in being good in respect R. And all these properties are such that a person may be ascribing one or another of them to A in saying the words "A is good". I will there-fore call them goodness properties.

The word "good" turns up in still other constructions, so we should allow that there are still other goodness properties.

But let us stop for a moment to take note of another construction that doesn't require us to add to that list of goodness properties.

What I have in mind is sentences of the form "It is good that S," where "S" is itself a declarative sentence—as it might be, "It is good that Alfred is paying his debts" or "It is good that Bert is going to move his rook" or "It is good that the barn didn't burn down." The word "good" does not function as an adjective in that sentence; rather "It is good that" is grammatically a sentence-operator, like "It is true that," "Smith knows that," "Jones regrets that," and "It is probable that".

Now sentence-operators differ. Some are factive: "It is good that S," "It is true that S," "Smith knows that S," and "Jones regrets that S" are true only if there is such a fact as the fact that S. Others are not factive: "It is probable that S" is not.

Consider the factive "Jones regrets that S." People who say that are ascribing a property to the fact that S, namely the property being regretted by Jones. And it might be said that the same is true of people who say the factive "It is good that S". Thus it might be said that even if there is no property that people who say "A is good" are all ascribing to A, still, people who say "It is good that S" are all ascribing a property—the property being good—to the fact that S.

But it won't do. We may well grant that people who say the sentence,

Jones regrets that the barn burned down,

are asserting exactly what they would have asserted if they had instead said the sentence,

The fact that the barn burned down is regretted by Jones;

and we may therefore conclude that they are ascribing the property being regretted by Jones to the fact that the barn burned down. We may equally well grant that people who say the sentence,

It is good that the barn burned down,

are asserting exactly what they would have asserted if they had instead said the sentence,

> The fact that the barn burned down is good.

But which property is it to be thought they would be ascribing to the fact that the barn burned down in saying those words? One of them might be ascribing the property being good for Smith. Another might be ascribing the property being good for us.

Indeed, let us give the name "A" to the fact that the barn burned down. Then they are ascribing to A exactly what they would have ascribed to A if they had instead said the sentence,

> A is good.

In short, the sentence "It is good that S" provides us with nothing new. If a person says those words, then we know that for some respect R, he is asserting that the fact that S is good in respect R— just as if a person says "A is good," then we know that for some respect R, he is asserting that A is good in respect R. But if the context does not tell us what that respect is, then we don't know what property he is ascribing. The one form of words is no more informative along that dimension than the other is.

10.

To return to the goodness properties. These include all properties that are instances of

> (I) being a good K_{gf}
> (II) being good-modified,
> (III) being good-modified for a K

or

> (IV) being a good K_{gf} for a K.

To ascribe any of those properties to a thing is to make a favorable evaluative judgment about the thing. The sample evaluative judgments I gave at the outset were: that D is a good person, E is a good tennis player, and F is a good toaster. These three are judgments in the making of which the judger ascribes an instance of (I), and all three are favorable evaluative judgments. The judgment that G is good at doing crossword puzzles is a judgment in the making of which the judger ascribes an instance of (II), and it too is a favorable evaluative judgment. Similarly for judgments in the making of which the judger ascribes an instance of (III) or (IV).

We will look at other kinds of favorable evaluative judgments. But we must first attend to an objection to the idea that there really are such properties as I am calling goodness properties.

III

Expressivism

1.

I take the following ideas to be true.

The kind umbrella is a goodness-fixing kind, since what being an umbrella is itself sets the standards that an umbrella has to meet if it is to be good *qua* umbrella. (We learn what being good *qua* umbrella is in the course of learning what being an umbrella is.) So there is such a property as being a good umbrella: it is an instance of

(I) being a good K_{gf}.

To ascribe being a good umbrella to a thing is to make a favorable evaluative judgment about the thing. So, for example, let DRY be a certain umbrella. Then judging that DRY is a good umbrella is making a favorable evaluative judgment about DRY. Indeed, judging that DRY is a good umbrella is making a favorable evaluative judgment about DRY that might very well be true.

Is there any reason to object to those ideas?

Simon Blackburn said:

The natural world is the world revealed by the senses, and described by the natural sciences: physics, chemistry, and notably biology, including evolutionary theory. However we think of it, ethics seems to fit badly into that world. Neither the senses nor the sciences seem to be good detectors of obligations, duties, or the order of value of things.[1]

---

[1] Simon Blackburn, *Ruling Passions* (Oxford: Clarendon Press, 1998), 49.

He must have had in mind by "ethics" something narrower than I refer to by that word: he must have been thinking of it as standing for something concerned with morality in particular. I say that partly because he thinks of ethics as concerned with obligations and duties, but also because what he says about it is so very implausible if taken to be about the evaluative in general. For surely it might be precisely by the senses—with the help of some elementary science—that I discover that DRY is a good umbrella.

It is not easy to say exactly, and in detail, what features are both necessary and sufficient for an umbrella to be a good one. It is necessary that the mechanism for opening the umbrella operate easily, and that the umbrella remain open unless the mechanism for closing it is activated. (An umbrella that closes on you when drizzle turns to rain is obviously not a good umbrella.) It is necessary that the cover be securely fastened to the ribs, and that the umbrella be sturdy—that is, that it be capable of surviving, for a considerable time, normal use for the purpose for which umbrellas are manufactured. Are those features sufficient? Well, we should presumably add a requirement on size and another on weight, and a requirement that the handle be graspable. There is nothing here that is not discoverable by the senses with the help of some elementary science.

Nor does it matter that, as I said, it is not easy to say exactly, and in detail, what features are both necessary and sufficient for an umbrella to be a good one. On the one hand, if you don't require detail, then it is easy to say what is necessary and sufficient for an umbrella to be a good one: it is necessary and sufficient that it be good for use for the purpose for which umbrellas are manufactured. On the other hand, we should not allow ourselves to be dazed by a demand for necessary and sufficient conditions. I am not able to produce exact, detailed, necessary and sufficient conditions even for merely being an umbrella, much less for being a good one; yet the senses and the sciences have often revealed to me that things are umbrellas.

So if a thing's being (or not being) a good umbrella is part of ethics, then anyway part of ethics fits comfortably into the world revealed by the senses and described by the natural sciences.[2]

---

[2] It is often said to be a deep and difficult question whether there is value in the world. I am therefore tempted to say, displaying two good umbrellas: "Here is one good umbrella and here is another. Therefore there *is* value in the world."

Blackburn is not the only person who has the impression he reported in the passage I quoted just above, and we should ask what lies behind it, in him and others. One possibility is that what lies behind it in them is entirely a difficulty about morality. If that is the case, then we should expect them to explain what on their view makes morality a special case—special in that it alone is only dubiously accessible to the senses and the sciences.

For it cannot be too strongly stressed that "good" does not mean something different in moral and nonmoral linguistic contexts. The adjective "good" is not ambiguous. It means the same in "good government" as it does in "good umbrella". (Just as the word "big" means the same in "big camel" and "big mouse".) It means the same in "morally good plan" as it does in "strategically good plan". "Morally good plan" means something different from "strategically good plan", of course, but that is not because "good" means something different in those two expressions; the difference is entirely due to the difference in what modifies "good" in them.

A second possibility is that what lies behind the impression Blackburn reported in the passage I quoted is a suspicion of all evaluation, whether evaluation of umbrellas or governments, or strategic or moral evaluation of plans.[3] We should have a closer look at this possibility.

2.

The suspicion I have in mind emerges as follows.

I said in chapter I that an Expressivist thinks (rightly) that there is no such property as goodness. He therefore thinks (rightly) that there is no such thing as believing that such and such a thing is good; and he therefore thinks (rightly) that if a (putative) evaluation of a thing consists in a person's believing that the thing is good, then there is no such evaluation. A fortiori, there is no such thing as finding out by use of the senses and the sciences that 'it' is true.

(I obviously borrow from the master here. See G. E. Moore, "Proof of an External World," *Proceedings of the British Academy* 25 (1939); reprinted in G. E. Moore, *Philosophical Papers* (London: Allen & Unwin, 1959).

[3] I do not accuse Blackburn himself of suspicion of all evaluation, though he may harbor it—I find it less than clear what exactly his view is.

Does the Expressivist also think that there is no such property as being a good umbrella? It is consistent to think both that there is no such property as goodness and that there is such a property as being a good umbrella—indeed, that is exactly the view I invite you to accept. If the Expressivist also holds this view, then he is not suspicious of all evaluation. He is suspicious only of (putative) evaluations that consist in believing that this or that is (simply) good.

But if he thinks that all is well with the property being a good umbrella, then what is distinctive about his Expressivism? There isn't much meat in it.

There *is* a meaty Expressivism. Its friends think, not merely that there is no such property as goodness, but also that there is no such property as being a good umbrella. They therefore think that there is no such thing as believing that DRY is a good umbrella. On their view, then, if a (putative) evaluation of DRY consists in a person's believing that DRY is a good umbrella, then there is no such evaluation. A fortiori, there is no such thing as finding out by use of the senses and the sciences that 'it' is true.

Similarly, there are no such properties as being a good tennis player or toaster, and no such properties as being good for England or being a strategically good plan, and so on and on. So these Expressivists are suspicious of evaluation generally. From here on, it is these philosophers whom I will throughout refer to by "Expressivists".

Their view is intuitively implausible. For consider being a good umbrella. As I said, the Expressivist says that there is no such property, and therefore that there is no such thing as believing that DRY is a good umbrella. But we certainly *say* that there is such a belief! The Expressivist replies that there certainly is a mental state that the vulgar call "believing that DRY is a good umbrella". But he says that that mental state is not really a belief. It contains a belief, namely the belief that DRY is an umbrella.[4] But it also contains something that is not a belief, but is instead a favorable attitude toward DRY. Thus

_____

[4] Might he instead say that the mental state contains no belief at all, but consists wholly in a favorable attitude toward DRY? If that were the case, then it would be possible to be in the mental state while not believing that DRY is an umbrella, and that can hardly be right. The mental state is, after all, the one that the vulgar call "believing that DRY is a good umbrella."

Compare Ayer on a person who says, "You acted wrongly in stealing that money." Ayer does not say that the speaker merely displays an unfavorable attitude:

the mental state is not itself believing something; it is, rather, a complex consisting partly in believing something and partly in having a favorable attitude.

Why might a person be inclined to say this? I suspect that one or more of four or five ideas lie behind saying it.

The first is the idea that if there were such a property as being a good umbrella, then it would be a conjunctive property, consisting in being an umbrella and being good. There plainly is no such conjunctive property since there is no such property as being good. So the mental state that the vulgar call "believing that DRY is a good umbrella" is not believing that DRY has that conjunctive property—there being no such thing—it is only partly believing something, namely that DRY is an umbrella, and for the rest is just having a favorable attitude.

I am sure that that idea really has been at work in Expressivists. But it is *wholly* due to nothing better than overlooking the fact that "good" is an attributive adjective.

The second idea is that evaluation is (as some people put it) inherently or essentially 'contestable': it may be that Smith and Jones are in complete agreement as to the facts about A, and yet that Smith evaluates A favorably and Jones evaluates it unfavorably—in which case there is nothing that would settle the dispute between Smith and Jones, and thus it is not the case that one speaks truly and the other falsely.

Which are 'the facts about A'? For these purposes, you obviously aren't allowed to suppose that there are any evaluative facts about A or anything else.

This second idea is on the face of it wrong. Suppose that Smith and Jones agree that the mechanism for opening DRY operates easily and that it remains open unless the mechanism for closing it is activated, that its cover is securely fastened to its ribs, that it is sturdy and not very heavy, and that its handle is graspable. Smith therefore says, "DRY is a good umbrella." Jones says, "Not so." Why? If Jones says, "The facts that Smith and I agree on do not count in favor of DRY's being a good umbrella"—or if he says, "Well look, DRY isn't red, and an umbrella is a good one only if it is red"—then

---

Ayer is aware that he must accommodate the fact that the speaker does anyway believe that the hearer stole the money. See Alfred Jules Ayer, *Language, Truth and Logic* (London: Victor Gollancz, 1950), 107.

he is mistaken. The dispute between him and Smith is not unsettleable: Jones speaks falsely.

The idea that evaluation is inherently contestable is normally held by people who are thinking of moral evaluation in particular, and not of evaluation in general. But what we are considering here *is* evaluation in general.

There is certainly room for unsettleable dispute about whether DRY is a good umbrella, for "good umbrella" is vague. But so after all are "big umbrella" and "red umbrella", yet no Expressivist is troubled about the properties big umbrella and red umbrella.

There is a third idea that I take to lie behind some Expressivist suspicion of evaluation. It is more interesting, and deserves a section of its own.

3.

The idea I have in mind issues from the fact of change across time. I don't think that umbrellas have improved much over the years, but cars have. Typewriters too. Let Teddy have been the best typewriter made in 1900; everybody said of it in 1900, "Teddy is a good typewriter." Let Teddy have survived undamaged in someone's attic, and have been discovered there in 2000. Is Teddy a good typewriter? Well, it is still usable as a typewriter, but its typeface is muddy and uneven. It types slowly; it jams whenever you try to type fast on it. It is hard to clean and needs frequent repair. So we say in 2000, "Teddy is a bad typewriter." If anyone now manufactures a duplicate of Teddy, you might buy it, out of a taste for what look like antiques. But we'd say you wouldn't be buying a good typewriter: you'd be buying a bad one.[5]

So here is the idea: those who (as the vulgar say) believed in 1900 that Teddy was a good typewriter were merely believing that Teddy was a typewriter and having a favorable attitude toward it; we who (as the vulgar say) believe in 2000 that Teddy is a bad typewriter are merely believing that Teddy is a typewriter and having an unfavorable attitude toward it. The difference between them and us is merely a difference in attitude.

---

[5] There are analogues of Teddy across space. I am told that English plumbing is no match for American plumbing, and that a shower said to be a good one in England would be said to be a bad one in America.

What should be noticed first, however, is that what emerged there is a special case of a general phenomenon that has nothing to do with goodness and badness. Suppose that Eddy is a plane built in 1935, and said at the time to be a big plane. Suppose that Eddy survived to this date, and is now in use on local routes. We would say now that Eddy is a small plane.

We may imagine that Eddy was also said at the time to be a fast plane. We would say now that it is a slow one.

The cross-temporal differences between what is said about Eddy issue from advances in technology in virtue of which there are bigger, faster planes now than there were in 1935. Similarly for Teddy: there are better typewriters now than there were in 1900.

I suggest that what we should say about these cases emerges as follows.

Consider the words:

(α) Eddy is a big plane.

Some people who said those words in 1935 may have thought that the technology for building planes would not advance much further, and thus that Eddy was about as big a plane as planes would ever be. What they meant, then, may have been that Eddy was, simply, a big plane. Alternatively put, what they were ascribing to Eddy may have been a property that is an instance of

(I*) being a big K*,

the instance that results for K* = the kind plane. If so, they were speaking falsely, as we know now.

Other people who said the words (α) in 1935 may have thought that plane-building technology might well improve, or that it might or might not improve, but in any case that Eddy was a big plane for a plane built in 1935. Alternatively put, what they were ascribing to Eddy may have been a property that is an instance of

(IV*) being a big K* for a K,

the instance that results for K* = the kind plane, and K = the kind plane-built-in-1935. If so, we may suppose that they were speaking truly.

I have already hinted at the suggestion I will make about Teddy. Consider the words

(β) Teddy is a good typewriter.

Some people who said those words in 1900 may have thought that the technology for making typewriters would not advance much further, and thus that Teddy was about as good a typewriter as typewriters would ever be. What they meant, then, may have been that Teddy was, simply, a good typewriter. Alternatively put, what they were ascribing to Teddy may have been a property that is an instance of

(I) being a good K_{gf},

the instance that results for K_{gf} = the kind typewriter. If so, they were speaking falsely, as we know now.

Other people who said the words (β) in 1900 may have thought that typewriter-making technology might well improve, or that it might or might not improve, but in any case that Teddy was a good typewriter for a typewriter made in 1900. Alternatively put, what they were ascribing to Teddy may have been a property that is an instance of

(IV) being a good K_{gf} for a K,

the instance that results for K_{gf} = the kind typewriter, and K = the kind typewriter-made-in-1900. If so, we may suppose that they were speaking truly.[6]

This analogy brings home that there is nothing special to, or problematic in, properties that are instances of (IV). We help our-

---

[6] Let Freddy be an IBM electric typewriter manufactured in 2000. It may well be that you would be speaking truly if you said, "Freddy is a good typewriter," ascribing to Freddy the instance of (I) that results for K_{gf} = the kind typewriter, as well as if you said those words ascribing to Freddy the instance of (IV) that results for K_{gf} = the kind typewriter, and K = the kind typewriter-made-in-2000. For with the development of computers, use of typewriters has been shrinking, and it is not likely that important further improvements will be made in them.

On the other hand, if my informants of footnote 5 were right, then a particular shower in England may be a good shower for a shower in England while not being (simply) a good shower.

selves everywhere to analogous properties. There is not only being a big K* for a K, there is being a fast K* for a K, being a comfortable K* for a K, being a well-cooked K* for a K, and being a disagreeable/happy/friendly/ignorant K* for a K. I draw attention only to a constraint on instances of (IV). A thing can be a good K* for a K only if there is such a property as being a good K*, and thus only if K* is a goodness-fixing kind. By contrast, a thing can be a big K* for a K even if K* is not a goodness-fixing kind. The kind plane is a goodness-fixing kind, but that is not crucial to there being such a property as: being a big plane for a plane-built-in-1935. The kind attic is not a goodness-fixing kind, but there is such a property as being a big attic for an attic-in-a-townhouse.

In sum, anyway, the history of the change in attitude toward Teddy, as between 1900 and now, is no reason at all for supposing that there is no such property as being a good typewriter, and therefore no such belief as that such and such is a good typewriter. What Teddy brings home to us is just that a person's saying the words "A is a good K_{gf}," does not by itself fix what property he is ascribing to A. He *may* be ascribing being a good K_{gf}; but the context in which he speaks may indicate that he is instead ascribing merely being a good K_{gf} for a K.

4.

I said I suspect that one or more of four or five ideas lie behind Expressivist suspicion of evaluation, and we have looked at three of them. The fourth issues from attention to motivation, and it emerges as follows.

Consider Teddy. The people who in 1900 said "Teddy is a good typewriter" bought a lot of Teddy's ilk. People who (as the vulgar say) believe that umbrellas of a certain kind are good ones buy them. People who (as the vulgar say) believe that a certain restaurant is a good one eat there. More generally, people who (as the vulgar say) believe that X is a good K do things in virtue of being in that state.

For brevity, I will mostly replace references to the vulgar with scare quotes. Thus I will abbreviate that generalization as follows: people who 'believe' that X is a good K do things in virtue of being in that state.

How come? Their 'beliefs' give them motives to act—they want to buy umbrellas they 'believe' to be good ones, they want to eat at restaurants they 'believe' to be good ones, and they have these wants in virtue of having those 'beliefs'. Thus:

> (Wants Generalization) People who 'believe' that X is a good
> K want to do things in virtue of being in that state.

Now many people go on from there to make a further claim, and it is this further claim that I had in mind by the fourth idea that lies behind Expressivist suspicion of evaluation: since the Wants Generalization is true, so also is

> (Containment Thesis) 'Believing' that X is a good K is a complex that contains a want to do something.

The step from the Containment Thesis to Expressivism is plainly a short one. For we already know—on any view it is true—that 'believing' that X is a good K contains the belief that X is a K. The Containment Thesis adds that it also contains a want to do something. If we add (i) that wanting to do something is having a favorable attitude toward something, and (ii) that 'believing' that X is a good K contains nothing else besides the belief that X is a K, and that favorable attitude, then the Expressivist is home free: 'believing' that X is a good K really is a mental state that consists partly in believing something and partly in having a favorable attitude.

Should we agree that since the Wants Generalization is true, so also is the Containment Thesis?

5.

Let us begin by asking whether

> (Wants Generalization) People who 'believe' that X is a good
> K want to do things in virtue of being in that state

is itself true.

Putative countercases of the following kind have often been pointed to. Surely, I might 'believe' that a certain umbrella that I see in a shop is a good one, and yet not want to buy it because it is too expensive. Surely I might 'believe' that a certain restaurant is a good one, and yet not want to eat there because my enemy Jones has taken to eating there lately.

Friends of the Wants Generalization are unmoved by such examples. They reply that if you don't buy the umbrella because it is too expensive, then that shows that you do want to buy it: you just don't want to buy it as much as you want to save the money it would cost. If you don't eat at that restaurant because Jones eats there, then that shows that you do want to eat there: you just don't want to eat there as much as you want to avoid Jones. And they add that they didn't say that the 'believer' greatly wants to do what he wants to do in virtue of being in the state: it is enough for the truth of the Wants Generalization that the 'believer' wants to do it a little.[7]

But suppose that, having nothing better to do while I wait for a friend, I wander into a nearby pet shop. There is a birdcage on a table by the door. I investigate it by use of the senses and some elementary science. "Very good birdcage," I conclude. But I don't want to buy that very good birdcage. I don't want to do *anything* to, with, or in respect of that birdcage—I don't have a bird! What is my little want here?

I fancy that the following reply may be made. "You *say* you believe it's a good birdcage. But if there is no want that you have in virtue of 'believing' that it's a good birdcage, then there is nothing in your behavior—nothing you are even disposed to do—that distinguishes you from someone who does not 'believe' that it's a good birdcage. So there is nothing that could be thought to give us a ground for thinking that you have the 'belief' and he does not." Not so. For one thing, if you ask, I'll say it's a good birdcage, and the other fellow, if he's honest, will not. For another, if you ask, I'll tell you why I say it's a good birdcage. (Big, sturdy, easy to clean, . . . , these being reasons for believing that it's a good birdcage.) He'll do no such thing.

People who want to buy birdcages typically want to buy good ones. That isn't a deep fact: the good ones are precisely those that serve well the purposes that birdcages serve. But that is no reason for believing that people who come to 'believe' a thing is a good birdcage want to buy it. Or want to do anything to, with, or in respect of it.

---

[7] This is one of the theses that I call Little Bit Theses. (If I 'believe' that DRY is a good umbrella, then I must at least a little bit want to buy DRY—or borrow or use or gaze at or photograph or . . . DRY.) It is a good heuristic to assume that the proponent of a Little Bit Thesis is in the grip of some theory, and try to figure out what it is. I will get to what I take to be the theory behind this one shortly.

When goodness is in question, it very often *is* the case that there are wants in the offing. People want to live, and moreover, to live well; it is therefore likely that they want to do a thing when convincingly told that doing it would be good for them. People who want to do a thing are likely to want to get a thing about which they are convincingly told that it is good for use in doing the thing. But why should we think that where goodness is in question there *always* are wants in the offing?

If we didn't have any wants at all, then of course we wouldn't have any interest in whether things are good umbrellas, restaurants, or birdcages, or in whether doing this or that would be good for us, or would help us do a thing. But if we didn't have any wants, we wouldn't have any interest in anything. Goodness is not a special case.

People who accept the Wants Generalization think it *must* be true, even in face of such examples as my example of the birdcage. (So I *must* have some want in respect of that birdcage, even if only a little want, a little want that I am not aware of having.) I suggest that they think this only partly on the ground of observation of human behavior. I suggest that the deep source of their finding the Wants Generalization attractive lies in their thinking that all there is to 'believing' that X is a good K is believing that X is a K and wanting to do something in respect of X. For it would only be if you thought that that *is* all there is to 'believing' that X is a good K that you would think that a person who 'believes' that X is a good K must therefore want to do something in respect of X.

For compare goodness with redness. Some people want to buy red umbrellas, red coffee mugs, and red hats, but nobody thinks that a person who believes that X is a red K must therefore want to do something in respect of X. Why should it be thought that 'believing' that X is a good K is different? There plainly is such a thing as believing that X is a red K. People who think that the Wants Generalization must be true think so because they think that there isn't any such thing as believing that X is a good K.

Alternatively put, people who think that the Wants Generalization must be true think so because they think that

> (Containment Thesis) 'Believing' that X is a good K is a complex that contains a want to do something

is true.

But if the Containment Thesis is your ground for thinking that the Wants Generalization must be true, then you cannot argue *from* the Wants Generalization *to* the Containment Thesis.

6.

Let us ask: suppose we accept

> (Wants Generalization) People who 'believe' that X is a good K want to do things in virtue of being in that state,

on whatever ground. (Thus we accept, in particular, that I do have a little want in respect of that birdcage, a little want that I am not aware of having.) Can we get from here to the Containment Thesis?

Suppose Alice saw an umbrella in a shop. Call it RIBS. She examined it, and concluded that it is a good umbrella; thus she now 'believes' that RIBS is a good umbrella. We are accepting the Wants Generalization, so we can conclude that she now wants to do something in virtue of being in that mental state. Let us suppose that there is no problem about what she wants to do: she wants to buy RIBS.

A friend of the Containment Thesis may now argue for the Containment Thesis as follows.

Well and good: Alice wants to buy RIBS in virtue of being in the mental state of 'believing' that it is a good umbrella. But how we are to understand that "in virtue of"? What does it come to for her to want to buy RIBS *in virtue of* being in the mental state of 'believing' that it is a good umbrella? There are only two available answers to this question.

The first, (i), is the answer that would be given by the vulgar. The vulgar would say: "'Believing' that a thing is a good umbrella is—simply, straightforwardly, literally—believing that it is a good umbrella. And Alice's coming to be in the state of believing that RIBS is a good umbrella caused her to start to want to buy it."

But that answer won't do, since, as Hume taught us, no belief can cause a want. More precisely, a person's coming to be in the mental state of believing something can't cause the person to start to want to do something.

The second available answer, (ii), is: "I grant you that the vulgar are mistaken: 'believing' that a thing is a good umbrella isn't believing that it is a good umbrella. But Alice's coming to be in the state of 'believing' that RIBS is a good umbrella did, all the same, cause her to start to want to buy it."

But anyone who opts for that second answer is thereby committed to the view that Alice's 'believing' that RIBS is a good umbrella is a complex that contains a want. For Hume didn't merely teach us that no belief can cause a want; he taught us, more strongly, that nothing can cause a want unless it itself contains a want. More precisely, a person's coming to be in a mental state can cause the person to start to want to do something only if the state is a complex that itself contains a want.

It might be thought that there is room for a third answer, (iii): "The state that Alice came to be in, namely 'believing' that RIBS is a good umbrella, is a complex that contains a quite particular want, namely wanting to buy RIBS. How are we to understand what it came to for her to want to buy RIBS *in virtue of* coming to be in the state of 'believing' that RIBS is a good umbrella? Her coming to be in that state did not cause, but contained, her coming to want to buy RIBS."

But that won't do, for the state of 'believing' that RIBS is a good umbrella cannot be thought to contain wanting to buy RIBS. Alfred, for example, might be in that very same state of 'believing' that RIBS is a good umbrella, but without wanting to buy it. He might instead want to steal it.

So only two answers are available, (i) and (ii). But Hume taught us that (i) is unacceptable. Hume taught us also that to accept (ii) is to be committed to the conclusion that Alice's 'believing' that RIBS is a good umbrella is a complex that contains a want.

By hypothesis, Alice is not unique, for we are assuming that the Wants Generalization is true. So given that the Wants Generalization is true, it follows that so also is

> (Containment Thesis) 'Believing' that X is a good K is a complex that contains a want to do something.

QED.

A friend of the Containment Thesis may well grant that a question remains: *which* want is contained in the complex state of 'believing' that RIBS is a good umbrella? A general, or abstract want? No matter for the moment, says the friend of the Containment Thesis. He says that it has anyway been established that the state of 'believing' that RIBS is a good umbrella is a complex that contains *a* want.

7.

Has that been established? It will be remembered that the first premise of the argument is the Wants Generalization, and we are merely assuming that it is true.

More important, the argument relied on two lessons that we were said to have been taught by Hume. I leave to Hume experts the question what exactly Hume's own views were, but I suggest that there is nothing in Hume that justifies accepting those two ideas, and indeed, that they arc both false.

The first was the idea that no belief causes a want. More precisely, a person's coming to be in the mental state of believing something can't cause the person to start to want to do something.

Suppose Bert wanted to buy a red umbrella, any red umbrella, and went to Umbrella Shop with that aim in view. There was only one red umbrella on offer; call it RED. Catching sight of RED, Bert came to believe that it is a red umbrella. In virtue of coming to be in that mental state, he wanted to buy RED. One might have thought that we could say:

> (S) Bert's coming to believe that RED is a red umbrella caused him to start to want to buy it.

Why is it to be thought that we can't?

I suggest that people who think that (S) must be false think so because they think that Bert wouldn't have wanted to buy RED in virtue of coming to believe that it is a red umbrella if he hadn't already wanted to buy a red umbrella.

Suppose that is true. Even so, it is a bad mistake to think that that fact warrants the conclusion that (S) is false. For by hypothesis, Bert *did* already want to buy a red umbrella. (That is why he went to Umbrella Shop.) And we can say: the fact that he did already want to buy a red umbrella is *why* (S) is true.

Charles's throwing a rock at my window caused my window to break. Well, it wouldn't have caused my window to break if my window hadn't been fragile. (If my window had been made of bulletproof glass, Charles's throwing a rock at it wouldn't have caused it to break.) But that fact does not warrant the conclusion that Charles's throwing a rock at my window didn't cause it to break. Rather, my window's having been fragile is *why* Charles's throwing a rock at it caused it to break.

We can put it like this: my window's having been fragile was among the background conditions that were present such that Charles's throwing a rock at my window caused it to break because of their presence.[8]

And we can say, similarly: Bert's having wanted to buy a red umbrella was among the background conditions that were present such that Bert's coming to believe that RED is a red umbrella caused him to want to buy it because of their presence.

But then the argument we looked at fails at its first step. By hypothesis, Alice wants to buy RIBS in virtue of being in the mental state of 'believing' that it is a good umbrella. What does it come to for her to want to buy RIBS *in virtue of* being in the mental state of 'believing' that it is a good umbrella? The first answer, (i), was the answer that would be given by the vulgar: "'Believing' that a thing is a good umbrella is—simply, straightforwardly, literally—believing that it is a good umbrella. And Alice's coming to be in the state of believing that RIBS is a good umbrella caused her to start to want to buy it." The reply made was that that is unacceptable, for as Hume taught us, no belief can cause a want—more precisely, a person's coming to be in the mental state of believing something can't cause the person to start to want to do something. But that is simply a mistake.

We should note now that if the (putative) first lesson that Hume taught us is a mistake, so also is the (putative) second lesson that Hume taught us. If a belief can cause a want (so that the first lesson is false), then a state that does not contain a want can cause a want (so that the second lesson is also false). So the argument also fails at its second step.

---

[8] The fact that it is not required for the truth of "C caused E" that C itself contains everything X such that E would not have come about if X had not been present is a lesson taught us by Davidson among others. See Donald Davidson, "Causal Relations," reprinted in his *Essays on Actions & Events* (Oxford: Clarendon Press, 1980).

8.

As I said, I leave to Hume experts the question what exactly Hume's own views were, but I confess to a strong suspicion that he wouldn't really have claimed that

> (S) Bert's coming to believe that RED is a red umbrella caused him to start to want to buy it

can't be true: I suspect that he would have reacted to that example, not by saying, strongly, that no belief can cause a want, but rather by saying, more weakly, that no belief can cause a want except in the presence of background conditions that include a want. Thus of course it can be true that Bert's coming to believe that RED is a red umbrella caused him to start to want to buy it—though only given that he already wanted to buy a red umbrella.[9]

Actually, that is over-strong. By hypothesis, Bert did want to buy a red umbrella. (That is why he went to Umbrella Shop.) But that might not have been the case. Suppose Charles idly wandered into Umbrella Shop just to pass the time while waiting for a friend. Catching sight of RED, Charles came to believe that it is a red umbrella. In virtue of coming to be in that mental state, he wanted to buy RED. Why? Well, his coming to believe that RED is a red umbrella caused him to remember that his daughter said she would love to have a red umbrella, and *that* caused him to want to buy it. So Charles's coming to believe that RED is a red umbrella caused him to want to buy it, but not because he already wanted to buy a red umbrella at the time at which he came to believe that RED is a red umbrella: rather by causing him to remember his daughter's desire for a red umbrella, *that* having caused him to want to buy it.

Still, I suspect Hume would say that Charles's remembering his daughter's desire for a red umbrella can have caused him to want to buy RED only given that he wanted to satisfy her desires. So quite generally: a person's coming to be in a mental state that does not contain a want can have caused him to have want W_2 only if he had *a* want W_1—some want or other—it being because he had W_1 that his coming to be in the state caused him to have want W_2.

---

[9] Whether we should accept even this weaker claim is a matter we will return to in chapter IX, section 8.

We might accept this claim. Arguably there is something even more general at work here. Learning that Smith won the chess tournament can presumably cause me to admire him only against a background of my admiring good chess players. Learning that Jones cheated on his exam can presumably cause me to regard him with distaste only against a background of my regarding cheaters with distaste. That is, a general fact about attitudes may be at work here.

The claim is anyway plausible. Suppose that David tells us that he came to believe that RED is a red umbrella, and that that caused him to want to buy it. We ask how come. Did he want to buy a red umbrella? Did his daughter express a desire for a red umbrella? What did he want such that his coming to believe that RED is a red umbrella caused him to want to buy RED? Suppose he says: "No, there wasn't anything I wanted. My coming to believe that RED is a red umbrella just, simply, caused me to want to buy it." That would certainly be an odd business!

But the same holds of good umbrellas. When I told you about Alice, I wrote:

> Suppose Alice saw an umbrella in a shop. Call it RIBS. She examined it, and concluded that it is a good umbrella; thus she now 'believes' that RIBS is a good umbrella. We are accepting the Wants Generalization, so we can conclude that she now wants to do something in virtue of being in that mental state. Let us suppose that there is no problem about what she wants to do: she wants to buy RIBS.

In short, I didn't tell you what want W she had such that her coming to 'believe' that RIBS is a good umbrella could be said to have caused her to start to want to buy RIBS against a background that included her having want W. But I fancy that you assumed that she did have such a want, namely a want to buy a good umbrella. Suppose we ask, and she says: "No, there wasn't anything I wanted. My coming to believe that RIBS is a good umbrella just, simply, caused me to want to buy it." That too would certainly be a very odd business! Coming to 'believe' that a thing is a good umbrella doesn't just, simply, cause a person to want to buy it—just as coming to believe that a thing is a red umbrella doesn't just, simply, cause a person to want to buy it. There are *lots* of umbrellas I 'believe' to be good ones that I don't want to buy—just as there are lots of umbrellas I believe to be red ones that I don't want to buy.

You could only think it impossible that I 'believe' a thing is a good umbrella (or good birdcage), but don't have any want in respect of it, if you thought that

> (Containment Thesis) 'Believing' that X is a good K is a complex that contains a want to do something

was true, and therefore thought that

> (Wants Generalization) People who 'believe' that X is a good K want to do things in virtue of being in that state

must be true. But there is nothing in the considerations we have been attending to that provides us with a good reason for accepting the Containment Thesis.

In sum, I invite the conclusion that there is nothing lying in facts about motivation that provides us with a good reason for accepting Expressivism.

9.

I said I suspect that one or more of four or five ideas lie behind Expressivist suspicion of evaluation, and we have looked at four of them. The fifth issues from attention to speech acts. I said that four or five ideas lie behind Expressivist suspicion of evaluation since while some Expressivists take the fifth idea to be a reason for opting for Expressivism, others take it to be a consequence of Expressivism. No matter. It is well worth our attention.

The idea I refer to is that people who say sentences of the form "X is a good K" are displaying a favorable attitude toward X. Some Expressivists take this to be a fact that we observe about people, and (as I said) take it to be a reason for opting for Expressivism. For if that is what people who say those words are doing in saying them, then surely that is reason for believing that the state that consists in 'believing' that X is a good K is a complex that contains a favorable attitude toward X. Others arrive at this idea from Expressivism as follows. There is no such thing as believing (as it might be) that DRY is a good umbrella. So anyone who says the words "DRY is a good umbrella" is not expressing a belief. What *is* he doing? 'Believing' that DRY is a good umbrella is believing that DRY is an umbrella and having a favorable attitude toward DRY. So a person who says the words "DRY is a good umbrella" is expressing the belief that DRY is an umbrella, and displaying that favorable attitude toward DRY.

Now that claim is clearly false. "Display" is factive: that is, you don't display an attitude unless you have it. Yet people may well say of DRY "It's good" or "DRY is a good umbrella" when they do not have a favorable attitude toward it. I might 'believe' that DRY is a terrible umbrella and yet say to Jones "It's a good one," hoping that Jones will rely on DRY and come to grief in the rain.

The Expressivist can of course retrench: he can say that a person who says "DRY is a good umbrella" ascribes the property being an umbrella to DRY and *purports to* display a favorable attitude toward DRY—that is, the speaker either displays or anyway purports to display a favorable attitude toward DRY. The need for this retrenchment has typically been overlooked by Expressivists. My hypothesis is that the reason why Expressivists typically make the false claim that one who says "DRY is a good umbrella" displays a favorable attitude toward DRY is that they confuse it with a very different claim which is true, namely that one who says "DRY is a good umbrella" praises DRY.

The first entry for "good" in the *Oxford English Dictionary* says that "good" is the most general adjective of commendation. Surely "good" is an 'adjective of commendation': that is, saying "It is good" about a thing is commending it. Or praising it, as I will mostly say. Similarly, saying "I promise" is promising. Moreover, these are semantic facts about those words. A person who does not know that saying "It is good" is praising, and that saying "I promise" is promising, does not know the meanings of those words. But it is one thing to perform the speech act of praising a thing and quite another to have anything that would ordinarily be regarded as a favorable attitude toward the thing praised—just as it is one thing to perform the speech act of promising to do a thing and quite another to have a favorable attitude toward doing the thing promised.

In particular, saying "DRY is a good umbrella" is praising DRY, whatever the speaker's attitudes toward DRY may happen to be.

Analogously, saying "DRY is a bad umbrella"—well, is what? Damning DRY? I will mostly say it is dispraising DRY. Just as one can praise a thing without having a favorable attitude toward it, one can dispraise a thing without having an unfavorable attitude toward it.

Moreover, there is nothing in the fact that one who says "DRY is a good umbrella" praises DRY that stands in the way of saying that the speaker ascribes to DRY the property being a good umbrella, for it is entirely possible that ascribing a certain property to a thing *is* praising it. So there is nothing in the fact that one who says "DRY is a good umbrella" praises DRY that stands in the way of saying that there is such a property as being a good umbrella.

Therefore there is nothing in the fact that one who says "DRY is a good umbrella" praises DRY that stands in the way of saying that there is such a belief as the belief that DRY is a good umbrella—not just that there is a state that the vulgar call "believing that DRY is a good umbrella", but that there is a state that really is believing that DRY is a good umbrella.

In short, this fifth idea does not provide us with any reason to reject the claim that there is such a property as being a good umbrella, and therefore does not provide us with any reason to reject the claim that there is such a thing as believing that DRY is a good umbrella.

And in sum, none of the five ideas we have looked at provide us with any reason for opting for Expressivism. I therefore take it that we are entitled from here on to omit the qualifier "what the vulgar call believing" and those tiresome scare quotes around the word "believing".

10.

But there is an issue that we need to have a look at. I take it to be clear that when a person says of a thing "It is good" he praises it. So also for saying the likes of "DRY is a good umbrella." So also for saying the likes of "Kasparov is a good chess player," "Olivier was good as Hamlet," and "Spring-form pans are good for use in making cheesecake."

It may be objected, however, that not just any sentence containing the word "good" is such that to say it is to praise a thing. Suppose I say of Smith, "He's a good liar." Or suppose I say of Jones, "He's good at avoiding responsibility for what he does." Can anyone plausibly think that I praise Smith and Jones in saying those things of them? Surely I dispraise them in saying those things of them!

I suggest that we should say that I both praise and dispraise them in saying those words of them.

We have to grant in any case that it is possible to both praise and dispraise a person in saying some words about him. If I am a professor of mathematics, and my letter of recommendation for my graduate student for a teaching position at Greatorex University consisted entirely of the words "He is good at doing arithmetic," then I have both praised and dispraised my student. I have praised him, since writing "He is good at doing arithmetic" *is* praising him. But the context in which I wrote those words makes it the case that I also dispraised him. As we say, you can damn with faint praise, and that is what I did here. But of course you can't damn with faint praise unless you (faintly) praise.

However, that phenomenon is different from what goes on when I say of Smith, "He's a good liar," and of Jones, "He's good at avoiding responsibility for what he does." In writing the words "He is good at doing arithmetic" of my student, I praised him; my writing those words *was* my praising him. What makes my writing those words also have been dispraising him is the context in which I wrote them. If my saying "He's a good liar" and "He's good at avoiding responsibility for what he does" is my praising Smith and Jones, then my saying those words is also, itself, my dispraising Smith and Jones. It is not the context in which I say those words that makes my saying them be my dispraising Smith and Jones. Rather it is the words I say that makes it the case that my saying the words is my dispraising Smith and Jones—the context in which I say the words is irrelevant. And how can it be that my saying the very same words is also my praising Smith and Jones?

Let us distinguish between 'praise *simpliciter*' and 'praise *qua*'. If I say of a man, "He's a saint," then I praise him *simpliciter*: I ascribe to him a property such that if he possesses it, then he is praiseworthy in virtue of possessing it. But if I say, "DRY is an umbrella," then I don't praise DRY *simpliciter*: DRY is by hypothesis an umbrella but is not praiseworthy in virtue of being an umbrella. It is creditable in a saint to be a saint; it is not creditable in an umbrella to be an umbrella.

Suppose I say, "DRY is a good umbrella." Do I praise DRY *simpliciter*? I will say no, on the ground that DRY is not praiseworthy in virtue of being an umbrella. More generally, saying "X is a good K" is praising X *simpliciter* if and only if it is or would be praiseworthy in X to be a K.

But if I say, "DRY is a good umbrella," then I praise DRY *qua* umbrella. What I say is that as umbrellas go, DRY is a good one,

More generally, saying "X is a good K" is always praising X *qua* K, since it is always saying that as Ks go, X is a good one. You may not think Ks go far or go well; all the same, *as* they go, X is a good one.

Similarly for the good-modifiers. A person is not praiseworthy in virtue of being a person who plays chess, so saying "Kasparov is good at playing chess" is not praising him *simpliciter*. But saying "Kasparov is good at playing chess" is saying that as people who play chess go, he is a good one, so saying that is praising him *qua* person who plays chess.

Analogously for dispraise. If I say of a man, "He's a villain," then I dispraise him *simpliciter*: I ascribe to him a property such that if he possesses it, then he is dispraiseworthy in virtue of possessing it. Similarly if I say of a man, "He's a liar" or "He's a thief." But if I say, "DRY is an umbrella," then I don't dispraise DRY *simpliciter*: DRY is not dispraiseworthy in virtue of being an umbrella.

Suppose I say, "DRY is a bad umbrella." Do I dispraise DRY *simpliciter*? I will say no, on the ground that DRY is not dispraiseworthy in virtue of being an umbrella. More generally, saying "X is a bad K" is dispraising X *simpliciter* if and only if it is or would be dispraiseworthy in X to be a K.

But if I say, "DRY is a bad umbrella," then I dispraise DRY *qua* umbrella. What I say is that as umbrellas go, DRY is a bad one. More generally, saying "X is a bad K" is always dispraising X *qua* K, since it is always saying that as Ks go, X is a bad one.

Similarly for what might analogously be called bad-modifiers. A person is not dispraiseworthy in virtue of being a person who plays chess, so saying "Kasparov is bad at playing chess" is not dispraising him *simpliciter*. But saying "Kasparov is bad at playing chess" is saying that as people who play chess go, he is a bad one, so saying that is dispraising him *qua* person who plays chess. (Wrongly, of course, since he is not only good at playing chess, but very good at playing chess.)

Let us now look again at "Smith is a good liar." My characterization of the notions 'praise/dispraise *simpliciter*' and 'praise/dispraise *qua*' yields the following. Saying "Smith is a good liar" is dispraising Smith *simpliciter*, since it is or would be dispraiseworthy in Smith to be a liar. But it is also praising Smith *qua* liar, since it is saying that as liars go, Smith is a good one.

So also for "Jones is good at avoiding responsibility for what he does." Saying that is dispraising Jones *simpliciter*, since it is or would be dispraiseworthy in Jones to avoid responsibility for what he does. But it is also praising Jones *qua* person who avoids responsibility for what he does, since it is saying that as people who do that go, he is good at it.

And that is exactly the view that I suggest we should take of those sentences.

Note, moreover, that my characterization of those two notions of praise yields that saying "Smith is a bad liar" is both dispraising him *simpliciter* and dispraising him *qua* liar. That too is as it should be. (I hope it is clear that it is no praise at all to say of a man that he is a bad liar.)

So I suggest that there is nothing in the sentences we have been looking at that stands in the way of our saying that anyone who ascribes a goodness—property to X—thus anyone who ascribes to X a property that is an instance of

(I) being a good K_{gf},
(II) being good-modified,
(III) being good-modified for a K,

or

(IV) being a good K_{gf} for a K,

praises X. Though we need to add that some of those properties are such that to ascribe them to X is also to dispraise X.

11.

We have been looking in this chapter at Expressivist suspicion of evaluation, and I have argued that it is without warrant. There is no good reason to reject the claim that there are properties that are instances of (I), (II), (III), and (IV), and that they are favorable evaluative properties—properties such that to ascribe them to a thing is to make a favorable evaluative judgment about the thing, a favorable evaluative judgment that might very well be true.

I have suggested also that all of those properties are such that to ascribe them to a thing is to praise the thing. This is an important fact for our purposes, and we will return to it later.

IV

Betterness Relations

1.

Let us now look at some relations.

"Good" is an attributive adjective. "Better than" is an attributive relation-term: what holds of it is analogous to what holds of "good". For let us remember that what marks "good" as an attributive adjective is the fact that there are pairs of kinds K_1 and K_2 for which the propositions that A is a good K_1 and that A is a K_2 do not jointly entail the proposition that A is a good K_2. Analogously, there are pairs of kinds K_1 and K_2 for which the propositions that A is a better K_1 than B and that A and B are K_2s do not jointly entail the proposition that A is a better K_2 than B. For example, it might be the case that A is a better tennis player than B, and A and B are chess players, though it is not the case that A is a better chess player than B.

Again, a person who says the words "A is good" may be ascribing to A either the property being a good tennis player, or the property being good for England; there is no such thing as *the* property that people are ascribing to A in saying those words. Analogously, a person who says the words "A is better than B" may be ascribing to A and B either the relation being a better tennis player, or the relation being better for England; there is no such thing as *the* relation that people are ascribing to A and B in saying those words.

That should strike us as independently plausible. Suppose a person asks us, "Was St. Francis better than chocolate?" What *can* he mean? In what respect 'better than' does he mean to be asking whether St. Francis was better in that respect than chocolate? If he says, "No, no, what I am asking is not for a certain respect R whether St. Frances was better in respect R than chocolate. What I am asking is just whether St. Francis was (simply) better than chocolate," then he hasn't asked us any question, so it is no wonder we can't answer it.

I said in chapter I that there is such a property as 'being a good K' just in case K is a goodness-fixing kind, thus just in case the property is an instance of

(I) being a good K_{gf}.

So while there are such properties as being a good toaster, being a good seeing eye dog, and being a good beefsteak tomato, there are no such properties as being a good pebble, or being a good smudge. Analogously, there is such a relation as 'being a better K' just in case K is a goodness-fixing kind, thus just in case the relation is an instance of

(I-R) being a better K_{gf}.

So while there are such relations as being a better toaster, being a better seeing eye dog, and being a better beefsteak tomato, there are no such relations as being a better pebble, or being a better smudge.

Again, just as there are properties that are instances of

(II) being good-modified,
(III) being good-modified for a K,

and

(IV) being a good K_{gf} for a K,

there are relations that are instances of

(II-R) being better-modified,
(III-R) being better-modified for a K

and

(IV-R) being a better K_{gf} for a K.

In chapter II, I said that the properties that are instances of (I), (II), (III), and (IV) are properties that consist, for some R, in being good in respect R, and I therefore called them goodness properties. Similarly, the relations that are instances of (I-R), (II-R), (III-R), and (IV-R) are relations that consist, for some R, in being better in respect R, and I will therefore call them betterness relations. It is surely clear that for every goodness property there is an analogous betterness relation, and vice versa.

Analogously for praise and dispraise. If I say, "Smith is a better chess player than Jones," I do not praise Smith *simpliciter*, for it is not praiseworthy in a person to be a chess player. But I do praise him '*qua* chess player relative to Jones'—I don't of course say that Smith is a good chess player as chess players go, for Jones may be a very bad chess player, but I do say that Smith is anyway a better one than Jones is, and that is some (if only faint) praise. If I say, by contrast, "Smith is a better liar than Jones," I dispraise Smith *simpliciter*. But I also praise him '*qua* liar relative to Jones'—I say that Smith is anyway a better liar than Jones is, and that is some (if only faint) praise. So just as the goodness properties are favorable evaluative properties, though some are also unfavorable evaluative properties, the betterness relations are favorable evaluative relations, though some are also unfavorable evaluative relations.

I said earlier that in the case of very many goodness properties, it is entirely possible to find out by the senses and the sciences that the properties really are possessed by the things a judger judges them to be possessed by. We are able to find out whether DRY is a good umbrella by the senses and the sciences. So also for finding out whether a certain apple would be a better baking apple than another, whether a certain antibiotic would be better than another to give to a child who has an ear infection, and whether your fertilizing your houseplants monthly would be better for them than your fertilizing them weekly.

2.

Let us now stop to take another look at Consequentialism.

I said in chapter I that Consequentialism is the thesis that what we ought to do is (very roughly) to maximize the amount of goodness in the world. We should be clearer now: the Consequentialist does not think that what we ought to do is to promote the existence of as many things as we can that are good in some respect or other. Since everything is good in some respect, to say that *that* is what we ought to do would be to say that what we ought to do is, simply, to promote the existence of as many things as we can. On the other hand, the Consequentialist cannot at all plausibly think that what we ought to do is to promote the existence of as many things as we can that have the property goodness—that is, the property that we ascribe to a thing when we say "It is good"—since there is no such property.

Here is the currently most popular interpretation of Consequentialism. Let A be any person and t any time. Let V_{act}-ing be any act-kind. Let α be the world that will be actual just in case A V_{act}s at t, and let β_1, β_2, . . . be the worlds that will be actual if A does, at t, any of the other things it is open to him to do at t. Then according to the Consequentialist, A ought to V_{act} at t just in case α is a better world than any of the βs are. That is still a rough statement of the theory, but will suffice for present purposes. I draw attention only to the fact that we are to take the worlds it speaks of to be, as it were, complete: we are to take them to include A's acts and not merely the consequences of A's acts. Thus suppose that A eats a banana at t. Then the world that is actual includes all of actual past history up to t, *and* A's eating the banana, *and* everything else that happens during and after A's eating of the banana.

I will take that to be what Consequentialism says. Then the Consequentialist does not need there to be such a property as goodness; it is enough for his purposes if there is such a relation as being a better world. Is there?

I said in the preceding section that there is such a relation as 'being a better K' just in case K is a goodness-fixing kind, thus just in case the relation is an instance of

(I-R) being a better K_{gf}.

But I said in chapter II, that the kind possible world is not a goodness-fixing kind: there is no such thing as being better *qua* world— no such thing as being a model, exemplar, paradigm, good specimen of a world. It follows that there is no such relation as being (simply) a better world. If that is right, then Consequentialism must be rejected.

That leaves room for variants on Consequentialism. Utilitarianism, for example, which I take to be the idea that what matters to whether A ought to V_{act} at t can be expressed, not in terms of the (alas, only putative) relation 'better world' but rather in terms of the relation 'happier world'. Thus the Utilitarian says that A ought to V at t just in case the people who live in α are happier than the people who live in the βs.

It is a familiar enough idea—and it is familiar enough what the difficulties are that confront it. I think it useful to divide them into four groups.

Group (i) contains difficulties that arise from differences in the 'objects' of happiness—that is, differences in what it is that the people in the worlds are happy *about*. John Stuart Mill drew attention to the fact that some people are happiest about small bodily pleasures, like those one gets from a warm bath; and he claimed that that happiness does not matter for purposes of assessing what one ought to do as much as the happiness one gets from reading good poetry. Again, some people are happiest only when in receipt of things that happen to be very expensive, such as caviar and diamonds. And we should take note of the fact that some people are happiest about the misfortunes of the people they envy.

Group (ii) contains difficulties that arise from differences in the causes of happiness. For example, a person's happiness may be a product of ignorance—as where he believes that he has accomplished great things, and is greatly loved, but is hopelessly, and perhaps willfully, mistaken.

Group (iii) contains difficulties that arise from differences in the distribution of happiness in different worlds. There might be a little more happiness in world W than in world W*; but what if the happiness in W is all possessed by a small minority, whereas the happiness in W* is equitably shared? Or if there are so enormously many people in W that, although the happiness in W is equitably shared, nobody in W gets more than just barely enough to make life worth living?

The Utilitarian needs to declare himself, one way or another, on how to respond to the difficulties in those three groups. Moreover, it is not clear how he is to respond to them, given that he can't help himself to the relation 'better world'. For example, suppose that there is a little more happiness in W than in W*, but the happiness in W is all possessed by a small minority, whereas the happiness in W* is equitable shared. The Utilitarian can't say that we ought to prefer bringing W* about on the ground that W* is a better world than W. If he wishes to say that we ought to prefer bringing W* about, then he has to make out (somehow!) that W* is a happier world than W. (How is he to make that out?)

Most serious, however, are the difficulties in group (iv), which arise when we ask exactly why it should be thought that whether a person ought to do a thing turns on whether people at large will be happier if he does it than if he does anything else it is open to him to do at the time. There are at least three very familiar reasons for thinking that that won't do.

(iv-a) There is first what a person is plausibly thought to be entitled to for himself. Suppose that A can save the lives of five only by volunteering to give up his own life. (In a familiar example, A can save the lives of five only by volunteering to give up his own organs—heart, kidneys, and lungs.)

We may suppose that people at large will be happier if he proceeds than if he does not, for four more will live if he proceeds than if he does not. Does it follow that he ought to proceed? It is hard to see how anyone could sensibly claim that this does follow.

We might describe that reason for objecting to Utilitarianism as issuing from the fact that the requirements of generosity are limited.

(iv-b) The second issues from requirements of justice. Suppose that A can save the lives of five only by killing an innocent bystander. (In a familiar example, A is a transplant surgeon who can save the lives of five only by killing a bystander and distributing his organs to the five.) We may suppose that people at large will be happier if he proceeds than if he does not, for four more will live if he proceeds. Does it follow that he ought to proceed? A would be acting unjustly if he did—and therefore ought not.

And (iv-c), the Utilitarian's ground for the conclusion that A ought to do a thing, whether the doing is an acting or refraining from acting, seems to slide by it on the wrong track. Why ought I help Smith, when I ought to? Because *he* needs me to. Why ought I refrain from harming Jones, when I ought to? Because of what my harming him is my doing to *him*. That people at large will be happier if I act or refrain from acting is no doubt relevant, but typically is not what makes the directive true.

So why does Utilitarianism strike so many people as plausible? It does so for two reasons. First, Consequentialism strikes them as true—indeed, it strikes them as an obvious truth. Whether a person ought to do a thing is *of course* fixed by whether the world will be better if he does it than if he does not. Even those who object to

Consequentialism are sensitive to its appeal. As I said in chapter I, it seems to many people that those who resist Consequentialism have the burden of proof. For how could it be perfectly all right to do what will issue in the world's being less good than you might make it be?

And second, they think that if the people who live in one world are happier than the people who live in another, then it follows that the one world is better than the other. After all, what ultimately matters to people is how happy they are, and what else could mark one world as better than another if *not* how happy the people who live in it are?

But if there is no such relation as being a better world, so that Consequentialism has to be rejected, then the Utilitarian cannot argue that we ought to do what will make the world happier on the ground that a happier world is a better world, and for *that* reason we ought to prefer it. He has to argue from the relative happiness of a pair of worlds directly to a conclusion about which we ought to prefer—an idea that is made at a minimum suspect by the four kinds of difficulty I have drawn attention to.

There is room for a Utilitarian to say that I have grossly oversimplified his view. He did not mean that we ought to prefer the world in which there is simply, quantitatively, *more* happiness. He meant that we ought to prefer the world in which there is more equitably-distributed-happiness. Or the world in which there is more equitably-distributed-higher-level-appropriately-caused-happiness. Or the world in which there is more equitably-distributed-higher-level-appropriately-caused-happiness and enough of it to make life more than merely just barely worth living. Or. . . . I stop surveying the possibilities here. It is not clear that *any* of them will enable the Utilitarian to overcome the difficulties of all of the four kinds I mentioned—and in particular, those of the fourth kind.

There is also room for theories that might be called versions of Constrained Utilitarianism. I have in mind here theories designed precisely to overcome some or all of the difficulties of the fourth kind. Thus a Constrained Utilitarian might say that we ought to prefer the happier world except where acting on that preference would require violating a right. Another might say that we ought to prefer the happier world except where acting on that preference would require *either* violating a right *or* doing more than is required by generosity. While these theories are in one way more plausible than

Utilitarianism, in that they respond to one or more of the difficulties of the fourth kind, they are in another way at a disadvantage: they supply no story about the connection between the two considerations they say are determinative, namely happiness on the one hand, and the constraint or constraints on the other. A Utilitarian might well ask why we should accept that what we ought to do is subject to those constraints—if the constraints cannot be justified by a showing that they are warranted in light of their conducing to happiness. (If they could be justified by such a showing, then Constrained Utilitarianism would be reducible to Utilitarianism.)

3.

Here, anyway, is where we are. The goodness properties include properties that are instances of

(I) being a good K_{gf}
(II) being good-modified,
(III) being good-modified for a K,

and

(IV) being a good K_{gf} for a K.

The betterness-relations include relations that are instances of

(I-R) being a better K_{gf}
(II-R) being better-modified,
(III-R) being better-modified for a K,

and

(IV-R) being a better K_{gf} for a K.

They are all favorable evaluative properties or relations, though some are also unfavorable properties and relations.

There are other favorable evaluative properties and relations. For example, if I say, "A is a great chess player," I ascribe a property that is surely a favorable evaluative property, but it is not an instance of (I), (II), (III, or (IV). If I say "A is a better chess player than B by more than C is a better chess player than D," I ascribe a favorable evaluative relation, but it is not an instance of (I-R), (II-R), (III-R), or (IV-R). No matter. These are not interestingly different from the properties and relations we have been attending to.

There are others, however, that are interestingly different. Let us look at some of them.

V

Virtue/Kind Properties

1.

What I will call "virtue/kind properties" are particularly important.

I begin with virtues. Mostly when we say that something is a virtue, what we are calling a virtue can be more narrowly described as a moral virtue. We say that justice, generosity, kindness, and so on, are virtues; that is because they are moral virtues. But we do sometimes use the word "virtue" more broadly.[1] For example, being sharp is a virtue in a carving knife. Having good eyesight is a virtue in a seeing eye dog. Being a fast typist is a virtue in a stenographer. But those are not moral virtues. Unless I make clear otherwise, I will throughout use the word "virtue" in the broader sense—the moral virtues I will mostly call exactly that, "moral virtues".

I take it that the form of an ascription of a virtue is "F is a virtue in a K," where F is some property and K is some kind. So we will need to re-express two of the three examples I gave.

My first example was "Being sharp is a virtue in a carving knife." Is there such a property as being sharp? A knife is sharp if it has a sharp edge. A pencil point is sharp if its point is sharp. Is "sharp" ambiguous? Is it an attributive? Let us bypass those questions. Let us say that the property we are concerned with here is (not being sharp

---

[1] Here is an early example from the *Oxford English Dictionary*: "If it bee the vertue of a horse to goe well; if it be the vertue of a knife to cut well, if it be the vertue of a Soldier to fight well" (1631). A later example is: "The virtue of a pipe is to be smooth and hollow" (1841–4). I am sure that those "the"s are out of order. No doubt it is *a* virtue of a soldier to fight well; another is to obey appropriate orders.

but) being a sharp carving knife. And let us say that it is *that* property that is a virtue in a carving knife—thus:

> (1) Being a sharp carving knife is a virtue in a carving knife.

My second example was "Having good eyesight is a virtue in a seeing eye dog." Is there a property 'having good eyesight' that is shared by some human beings, seeing eye dogs, mice, fish, and cockroaches? Let us bypass this question too. Let us say that the property we are concerned with here is (not having good eyesight but) being a seeing eye dog that has good eyesight for a seeing eye dog. And let us say that it is that property that is a virtue in a seeing eye dog—thus:

> (2) Being a seeing eye dog that has good eyesight for a seeing eye dog is a virtue in a seeing eye dog.

I take it that my third example is not problematic in that way. That is, I take it that there is such a property as being a fast typist. No doubt that is vague. (How fast a typist does a typist have to be if he or she is to be a fast typist?) But so is being a sharp carving knife, and so also are almost all of the properties we have been and will be dealing with. So I take it that we can say:

> (3) Being a fast typist is a virtue in a stenographer.

And now: what makes (1), (2), and (3) true?

2.

The kinds 'carving knife', 'seeing eye dog', and 'stenographer' are goodness-fixing kinds, and that suggests an idea, namely that we should say, quite generally, that F is a virtue in a K only if K is a goodness-fixing kind. It is plain, after all, that a property's being a virtue in a K issues from considerations having to do, in *some* way, with what marks a K as a good K.

How should those considerations be accommodated? Being a sharp carving knife is surely among the properties that a carving knife has to have if it is to be a good carving knife.[2] Being a seeing

---

[2] What is required of a carving knife if it is to be a good one is presumably not

eye dog that has good eyesight for a seeing eye dog is surely among the properties that a seeing eye dog has to have if it is to be a good seeing eye dog. Being a fast typist is surely among the properties that a stenographer has to have if he or she is to be a good stenographer. So let us try:

> For F to be a virtue in a K is for it to be the case that
> (i) K is a goodness-fixing kind, and
> (ii) a K is a good K only if it has F.

That won't really do, however, for an obvious reason. What I have in mind is that accepting it commits us to the conclusion that being a carving knife is a virtue in a carving knife. For (i) the kind carving knife is a goodness-fixing kind, and (ii) a carving knife is a good carving knife only if it has being a carving knife. But that conclusion can hardly be right.

The simplest way to avoid that difficulty is to revise what we have so far by adding a third clause that rules it out. Thus let us say, instead:

> For F to be a virtue in a K is for it to be the case that
> (i) K is a goodness-fixing kind, and
> (ii) a K is a good K only if it has F, and
> (iii) it is possible for there to be a K that lacks F.

It is not possible for a carving knife to lack being a carving knife, so this account of the matter does not yield that being a carving knife is a virtue in a carving knife. At the same time, the revision makes no trouble for the truth of (1), (2), and (3).

A more interesting objection is not avoided by making that revision. I am sure that the following should turn out to be true:

> (4) Being capable of creating great mathematics is a virtue in a mathematician.

---

being a sharp carving knife throughout its life, but rather: being a carving knife that is capable of holding a sharp edge for a considerable time through normal use for the purpose for which carving knives are manufactured. (Carving meat, not wood.) But I will abbreviate: it will be that complex property that I refer to by the words "being a sharp carving knife".

On the other hand, I should think that one can be a good mathematician without being capable of creating great mathematics; and
that means that for this example, clause (ii) is false.

So we must weaken clause (ii). Here is an intuitively plausible
way of doing so:

> For F to be a virtue in a K is for it to be the case that
> (i) K is a goodness-fixing kind, and
> (ii) a K is as good a K as a K can be only if it has F, and
> (iii) it is possible for there to be a K that lacks F.

For this allows us to have that (1) through (4) are all true. It allows
us to have that being a sharp carving knife is a virtue in a carving
knife, since a carving knife is as good a carving knife as a carving
knife can be only if it has being a sharp carving knife. A seeing eye
dog is as good a seeing eye dog as a seeing eye dog can be only if
it has good eyesight for a seeing eye dog. A stenographer is as good
a stenographer as a stenographer can be only if he or she is a good
typist. And a mathematician is as good a mathematician as a mathematician can be only if he or she is capable of creating great mathematics.

It might pay to notice that this analysis also yields:

> (5) Being capable of creating good mathematics is a virtue in
>   a mathematician.

Being capable of creating good mathematics doesn't mark you as a
great mathematician; but a mathematician is as good a mathematician as a mathematician can be only if he or she is capable of creating good mathematics. But that is all to the good: we should
welcome (5) along with (4).

A difficulty remains. I should think that there are possible worlds
in which some seeing eye dogs are able to read street signs and
subway maps for their masters. Surely the seeing eye dogs in that
world that have that ability are better seeing eye dogs than those
that lack it. But then we had better grant that a seeing eye dog in
our world is as good a seeing eye dog as a seeing eye dog *can* be
only if it is able to read. Alas, the analysis we are looking at therefore yields:

(6) Being able to read is a virtue in a seeing eye dog—

at best an unfortunate outcome of an analysis of the virtues.

I don't know of any wholly happy way of avoiding that difficulty. Should we add a clause to the effect that there actually are Ks that have F? That would rule out (6). But that is arguably too strong a requirement. Mightn't it be the case that F is a virtue in a K, but alas, things being as they sadly are in our imperfect world, no Ks actually have that virtue?

On the other hand, I don't think that this is a deep difficulty, and that we should opt for a way of avoiding it that is suggested by the case that generated it. I take it that although it is (metaphysically) possible for there to be a dog that can read, that is not nomologically possible, dogs being what they are. Thus that we should opt for:

> (Virtues Analysis) For F to be a virtue in a K is for it to be the
> case that
> (i) K is a goodness-fixing kind, and
> (ii) a K is as good a K as a K can be only if it has F, and
> (iii) it is possible for there to be a K that lacks F, and
> (iv) it is not nomologically impossible for there to be a K
> that has F.

That does not yield (6)—while still allowing us to have (1) through (5).

At the same time, opting for this analysis allows us to have that being able to read *would* be a virtue in a seeing eye dog if it *were* nomologically possible for dogs to read: it allows us to have that in any possible world in which seeing eye dogs *are* able to read, being able to read *is* a virtue in a seeing eye dog. So it allows us to have that, although (6) isn't in fact true, it could have been. Thus on this account of the matter, the proposition that F is a virtue in a K is contingent—which I think is as it should be.

On the other hand, the analysis yields that nothing is a virtue in a pebble or a smudge or a cloud, and that too is as it should be.

3.

It pays us to spread the net and take note of some more examples.

First, some that are obvious: being a good carving knife is a virtue in a carving knife, and being a good seeing eye dog is a virtue in a seeing eye dog. Quite generally, being a good K is a virtue in a K.

More interesting, being a witty comedy is a virtue in a comedy. Being a witty joke is a virtue in a joke. Being a pleasant receptionist is a virtue in a receptionist. Being such as to taste good if eaten raw is a virtue in an eating apple.

On the other hand, being a witty funeral oration is not a virtue in a funeral oration. Being a pleasant plumber is not a virtue in a plumber. (Pleasantness is very welcome in a plumber, but a disagreeable plumber may be a better plumber than any pleasant plumber.) Being able to create great mathematics is not a virtue in a poet. And being such as to taste good if eaten raw is not a virtue in a receptionist, plumber, or poet.

Here are some more examples. On the assumption I invited you to make, namely that the kind 'human being'—for brevity, the kind 'person'—is a goodness-fixing kind, being a just person is a virtue in a person. Being a generous person is a virtue in a person. Being a just government is a virtue in a government. Being a courageous person—a conscientious person, a loyal person, a prudent person—is a virtue in a person. These are moral virtues, of course, but it is worth noticing that they are, also, (simply) virtues in their possessors, and that they are so in light of meeting the very same condition the meeting of which marks being a sharp carving knife as a virtue in a carving knife.

We should notice, finally, that, on this account of the matter, being a clever liar is a virtue in a liar. (The following is plainly true: a liar is as good a liar as a liar can be only if he or she is a clever liar. And it hardly needs saying that some liars are clever liars.) So be it. Being a clever liar is certainly not a moral virtue in a liar. But our use of "virtue" here is the broad one, and being a clever liar *is* in that broad use a virtue in a liar—just as while being a sharp carving knife is not a moral virtue in a carving knife, it is a virtue in a carving knife.

4.

Let us now say that a property is a virtue/kind property just in case it is an instance of

(V) being a K that has F,

where F is a virtue in a K.

Here is an example. Since being a sharp carving knife is a virtue in a carving knife, the property 'being a carving knife that has being a sharp carving knife' is a virtue-kind property. Since the property 'being a carving knife that has being a sharp carving knife' is identical with the property 'being a sharp carving knife', the property 'being a sharp carving knife' is a virtue/kind property.

Again, since being a seeing eye dog that has good eyesight for a seeing eye dog is a virtue in a seeing eye dog, the property 'being a seeing eye dog that has being a seeing eye dog that has good eyesight for a seeing eye dog' is a virtue-kind property. Since the property 'being a seeing eye dog that has being a seeing eye dog that has good cycsight for a seeing eye dog' is identical with the property 'being a seeing eye dog that has good eyesight for a seeing eye dog', the property 'being a seeing eye dog that has good eyesight for a seeing eye dog' is a virtue-kind property.

So here are two virtue/kind properties:

> being a sharp carving knife
> being a seeing eye dog that has good eyesight for a seeing
> eye dog.

Similar reasoning yields that the following are also virtue/kind properties:

> being a witty comedy
> being a witty joke
> being a pleasant receptionist
> being a just person
> being a generous person
> being a good carving knife
> being a good seeing eye dog.

Consideration of the last two examples on that list suggests a small thesis. Let K be any goodness-fixing kind. It follows that there is such a property as being a good K. Being a good K is a virtue in a K. Then the property 'being a K that has being a good K' is a virtue-kind property. That property is identical with the property 'being a good K'. It follows that the property 'being a good K' is a virtue-kind property. In short, every property that is an instance of

(I) being a good K_{gf}

is also an instance of (V), and thus is also a virtue/kind property.

5.

Let us now return to the evaluatives. I suggest that we should accept a larger thesis: all virtue/kind properties are favorable evaluative properties.

We already know that some virtue/kind properties are favorable evaluative properties, for the small thesis we just looked at says that every goodness property that is an instance of (I) is a virtue/kind property. But every goodness property is a favorable evaluative property. So *some* virtue/kind properties are favorable evaluative properties.

It is intuitively clear that being a just person and being a generous person are favorable evaluative properties. Presumably it is also intuitively clear that being a seeing eye dog that has good eyesight for a seeing eye dog is a favorable evaluative property. What warrants those intuitions? Saying

> A is a just person
> B is a generous person
> C is a seeing eye dog that has good eyesight for a seeing eye
>   dog

is *praising* A, B, and C.
   Similarly, I suggest, for saying

> A is a sharp carving knife
> B is a witty comedy
> C is a pleasant receptionist.

Saying these things is not praising A, B, and C *simpliciter,* for there is nothing praiseworthy in a thing in that it is a carving knife, comedy, or receptionist. But saying those things is praising A *qua* carving knife, B *qua* comedy, and C *qua* receptionist.

It is worth stress that saying those words *is* praising A *qua* carving knife, B *qua* comedy, and C *qua* receptionist—it cannot with any degree of plausibility be said that since a person who says those words does not use the word "good", his saying what he says is his merely supplying ground for praise. If the movie critic of a newspaper writes of a movie just out, "It's a witty comedy," it won't do at all to say that he hasn't praised it, on the ground that he didn't write the words, "It's a good comedy." A letter of recommendation for a student might contain no occurrence of the word "good" and yet be rightly regarded by its recipients, not merely as a ground for praise of the student but as, itself, praise of the student—as for example, a letter that ascribes "ingenious", "imaginative", "deep", and so on. "Good", says the *Oxford English Dictionary*, is the most general adjective of commendation, but it is not the only one. There are any number that are less general.

Compare dispraise. Consider: "Shelley's poetry is repetitive, vaporous, monotonously self-regarding, and often emotionally cheap, and so, in no very long run, boring, . . ."[3] Anyone who thinks that since that sentence does not contain the word "bad", the writer is not dispraising Shelley's poetry should really think again. We don't just *happen to* mind being bored, as we might happen to dislike carrots.

We can go deeper: we can explain why saying

   A is a sharp carving knife
   B is a witty comedy
   C is a pleasant receptionist

is praising A *qua* carving knife, B *qua* comedy, and C *qua* receptionist: saying those words is ascribing virtue/kind properties to A, B, and C. If 'being a K that has F' is a virtue/kind property, then (according to the Virtues Analysis) ascribing it to a K is ascribing to the K a property such that a K isn't as good a K as a K can be unless it has the property. No wonder ascribing the property 'being a K that has F' to a K is praising it.

In sum, ascribing *any* virtue/kind property is praising, and thus all of them are favorable evaluative properties.

6.

We might do well to stop for a moment for a glance back at G. E. Moore. I said in the preceding section that being a pleasant recep-

---

[3] F. R. Leavis, *The Common Pursuit* (London: Chatto & Windus, 1952), 221.

tionist is a virtue/kind property, and therefore a favorable evaluative property. Pleasant? Being pleasant was one of Moore's paradigm examples of a natural property!

There is a question that arises straightway: what is the property Moore had in mind by "being pleasant"? Is there a property 'being pleasant' that is shared by pleasant receptionists, pleasant movies, and pleasant experiences? (Compare: is there a property 'being witty' that is shared by witty comedies and witty people? Indeed, is there a property 'being just' that is shared by just people, just acts, and just governments?) Having asked that question, I now recommend that we bypass it. There is anyway such a property as being a pleasant receptionist.

Let us ask instead: what is a natural property? I drew attention in footnote 6 of chapter I to the very dark characterization of that notion that Moore supplied in *Principia*. In the second preface to *Principia*, which Moore later wrote but never finished, he said that what he had had in mind at the time of writing *Principia* was that a natural property is a "property with which it is the business of the natural sciences or Psychology to deal, or which can be completely defined in terms of such" (*Principia*, 13). This is less dark but puzzling all the same. I take it that being a carving knife, an umbrella, a bathtub, are not properties it is the business of the natural sciences or Psychology to deal with, or which can be completely defined in terms of properties they do deal with; are we to conclude that they are not natural properties? (And are we to conclude that, like goodness, they are nonnatural properties?)

An idea that Moore came to find more attractive in post-*Principia* writing was this: a natural property is a property such that to ascribe it to a thing is to describe the thing.[4]

But if a natural property is a property such that to ascribe it to a thing is to describe the thing, then there is no inconsistency in a property's being a natural property and its also being such that to

---

[4] Though Moore was markedly more cautious about this idea than the others who opted for it were. In his "A Reply to My Critics," he said that the idea was not clear, and that "to make it clear it would be necessary to specify the sense of 'describe' in question,"—and he said he was no more able to do this in 1942 than he had been in 1922, when he first considered the idea (G. E. Moore, "A Reply to My Critics," *The Philosophy of G. E. Moore*, ed. P. A. Schilpp [Evanston, IL: Northwestern University Press, 1942], 591).

ascribe it to a thing is to praise the thing. For there is no inconsistency in a property's being such that to ascribe it to a thing is to describe the thing, and its being such that to ascribe it to the thing is to praise the thing. Being a sharp carving knife, being a witty comedy, and being a pleasant receptionist are examples of properties of which both are true.

7.

We looked in section 2 at what it comes to for a property F to be a virtue in a K. Among the virtues in a person are being a just person and being a generous person. However these are commonly said to be, not merely virtues in a person, but moral virtues in a person. And there are virtues of other kinds too.

Let us say that for any property F and kind K,

> F is a *moral* virtue in a K just in case:
> (ii) a K is morally as good a K as a K can be only if it has F, and
> (iii) it is possible for there to be a K that lacks F, and
> (iv) it is not nomologically impossible for there to be a K that has F.

Being a just person and being a generous person obviously pass this test for being moral virtues in a person. So also do all of the other virtues-that-are-moral-virtues that I mentioned in section 3 above.[5] Being a highly intelligent person, however, does not—and rightly so.

It will hardly have been overlooked that that definition of "moral virtue in a K" omits the requirement (i) that K be a goodness-fixing

---

[5] I add a word in passing about prudence. Some people say that being a prudent person isn't a moral virtue in a person. That is because they think of prudence as entirely self-regarding; that is, they take it that the prudent person is one who is careful about and only about his or her own interests, and that morality has nothing to say about that. That strikes me as a very odd idea. On the one hand, it seems to me plain that prudence in respect of one's own interests really is morally called for. On the other hand, prudence in respect of the interests of others is surely morally called for on any plausible view of the deliverances of morality. (It is a strong moral count against a person that he or she is an imprudent parent or trustee.)

kind. And so it should. The kind 'act' is not a goodness-fixing kind, yet we can surely say that being a just act and being a generous act are moral virtues in an act.

What is at work here is the fact that "morally good" is a good-modifier, just as "good for Jones to use to replace the pawn he just lost" is a good-modifier. So while a thing can be a good K only if K is a goodness-fixing kind, a thing can be a K that is morally good, or a K that is good for Jones to use to replace the pawn he just lost, even if K is not a goodness-fixing kind.

People also have virtues of other kinds. Being a highly intelligent person is an intellectual virtue in a person, and so also is being a rational person. Being an ingenious, imaginative, deep mathematician are intellectual virtues in a mathematician. That they are is yielded by

> F is an *intellectual* virtue in a K just in case:
>> (ii) a K is intellectually as good a K as a K can be only if it has F, and
>> (iii) it is possible for there to be a K that lacks F, and
>> (iv) it is not nomologically impossible for there to be a K that has F.

Note that this yields, as it should, that being a clever liar is an intellectual virtue in a liar.

Being a healthy person is a physical virtue in a person, and so also are being a strong person, and being a person who has good eyesight, and being a person who has good hearing. That they are is yielded by

> F is a *physical* virtue in a K just in case:
>> (ii) a K is physically as good a K as a K can be only if it has F, and
>> (iii) it is possible for there to be a K that lacks F, and
>> (iv) it is not nomologically impossible for there to be a K that has F.

Being a pleasant person is a social virtue in a person, and so also are being a charming, witty, courteous person. That they are is yielded by

F is a *social* virtue in a K just in case:
>   (ii) a K is socially as good a K as a K can be only if it has
>   F, and
>   (iii) it is possible for there to be a K that lacks F, and
>   (iv) it is not nomologically impossible for there to be a K
>   that has F.[6]

Note that there is overlap here. I should think that being a courteous person, for example, is a moral virtue in a person as well as a social virtue in a person. (Not so being a charming person.) No matter. Exclusiveness is not a virtue in the list we are constructing.

We can in a similar way accommodate esthetic virtues: being a graceful dancer is an esthetic virtue in a dancer, and being an interesting novel is an esthetic virtue in a novel. (On a broad construal of the category of the esthetic, we can also say that being an enjoyable experience is an esthetic virtue in an experience.) Similarly, there may be strategic, tactical, and political virtues in a plan or act.

No doubt there are other kinds of virtue; I leave it to intuition which they are.

We can call the moral, intellectual, physical, . . . virtues "virtue-modifiers". (Compare a thing's being 'good-modified'.) With them in hand, we can single out what we might call "virtue-modified/kind properties", as we singled out virtue/kind properties. I omit the details.

8.

In sum, we have in hand an analysis of what it is for a property to be a virtue in a K, and thereby what it is for a property to be a virtue/kind property—and it is clear that virtue/kind properties are favorable evaluative properties. Thus the favorable evaluative properties we have looked at so far include not only all instances of

>   (I) being a good K_{gf},
>   (II) being modified-good,
>   (III) being modified-good for a K,

---

[6] Hume characterizes these properties as "immediately agreeable to others"—see his "Of Qualities Immediately Agreeable to Others," *An Enquiry Concerning the Principles of Morals*, section VIII—and includes them among the virtues.

and

(IV) being a good K_{gf} for a K,

they also include all instances of

(V) being a K that has F,

where F is a virtue in a K.

There are relations in the offing here too. For example, we might call

being a sharper carving knife

a virtue-kind relation. These are favorable evaluative relations. But they raise no interesting new questions, so I do not stop to discuss them.

The fact that our thinking is so rich in normativity does not issue just from the fact that we ascribe such a wide range of properties by use of the word "good": it issues also from the enormous variety of virtue/kind properties that we ascribe to the things around us. We turn to a particularly interesting group of virtue/kind properties in the following chapter.

VI

Correctness Properties (Acts)

1.

If a person says, "A is correct," does he ascribe a property to A? What property? Correctness? Consider a certain map. It may be a map of the highway system of England, and also a map of the railway system of England. Suppose it is a correct map of the highway system. That is compatible with its not being a correct map of the railway system. So there are kinds K_1 and K_2 such that: A is a K_1 and a K_2, and A is a correct K_1 but not a correct K_2. We should therefore conclude that "correct" is—like "good"—an attributive adjective.

By way of reminder, K is a goodness-fixing kind just in case what being a K is itself sets the standards that a K has to meet if it is to be good *qua* K. The kinds toaster, seeing eye dog, and tennis player are goodness-fixing kinds. Let us now say that K is a correctness-fixing kind just in case what being a K is itself sets the standards that a K has to meet if it is to be correct *qua* K. Being a map of England is being a representation of England, and that itself sets the following standard for being correct *qua* map of England: being a map of England such that the propositions it represents as true of England *are* true of England. So the kind 'map of England' is a correctness-fixing kind.

Again, consider the kind 'performing of Mozart's C Major Sonata (k. 545)'. I from here on abbreviate that expression as: performing of Mozart's S. What being a performing of Mozart's S is itself set the standards that a performing of Mozart's S has to meet if it is to be correct *qua* performing of Mozart's S: the performer has to perform it correctly—that is, in accord with Mozart's choices in composing S. Again, what being a spelling of the word "chiaroscuro" is itself sets

83

the standards that a spelling of that word has to meet if it is to be correct *qua* spelling of that word: the speller has to spell it correctly—that is, in accord with the then current practice.[1] (As things now stand, that requires him to spell it as follows: c-h-i-a-r-o-s-c-u-r-o. Spellings of words change, however, and there might come at time at which spelling it correctly requires spelling it differently.) So the kinds 'performing of Mozart's S' and 'spelling of the word "chiaroscuro"' are also correctness-fixing kinds.

In chapter II, I argued that there is such a property as being a good K just in case K is a goodness-fixing kind, thus just in case it is an instance of

(I) being a good K_{gf}.

I suggest that we should agree, for analogous reasons, that there is such a property as being a correct K just in case K is a correctness-fixing kind, thus just in case it is an instance of

(VI) being a correct K_{cf}.

There are such properties as being a good toaster, but no such property as being a good pebble; similarly, there are such properties as being a correct map of England, but no such properties as being a correct pebble, or being a correct toaster.

I called properties that are instances of (I) goodness properties; let us call properties that are instances of (VI) correctness properties.

Correctness properties differ from each other, and from goodness properties, in a variety of interesting ways. I will bring out one in particular, namely that while all goodness properties are favorable evaluative properties, some correctness properties are and some are not.

2.

The kinds 'map of England', 'performing of Mozart's S', and 'spelling the word "chiaroscuro"' are correctness-fixing kinds, so here are three properties that are instances of (VI):

---

[1] These two examples come from Gideon Rosen's "Brandom on Modality, Normativity and Intentionality," *Philosophy and Phenomenological Research* 63, no. 3 (November 2001). He points out that examples such as these show that "'correct' has application where 'true' does not."

being a correct map of England
being a correct performing of Mozart's S
being a correct spelling of the word "chiaroscuro".

These correctness properties are favorable evaluative properties. That they are follows from the fact that they are virtue/kind properties—and that they are virtue/kind properties emerges as follows. First, consider again:

> (Virtues Analysis) For F to be a virtue in a K is for it to be the case that
> (i) K is a goodness-fixing kind, and
> (ii) a K is as good a K as a K can be only if it has F, and
> (iii) it is possible for there to be a K that lacks F, and
> (iv) it is not nomologically impossible for there to be a K that has F.

We cannot say that correctness is a virtue in a map of England, since there is no such property as correctness. But we can say that being a correct map of England is a virtue in a map of England. For (i) the kind 'map of England' is not only a correctness-fixing kind, it is also a goodness-fixing kind. That is because what being a map of England is itself sets the standards that a map of England has to meet if it is to be good *qua* map of England. It is not easy to say in detail what exactly those standards are. (By contrast, it was easy to say what being correct *qua* map of England requires.) But it is clear enough that those standards include being a correct map of England. Better: being a close-enough-to-correct map of England. For a map of England might be a good one even if it is not the case that *everything* it represents about England is true of England. Its being good enough in other ways—informative, easy to understand, and so on—might outweigh the fact that it gets a small detail wrong. No matter: (i) the kind 'map of England' is a goodness-fixing kind.

Moreover, (ii) a map of England is as good a map of England as a map of England can be only if it does have 'being a correct map of England'. Also (iii) it is possible for there to be a map of England that lacks 'being a correct map of England', and (iv) it is not nomologically impossible for there to be a map of England that has 'being a correct map of England'. It follows that being a correct map of England is a virtue in a map of England.

It will be remembered, second, that a property is a virtue/kind property just in case it is an instance of

(V) being a K that has F,

where F is a virtue in a K. Since being a correct map of England is a virtue in a map of England, the following is a virtue/kind property:

> being a map of England that has being a correct map of England.

That property is identical with being a correct map of England. So being a correct map of England is a virtue/kind property.

And as I said, it follows that being a correct map of England is a favorable evaluative property.

Similar reasoning yields that the following are also favorable evaluative properties: being a correct performing of Mozart's S, and being a correct spelling of the word "chiaroscuro".

3.

Two of the kinds we just looked at, namely

> performing of Mozart's Sonata S
> spelling of the word "chiaroscuro",

are kinds whose members are acts. Let us look at a particularly interesting group of kinds whose members are acts, namely assertings. Suppose that A asked, "Who is Alice's brother?" and that several people answered. Suppose that some of them answered by asserting that Bert is Alice's brother. If so, then there were acts of the kind

> asserting that Bert is Alice's brother.

Is that a correctness-fixing kind? Yes. But we need to notice that there are two ways in which an asserting that Bert is Alice's brother can be correct *qua* asserting that Bert is Alice's brother. We might call them internal correctness and external correctness.

Internal correctness and incorrectness in assertings are of special interest in language classes. Suppose that A is the teacher of a class in English as a Second Language. She asked, "Who is Alice's brother?" Smith and Jones both asserted that Bert is Alice's brother, but while Smith did so by saying the words, "Bert is Alice's brother," Jones (a slower student) did so by saying the words, "Bert are Alice's brother." Then A may report what happened by saying the words:

(1) Smith asserted that Bert is Alice's brother correctly,

but

(2) Jones asserted that Bert is Alice's brother incorrectly.

We may suppose that the propositions that A asserts by saying those words are like propositions to the effect that so and so performed Mozart's S correctly, or incorrectly, and propositions to the effect that so and so spelled the word "chiaroscuro" correctly, or incorrectly, in the following respect: their truth turns on *how* the agent did what he did. Did the agent, or didn't he, carry out the enterprise of asserting X, performing Y, or spelling Z correctly? Then by hypothesis, A is right: the propositions she asserts by saying (1) and (2) are both true.

I stress that it doesn't matter to the truth of the propositions A asserts by saying (1) and (2) whether Bert is Alice's brother. The proposition she asserts by saying (1) is true even if Bert isn't Alice's brother, and the proposition she asserts by saying (2) is true even if Bert is Alice's brother.

Now though asserting is like performing and spelling in being an enterprise that one can carry out correctly or incorrectly, it is unlike performing and spelling in having a propositional content, and that opens an agent's engaging in it to assessment of correctness or incorrectness of a different kind, which I am calling external. Suppose that Bert isn't Alice's brother. Knowing that, and wanting to make a point of it, *we* may say the words:

Smith and Jones both asserted, incorrectly, that Bert is Alice's brother.

By hypothesis, we too are right: the proposition we thereby assert is true.

In order to signal the difference between the propositions asserted by A, on the one hand, and the proposition asserted by us, on the other hand, I made use of a syntactical device English provides us with for signaling that difference. But it is a rather delicate device, and people don't always make use of it. It would not really have been a misuse of language on our part if to make the point we had wanted to make, we had instead said the words:

> Smith and Jones both asserted that Bert is Alice's brother incorrectly.

So there is in fact an ambiguity here. To avoid it, let us from here on say

> X asserted that Bert is Alice's brother internal-correctly

when we wish to assert the proposition that is true just in case X asserted that Bert is Alice's brother, and carried out the enterprise of doing so correctly; and let us from here on say

> X asserted that Bert is Alice's brother external-correctly

when we wish to assert the proposition that is true just in case X asserted that Bert is Alice's brother, and the propositional content of his act of asserting—namely the proposition that Bert is Alice's brother—is true.

We will look at some other kinds whose members are speech acts. But we need to stop first to discuss an objection to what I have just said about correctness in asserting.

4.

Timothy Williamson has argued that the following normative constraint governs asserting:

> (Knowledge Rule) One must: assert that p only if one knows that p.[2]

---

[2] Timothy Williamson, *Knowledge and Its Limits* (Oxford: Oxford University Press, 2000), ch. 11.

A startling thesis! For "must" is a very strong normative term: judgments to the effect that someone must do a thing are strong directives—stronger than the examples I gave at the outset, which were judgments to the effect that someone ought to do a thing. We will start looking at the directives in chapter VIII, and it might therefore be thought that we should postpone discussion of the Knowledge Rule.

Not so. I suggest that Williamson's argument for the Knowledge Rule does not support it. What it supports is at most the markedly weaker

> (Weak Knowledge Rule) An act of asserting that p is a correct asserting that p only if the asserter knows that p,

and that is immediately relevant to our concerns here, since neither of the two ways in which I said an asserting that p can be correct requires that the asserter know that p. For what I call internal-correctness requires only correctness in carrying out the asserting enterprise, and what I call external-correctness requires only truth.

I begin by bringing out that (i) Williamson's argument for the Knowledge Rule supports, at most, the Weak Knowledge Rule. I will then argue that (ii) the Weak Knowledge Rule should be rejected.

5.

To begin with (i). Williamson says about the role of the word "must" in the Knowledge Rule: "As used here, 'must' expresses the kind of obligation characteristic of constitutive rules." An example of what he has in mind by "constitutive rules" is the body of rules that govern the playing of a game—in particular, the rules such that what the game is is fixed by those rules. Tennis, for example. Or chess. Among the constitutive rules of chess, for example, is the rule that a bishop moves only on a diagonal, not either horizontally or vertically. And Williamson says: we should think of asserting as like a game. A person who asserts that p when he does not know that p breaks a rule of asserting just as a person who moves a bishop horizontally while playing chess breaks a rule of chess.

Alas for that idea, the rules of a game impose *no obligation of any kind* on the players. The rules of chess do not tell you what you are under an obligation to do. They do not tell you what you must, or even what you ought to do. Suppose you are playing chess, and it is your turn to move. You then learn that if you don't move your bishop horizontally, hundreds will die! Are you all the same under an obligation to not do so? Must you, ought you not do so? That idea is just silly.

We can say that the rules of chess tell us what counts as a move in chess. Or what counts as a legal move in chess. Or what counts as a correct move in chess. (Being a correct move in chess is not the same as being a strategically correct move in chess: a move that is a correct chess move may be a strategically incorrect chess move.) What we cannot say is that they are, or that they themselves license, directives. It is entirely consistent to say that a certain move would be correct though you ought not make it, and that a certain move would be incorrect though you ought to make it.

And so also for assertings. If asserting is governed by constitutive rules, as chess is, then those rules tell us at most what counts as asserting correctly or incorrectly.

In sum, then, (i) Williamson's argument for the Knowledge Rule supports, at most:

> (Weak Knowledge Rule) An act of asserting that p is a correct asserting that p only if the asserter knows that p.

6.

I suggest now that (ii) the Weak Knowledge Rule should be rejected.

In order to give the Weak Knowledge Rule the best run for its money, we should take it to be restricted to assertings of a special kind.

For there are any number of assertings about which it would be most implausible to say that they are incorrect assertings on the ground that the asserter does not know that what he asserts is true. Consider the jury in a civil suit. On the jury's return to the courtroom, the foreman, on request by the judge for the jury's verdict, asserts that the defendant is guilty. The foreman, we may suppose, does not know that the defendant is guilty. (The standard of proof in a civil suit is more-probable-than-not.) If the defendant turns out to not have been guilty, then we may well want to say that the foreman asserted, incorrectly, that the defendant was guilty. But it cannot plausibly be thought to follow from the fact that the foreman did not *know* that the defendant is guilty that the foreman's asserting that he is guilty was an incorrect asserting.

Again, consider exams. One of the questions on my history orals was, "Who won the battle of Shiloh?" I wasn't sure, but I took a stab at it and asserted that Grant won the battle of Shiloh. It cannot plausibly be thought that my asserting that Grant won the battle of Shiloh on that occasion was an incorrect asserting of that proposition, on the ground that I didn't *know* that Grant won it.

I am sure that Williamson would agree that the fact that the foreman and I did not know that what we asserted was true does not entail that our assertings were incorrect. He would say that these were not "flat-out" assertings—that is his term—and that it is only those that he had in mind.[3] I think that what he had in mind were what we might call "word-givings"—thus that the Weak Knowledge Rule is to be understood to apply to and only to assertings such that in asserting what he asserts an asserter is giving his word that what he asserts is true. I was not giving my word that Grant won the battle of Shiloh in asserting that he did in my history exam. (I wasn't merely guessing, but I was close to it.) And the foreman wasn't giving his word that the defendant was guilty. (He was delivering a verdict on the ground that it was more probable than not.) By contrast, if in saying "I will be in my office at 3" I am promising you that I will, then I am giving you my word that I will. If in saying "I saw Jones in the park yesterday" I mean for you to take my word for it that I did, then I am giving you my word that I did. So it is only assertings that are word-givings about which we should be asking whether the Weak Knowledge Rule is true.

Is it? Williamson argues for the Weak Knowledge Rule as follows. You bought a ticket in a large lottery. The drawing has by now been made. But the result of the drawing is still a secret—in particular, I do not know that your ticket did not win. Nevertheless, in light of the high probability that your ticket did not win, I assert to you, flat-

---

[3] Suppose we are French and are taking our first course in English. The teacher invites you, in French, to say, in English, that apples grow underground. You know perfectly well that apples grow on trees, but you nevertheless say the English sentence "Apples grow underground." I am sure that Williamson would say that you did not flat-out assert that apples grow underground. And perhaps we would do well to say that you not only did not flat-out assert that they do, you did not even assert that they do. You *said* they do, but you did not mean to commit yourself to their really doing so.

out, giving you my word: "Your ticket did not win." Let us suppose that what I asserted is true. Nevertheless, Williamson says,

> You will still be entitled to feel some resentment when you later dis-
> cover the merely probabilistic grounds for my assertion. I was repre-
> senting myself to you as having a kind of authority to make the flat-out
> assertion which in reality I lacked.[4]

What "kind of authority"? "Evidential authority". That is, I represented myself as having inside information, as knowing that your ticket did not win, whereas my evidence for the proposition that your ticket did not win was merely its high probability. Williamson concludes that my not having known that your ticket did not win shows that my asserting that it did not win was an incorrect asserting.

Williamson is surely right to say that you are entitled to feel resentment, given that I asserted, on merely probabilistic grounds, that your ticket did not win. And many people have been moved by Williamson's example to agree with the conclusion that he draws from it.

I suggest, however, that we shouldn't join them. We should say:

> (α) My asserting that your ticket did not win was a correct
> asserting,

since as a matter of fact your ticket did not win. However, to accom-
modate, the fact that you are entitled to feel resentment—indeed, to explain what makes it true that you are entitled to feel resentment—we should also say:

> (β) I ought not have asserted that your ticket did not win.

To begin with, it must be granted that (α) is consistent with (β). I said earlier that it is consistent to say that a certain chess move would be a correct chess move though you ought not make it. So also: it is consistent to say that an asserting was a correct asserting though the asserter ought not have asserted what he asserted.

Indeed, we must make room for that possibility. The gravamen of the charge against Smith might be the very fact that he asserted,

---

[4] Williamson, *Knowledge and Its Limits*, 246.

correctly, that Jones is hiding in the basement, despite the fact that those to whom Smith addressed himself were villains in search of Jones, to whom Smith ought to have said nothing or lied.

Nor is it only in cases where chess moves and speech acts are in question that we need to be able to say that a person did a thing correctly though he ought not have done what he did. We must make room for the possibility that a person performed Mozart's S correctly, or spelled the word "chiaroscuro" correctly, though— things being as they then were—he ought not have performed the sonata, or spelled the word.

I add now that we should not only grant that (α) is consistent with (β), we should say (α). For we should remember that a person may perform other speech acts *by* asserting something. Suppose that the reason why I asserted to you that your ticket did not win was that you had asked me whether your ticket won, thinking I had inside information about the drawing. In fact I had no inside information. Was my act of answering your question therefore an incorrect answering of it? Since by hypothesis, your ticket did not win, I take it that my answering your question was a correct answering of it—I take it to be a *datum* that it was. But it can't be thought that my answering was a correct answering, though the asserting, *by* which I answered, was an incorrect asserting.

Again, consider describing. Suppose it is important for you to find out what Smith looks like. Thinking that I know him, you ask me to describe him. I haven't the least idea what he looks like, but I describe him as follows: "He has brown hair and big teeth." In fact he does have brown hair and big teeth. Then I did describe Smith correctly—this is yet another *datum*. But it can't be thought that my describing of Smith was a correct describing of Smith though the asserting, *by* which I described Smith, was an incorrect asserting.

On the other hand, though my answering of your question was a correct answering of it, I ought not have answered as I did, since in answering as I did, I gave you the impression, not merely that your ticket did not win, which is true, but also that I knew it did not win, which is false. Though my describing of Smith was a correct describing of him, I ought not have described him as I did, since in describing him as I did, I gave you the impression, not merely that he has brown hair and big teeth, which is true, but also that I knew it, which is false. So also for the assertings I did, by the doing of which I answered and described.

Williamson's example is of great interest, but not because it shows that an asserting that p is a correct asserting that p only if the asserter knows that p. Rather because the example draws attention to something not typically noticed by moral theorists. It is a familiar enough fact that if you give a person your word that p, then he has a ground for complaint against you if not-p; and there is a substantial moral theoretic literature on the hard question what exactly makes that so—in short, on *how* giving a person your word that p gives him a ground for complaint against you if not-p. Williamson's example makes the further point that if you give a person your word that p, then he doesn't merely have a ground for complaint against you if not-p: he also has a ground for complaint against you if, although p, you don't know that p. What explains the familiar fact should also explain this further fact. (Neither is due to the constitutive rules of asserting, assuming that asserting has such rules.) This issue calls for closer attention than I can give it here, but whatever its resolution may be, we should in any case say:

(β) I ought not have asserted that your ticket did not win.

More important for our purposes, however, we should say:

(α) My asserting that your ticket did not win was a correct
asserting,

since as a matter of fact your ticket did not win. So we should reject the Weak Knowledge Rule.

We can have been tempted by that rule only if we were blind to the richness of the stock of concepts that we make use of in normative thinking. The idea that the concepts 'must', 'obligation', 'correct', and 'ought' come to pretty much the same—a smooth, warm, conceptual pudding—is just a mistake.

7.

We looked in section 3 at the following speech act kind:

asserting that Bert is Alice's brother.

And I said that it is a correctness-fixing kind, but that we need to distinguish between the properties 'being an internal-correct asserting that Bert is Alice's brother' and 'being an external-correct asserting that Bert is Alice's brother'.

Let us now look at some other speech act kinds, those that I will call *asserting-based speech act kinds*. What acts of these kinds have in common is that they are performed by asserting a proposition. I mentioned answerings and describings in the preceding section; let us also look at reportings and explainings. Thus let us focus on the kinds

> answering A's question
> describing B
> reporting what C did to D
> explaining why E kicked his cat.[5]

There are limits to the ranges of propositions P such that one can do these things by asserting P. In order to say what the range is for the first of those kinds, we need to be told what A's question *is*. Very well, suppose that A's question is, "Who is Alice's brother?" A person answers that question just in case he does so by asserting a proposition to the effect that so and so is Alice's brother. (If you say that nobody is Alice's brother since Alice doesn't have a brother, then you don't answer A's question, you reject it.) A person describes B just in case he does so by asserting a proposition to the effect that B has such and such a property. A person reports what C did to D just in case he does so by asserting a proposition to the effect that C did such and such to D. A person explains why E kicked his cat just in case he does so by asserting a proposition to the effect that E kicked his cat because of such and such. All the same, anyone who does any of these things does so by asserting a proposition.

They are plainly correctness-fixing kinds, and we need to distinguish here too between internal and external correctness.

Let us begin with internal correctness. Let "V_{act}-ing" be schematic for answering A's question, describing B, reporting what C did to D, and explaining why E kicked his cat. Then I take it we can say:

---

[5] By contrast, asking a question, reciting such and such poem, nominating Smith for president, ordering Jones to open the door, giving so and so permission to use your computer, and naming your dog "Fido" are speech act kinds, but they are not asserting-based speech act kinds, for acts of *these* kinds are not performed by asserting a proposition. We could call them noncommittal speech act kinds.

Smith V_{act}s internal-correctly at a time just in case he then asserts internal-correctly the proposition such that he then V_{act}s by asserting it.

That fact calls for explanation, however, since it is not due wholly to the fact that a person V_{act}s *by* asserting a proposition. People typically assert propositions *by* saying some words; yet it might be the case that a person says some words correctly (that is, he carries out his saying of them correctly), and thereby asserts a proposition, but does not assert the proposition internal-correctly. We met an example earlier. We supposed that A asked her students "Who is Alice's brother?" and that Jones said the words "Bert are Alice's brother." We may suppose that he said the words correctly (that is, he pronounced them correctly). By saying those words, he asserted the proposition that Bert is Alice's brother. But he did not assert that proposition internal-correctly.

Whether one asserts something by doing something, and if so what one thereby asserts, is fixed by an elaborate convention. It is due to the convention that a person who says the words "Bert is Alice's brother" thereby asserts that Bert is Alice's brother. It is also due to the convention that if you are asked who Alice's brother is, and you point to Bert by way of reply, then you have thereby asserted that Bert is Alice's brother. (The convention I refer to is the default convention. We might agree that for the rest of this evening, if one of us says the words "Bert is Alice's brother" to the others, he will thereby assert that the time has come for us to go home.)

We have to think of the convention as having two parts. One part fixes what counts as asserting this or that internal-correctly. The other part allows for misperformances. There is no sharp line to be drawn between asserting P but doing it incorrectly, and not asserting P at all. But some acts fall clearly on one side or the other. The child or the language student who says "Bert are Alice's brother" thereby asserts the proposition that Bert is Alice's brother, though he asserts it internal-incorrectly; specially adopted conventions apart, no one who says "Bert loves bananas" thereby asserts the proposition that Bert is Alice's brother.[6] (Compare the difference between

---

[6] Some, though I should think not all, legal conventions do not allow for mistakes in performance. Thus, if you haven't followed the convention for conveying title correctly, then you haven't conveyed title at all. Or married the couple before

performing Mozart's S incorrectly, and not succeeding in performing it at all.)

In short, it is in consequence of the fact that whether a person asserts P by saying some words is fixed by a convention that allows for misperformances that the following can happen: a person says such and such words correctly, and by saying them, asserts P, but he nevertheless asserts P internal-incorrectly.

To return to V_{act}-ings. Consider answering A's question. Suppose that A's question was Q. Whether a person answers Q by asserting P isn't fixed by a convention at all. A fortiori, it isn't fixed by a convention that allows for misperformances. Whether you answer Q by asserting P is fixed *wholly* by what Q and P are. And therefore if you answer Q by asserting P, then there is nothing that could mark your answering as internal-incorrect if your asserting is internal-correct.

Similarly for describing B, reporting what C did to D, and explaining why E kicked his cat. A person explains why E kicked his cat if and only if he does so by asserting a proposition to the effect that E kicked his cat because of such and such. So if you explain why E kicked his cat by asserting such a proposition, then there is nothing that could mark your explaining as internal-incorrect if your asserting is internal-correct.

To repeat, then,

> Smith V_{act}s internal-correctly at a time just in case he then asserts internal-correctly the proposition such that he then V_{act}s by asserting it.

What marks V_{act}-ings as *external*-correct is obvious:

> Smith V_{act}s external-correctly at a time just in case the proposition such that he then V_{act}s by asserting it is true.

8.

I have been using the nouns "asserting", "answering", "describing", "reporting", and "explaining" instead of the less clumsy nouns "asser-

---

you. Or registered to vote. Or nominated Jones for president. By contrast, we cut each other a considerable amount of slack in assertings in ordinary life. We have to—getting along in ordinary life requires it.

tion", "answer", "description", "report", and "explanation" for a reason. Following Jonathan Bennett, I will call the former imperfect
nominals and the latter perfect nominals.[7]

The imperfect nominals are unambiguous. "Smith's asserting that
p" always refers to an act of asserting by Smith, and similarly for
"Smith's answering A's question/describing B/reporting on what C
did to D/explaining why E kicked his cat". It was because I wished
to make clear in the preceding sections that it was acts that we were
talking about, that I used imperfect nominals to refer to them. The
perfect nominals, by contrast, are ambiguous.

Suppose Smith asserted that p. Then "Smith's assertion that p"
may be used to refer to his act of asserting; but it may be used to
refer instead to *what* Smith asserted—that is, it may be used to refer
to the propositional content of his act of asserting, thus to the
proposition that p. Again, suppose Smith answered A's question.
Then "Smith's answer to A's question" may be used to refer to his
act of answering; but it may be used to refer instead to what he
asserted, by the asserting of which he answered A's question—that
is, it may be used to refer to the propositional content of his act of
asserting, and thereby of his act of answering. Similarly for "Smith's
description of B/report on what C did to D/explanation of why E
kicked his cat".

For the sake of clarity, then, I will continue to use the imperfect
nominals to refer to acts, and I will from here on use the perfect
nominals to refer to and only to the propositional contents of acts—
thus to propositions.

We looked in the preceding section at what it is for assertings/
answerings/describings/reportings/explainings to be internal-correct
and external-correct. What about assertions/answers/descriptions/
reports/explanations? Since these things are propositions, there is no
such thing as their being internal-correct or internal-incorrect.
Correctness in these things is entirely external—and it obviously
consists in truth. Thus we can say: Smith's assertion/answer/descrip-
tion/report/explanation is a correct assertion/answer/description/
report/explanation just in case it is true.[8]

---

[7] Jonathan Bennett, *The Act Itself* (Oxford: Clarendon Press, 1995), 31.
[8] For further discussion of this claim, see Addendum 2 on Correctness.

9.

We should stop for a moment for a reminder of the main positive points that have emerged so far. I said in section 1 that the following are correctness-fixing kinds: 'map of England', 'performing of Mozart's S', and 'spelling of the word "chiaroscuro"'. In section 2, I showed that the following are virtue/kind properties:

> being a correct map of England
> being a correct performing of Mozart's S
> being a correct spelling of the word "chiaroscuro".

It follows that they are favorable evaluative properties.

We then turned to speech act kinds. In section 3, I said that the speech act kind 'asserting that p' is a correctness-fixing kind and I distinguished between:

> being an internal-correct asserting that p

and

> being an external-correct asserting that p.

In section 7, we turned to some asserting-based speech-act kinds, namely 'answering A's question', 'describing B', reporting what C did to D', and 'explaining why E kicked his cat'. These are also correctness-fixing kinds, and here too we need to distinguish between internal and external correctness. Thus letting "V_{act}-ing" be schematic for answering A's question, describing B, reporting what C did to D, and explaining why E kicked his cat, we need to distinguish between

> being an internal-correct V_{act}-ing

and

> being an external-correct V_{act}-ing.

In short, an instance of one or other of these speech act kinds is internal-correct just in case the speaker carries out the speech enterprise correctly, and external-correct just in case the propositional content of his act is true.

We have now to ask whether these properties too are favorable evaluative properties.

10.

Let us begin with V_{act}-ings.

It is easy to see that properties that are instances of

being an internal-correct V_{act}-ing

are favorable evaluative properties since it is easy to see that they are virtue/kind properties.

Consider answerings of A's question. Being an internal-correct answering of A's question is a virtue in an answering of A's question. For (i) the kind 'answering A's question' is not merely a correctness-fixing kind, it is a goodness-fixing kind. That is because what being an answering of A's question is itself sets the standards that an answering of A's question has to meet if it is to be good *qua* answering of A's question: the answerer has to answer A's question well. Also, (ii), an answering of A's question is as good an answering of A's question as an answering of A's question can be only if it has 'being an internal-correct answering of A's question'. And (iii) it is possible for there to be an answering of A's question that lacks 'being an internal-correct answering of A's question', and (iv) it is not nomologically impossible for there to be an answering of A's question that has 'being an internal-correct answering of A's question'.

Since being an internal-correct answering of A's question is a virtue in an answering of A's question, being an answering of A's question that has 'being an internal-correct answering of A's question' is a virtue/kind property. Being an answering of A's question that has 'being an internal-correct answering of A's question' is identical with being an internal-correct answering of A's question. So being an internal-correct answering of A's question is a virtue/kind property.

Similarly for describings, reportings, and explainings, since describing/reporting/explaining well requires internal-correctness in one's describing/reporting/explaining.

It is also easy to see that properties that are instances of

being an external-correct V_{act}-ing

are also favorable evaluative properties since it is easy to see that they too are virtue/kind properties.

Consider answerings of A's question. Being an external-correct answering of A's question is a virtue in an answering of A's question. For (i) the kind 'answering A's question' is a goodness-fixing kind, and (ii) an answering of A's question is as good an answering of A's question as an answering of A's question can be only if it has 'being an external-correct answering of A's question, and it is obvious that conditions (iii) and (iv) are also satisfied. So being an external-correct answering of A's question is a virtue/kind property.

Similarly for describings, reportings, and explainings, since describing/reporting/explaining well requires external-correctness in one's describing/reporting/explaining.

(It might pay to mention that answering A's question well requires more than internal and external correctness—it also requires, in particular, being adequately informative in the circumstances. Thus if A's question was "Who is Alice's brother?" and Smith answers by saying "The person I kicked last month is Alice's brother," then what he says may be true, in that that person *is* Alice's brother, but unhelpful, and thus not a good answering, in that A has no idea which person Smith kicked last month. Analogues hold also of describing, reporting, and explaining.)

We can be brief about the perfect nominals. Similar reasoning yields that being a correct—that is, true—answer to A's question is a virtue in an answer to A's question, since an answer to A's question is as good an answer to it as an answer to it can be only if it is a true answer to it. So being a correct answer to A's question is also a virtue/kind property. Similarly for being a correct description of B, being a correct report on what C did to D, and being a correct explanation of why E kicked his cat.

11.

We now turn to assertings, and here a difference emerges. Of the pair

being an internal-correct asserting that p

being an external-correct asserting that p,

only the first is a favorable evaluative property.

We can easily see that the first is a virtue in an asserting that p. (i) The kind 'asserting that p' is not merely a correctness-fixing kind, it is a goodness-fixing kind. That is because what being an asserting that p is itself sets the standards that an asserting that p has to meet if it is to be good *qua* asserting that p: the asserter has to assert that p well. (ii) an asserting that p is as good an asserting that p as an asserting that p can be only if it has 'being an internal-correct asserting that p'. It is obvious that conditions (iii) and (iv) are also satisfied. So being an internal-correct asserting that p is a virtue/kind property and therefore is a favorable evaluative property.

Not so being an external-correct asserting that p: *that* is not a virtue in an asserting that p. Condition (i) is met, for as I said, the kind 'asserting that p' is a goodness-fixing kind; and as I said, for an asserting that p to be good *qua* asserting that p, the asserter has to assert that p well. But condition (ii) is not met. Suppose I asserted that apples grow underground, and did so by asserting, clearly and distinctly, the sentence "Apples grow underground." Then I asserted that apples grow underground as well as it is possible to assert that proposition, despite the fact that it is false. Not only can you not have asserted that proposition better than I did, my asserting of it would not have been a better asserting of it if it had been true. So as I say, condition (ii) is not met: it is not the case that an asserting that p is as good an asserting that p as an asserting that p can be only if it has 'being an external-correct asserting that p'.

It might be argued that things are otherwise when it comes to

being an external-correct asserting.

For suppose you asserted that apples grow on trees. It might be said that your asserting that apples grow on trees was a better asserting than my asserting that apples grow underground, since the content of your asserting is true and the content of my asserting is false. And it might be said that my asserting that apples grow underground would have been—not a better *asserting that apples grow underground*, but—a better *asserting* if it had been true that apples grow underground.

Why so? A reason might be thought to lie in an idea that many people find attractive, namely that the purpose or function of asserting is to convey or communicate information. Indeed, that we would not have had the practice of asserting if we had not generally or typically aimed to convey information by asserting things. Some people abuse the practice. They lie. But liars would not succeed in the private purposes for which they lie if it had not been generally or typically assumed that people who assert things do so in order to convey information. So it might be thought to follow that a person asserts well only if he does thereby convey information—thus only if his asserting is external-correct.

Should we agree? I leave aside the question what exactly it comes to to say that 'the purpose' of asserting is to do this or that; I leave it to intuition. And it does seem intuitively plausible to think that the purpose of asserting is to convey information, so let us grant that it is. What we should ask is whether its being so warrants us in concluding that a person asserts well only if he does thereby convey information—thus only if his asserting is external-correct.

Let us look at some other speech acts about which it is intuitively as plausible to think that their purpose is to convey information. I have in mind answering, describing, reporting, and explaining.

Every answering has an object O, which is the question that the answerer answers. Similarly, every describing has an object O, which is the thing that the describer describes. Similarly for reporting and explaining. ("To answer", "to describe", "to report", and "to explain" are transitive verbs.)

Suppose Smith and Jones answered on an occasion. Then both answered questions on that occasion. Moreover, how well an answerer answers on a given occasion turns entirely on how well he answers the question that he answers on that occasion. So Smith answered better than Jones did if and only if Smith answered the question he answered better than Jones answered the question he answered. Similarly for describing, reporting, and explaining.

There is no reason for thinking otherwise of asserting. Every asserting has an object O, which is the proposition that the asserter asserts. ("To assert" is also a transitive verb.) Suppose you and I asserted on an occasion. Then we both asserted propositions on that occasion. Moreover, how well an asserter asserts on a given occasion turns entirely on how well he asserts the proposition that he asserts on that occasion. So you asserted better than I did if and only if you asserted the proposition you asserted better than I asserted the proposition I asserted.

But then the idea about asserting that we are looking at won't do. Your asserting that apples grow on trees was a better asserting than my asserting that apples grow underground if and only if you asserted the proposition that apples grow on trees better than I asserted the proposition that apples grow underground—and the truth-value of the former proposition is irrelevant to how well you asserted it, and the truth-value of the latter proposition is irrelevant to how well I asserted it. And I would not have asserted the latter proposition better if it had been true than I did in fact assert it.

There is something here that calls for explanation, however. Asserting is like answering/describing/reporting/explaining in the following three respects among others. First, every asserting, like every answering/describing/reporting/explaining, has an object O. Second, every asserting, like every answering/describing/reporting/explaining has a content C, which is a proposition. And third, the purpose of asserting, like the purpose of answering/describing/reporting/explaining is to convey information.

But despite the fact that the purpose of asserting, like the purpose of answering/describing/reporting/explaining, is to convey information, the truth-value of the content C of an asserting is irrelevant to whether the asserter asserts O well, whereas the truth-value of the content C of an answering is relevant to whether the answerer answers O well—and similarly for describing, reporting, and explaining. That difference is what calls for explanation.

I suggest that the difference issues from the following further difference between asserting on the one hand and answering/describing/reporting/explaining on the other hand: the content of an asserting just *is* its object, whereas the contents of answerings/describings/reportings/explainings never are their objects. Alice answers O well only if the content C of her answering is true, and similarly for describing, reporting, and explaining. We cannot say that Bert asserts O well only if the content C of his asserting is true, for in his case, C just *is* O, and the truth-value of O is irrelevant to whether Bert asserts O well.

I stress that that is compatible with its being the case that the purpose of asserting is to convey information. Indeed, with the fact that all conveying of information proceeds by way of asserting. If I convey information by answering/describing/reporting/explaining O, then I do so by asserting a true proposition O*, O* being not merely the object of my asserting, but also the content of my asserting, the content of my answering/describing/reporting/explaining, and the information I convey. For suppose I answered the question O ("How old is Alfred?") by asserting O^*_1 (the proposition that Alfred is 32 years old). Then O^*_1 was the content of my answering. Suppose you answered the same question O by asserting O^*_2 (the proposition that Alfred is 47 years old). Then O^*_2 was the content of your answering. (The possibility that both of our answerings had the same object but different contents is due to the fact that the content of an answering is not identical with its object.) Suppose that O^*_1 is false and O^*_2 is true. Then the purpose of answering being what it is, I did not answer O well—you answered O better than I did.

Not so for asserting. By hypothesis, I asserted O^*_1. Then O^*_1 was the content of my asserting O^*_1. By hypothesis, you asserted O^*_2. Then O^*_2 was the content of your asserting. It follows that our assertings did not have the same object. (The impossibility of our assertings having had the same object but different contents is due to the fact that the content of an asserting is identical with its object.) The purpose of asserting being what it is, and O^*_2 being true and O^*_1 being false, you succeeded in doing what it is the purpose of asserting to do and I did not. But our assertings having had different objects, there is nothing such that you asserted it better than I did.

In sum, we should conclude that

> being an external-correct asserting that p

and

> being an external-correct asserting

are not favorable evaluative properties.

Similarly for the perfect nominals:

> · being a correct assertion that p

is not a favorable evaluative property since an assertion that p is not a better assertion that p if it is true than it would have been if it had been false, and so also for being a correct assertion.

12.

The fact that those four properties are not favorable evaluative properties has a bearing on an issue that has come in for discussion in recent years, namely whether (as the idea is put) 'Truth is normative'.

What *can* that be thought to mean? Nobody, I am sure, thinks that ascribing 'being a true proposition' to (as it might be) the proposition that snow is white is making a favorable evaluative judgment about that proposition. The kind 'proposition' is plainly not a goodness-fixing kind: no proposition is good *qua* proposition—no proposition is a better specimen of the kind 'proposition' than any other. A fortiori, true propositions are not better specimens of the kind 'proposition' than false ones are.

A strong interpretation of the idea that truth is normative that has appeared in the literature is this: if p, then one ought to assert that p. But that will certainly not do. It just isn't the case that a person ought to assert every truth. A weaker interpretation is this: if not-p, then one ought not assert that p. That too won't do. We sometimes ought to assert what is not true.

Huw Price supplies an interpretation of a different kind, an interpretation according to which a (putative) evaluative rather than a directive does the normative work:

> if not-p, then it is incorrect to assert that p.[9]

Now I am sure that *that* is true, indeed necessarily true. Or anyway, I am sure that it is necessarily true under the following interpretation of it:

> if not-p, then anyone who asserts that p asserts that p external-incorrectly.

The trouble for Price's purposes, however, is that 'being an external-correct asserting that p' is not a favorable evaluative property, and

---

[9] Huw Price, "Three Norms of Assertibility," *Philosophical Perspectives* 12 (1998): 246.

no more is 'being an external-incorrect asserting that p' an unfavorable evaluative property. So neither property is such that to ascribe it to an asserting is to make an evaluative judgment about the asserting. So if this is what the (putative) normativity of truth consists in, then truth is not normative.

Price could have said:

> if not-p, then it is incorrect to answer a question by asserting that p.

Alternatively put: if Q is the question "Is it the case that p?" and if, also, it is not the case that p, then any answering of Q by asserting that p is an external-incorrect answering of Q. 'Being an external-correct answering of Q' is a favorable evaluative property, and by the same token, 'being an external-incorrect answering of Q is an unfavorable evaluative property. So ascribing either of these properties to an answering is making an evaluative judgment about it. But it is hard to see why anyone would feel inclined to report *that* fact in the words "Truth is normative." Truth does figure in some evaluative properties, for an external-correct answering is a better answering than an external-incorrect answering. But on the other hand, a true proposition isn't a better proposition than a false one. Similarly, a sleeping pill that induces sleep is a better sleeping pill than one that doesn't, but I don't feel in the least inclined to report that fact in the words "Sleep-inducingness is normative"—after all, a sleep-inducing lecturer isn't a better lecturer than an interesting one.[10]

---

[10] I mention in passing another issue that has come in for discussion in recent years, namely whether (as the idea is put) 'Meaning is normative'. Or, on some views, what follows from the fact that meaning *is* normative. Here is Paul A. Boghossian:

> Suppose the expression 'green' means *green*. It follows immediately that the expression 'green' applies *correctly* only to *these* things (the green ones) and not to *those* (the non-greens). The fact that the expression means something implies, that is, a whole set of *normative* truths about my behavior with that expression: namely that my use of it is correct in application to certain objects and not in application to others. . . . The normativity of meaning turns out to be, in other words, simply a new name for the familiar fact that . . . meaningful expressions possess conditions of *correct use*. ("The Rule-Following Considerations," *Mind* 98 [October 1989]: 513)

There is a widespread tendency to take it that the appropriateness of the word "correct" or "incorrect" in a context is, by itself, a conclusive sign that there is normativity at work in that context.[11] I am sure that is due to the idea I mentioned earlier, namely that the concepts 'must', 'obligation', 'correct', and 'ought' come to pretty much the same. As I said, however, that idea is a mistake.

13.

I have focused in this chapter primarily on correctness in acts, speech acts in particular. Let us turn now to correctness in mental states.

Boghossian then goes on to discuss the question whether accepting that meaning is normative commits one to scepticism about what a person means by a word. I bypass that question. What I do is only to draw attention to the bearing on that idea of the distinction I have drawn between internal and external correctness. (i) For "green" to mean *green* is for the operative convention to say that if one says "A is green," then one thereby asserts that A is green. Moreover, the convention says that if one says "A is green" internal-correctly, then one thereby asserts that A is green internal-correctly. So there is normativity in the offing here, since 'being an internal-correct asserting that A is green' is a favorable evaluative property. (ii) But whether A *is* green is quite another matter, for 'being an external-correct asserting that A is green' is not a favorable evaluative property.

What about correct *use* of a word? We must surely grant that correctness in use turns on speakers' intentions. (Whatever it is that might be thought to warrant ascribing the relevant intention to a person. As I say, I bypass that question.) For suppose that Smith says on an occasion "A is green." Then Smith's use of "green" on that occasion is a correct use of it if and only if he intends to be asserting thereby that A is green. The fact that A is not green, if it is not green, makes no difference. (He may be genuinely mistaken, or he may be lying.) Smith's use of "green" on that occasion is an incorrect use of it if and only if he intends to be asserting something other than that A is green. What he in fact asserts is, as the convention says, that A is green; he uses the word incorrectly if what he intends to be asserting is (as it might be) that A is red. So there is normativity in the offing here too, for 'being an incorrect use of the word "green"' is an unfavorable evaluative property—just as 'being an incorrect use of an adding machine' is. It remains the case, however, that whether A *is* green has no bearing on the question whether a person who says "A is green" uses "green" correctly.

[11] The appropriateness of the word "success" in a context is also often regarded as a conclusive sign that there is normativity at work in that context. ("He succeeded in proving Bloggs's Conjecture!") I therefore offer the reader what I call The Deflationary Theory of Success (alternatively, Minimalism About Success): a person V_{act}s successfully if and only if he V_{act}s.

VII

Correctness Properties (Mental States)

1.

We begin with believings and beliefs. I say "believings *and* beliefs" for here too we need to settle on a terminology.

To go back. Asserting that p is an enterprise that a person can engage in. Suppose that Smith asserted that p. It follows that there was an act that consisted in Smith's asserting that p. That act is a member of the kind 'asserting that p'. It is also a member of the kind 'asserting'.

Believing that p is not an enterprise that a person can engage in; it is a mental state. Suppose that Jones believed that p. Does it follow that there was something that consisted in Jones's believing that p? What might that be? Let us say that mental states have *people-indexed instances*. Thus since Jones believed that p, there was such a thing as Jones's instance of believing that p. If you and I also believed that p, then there were such things as your instance of believing that p and mine, and there therefore were at least three different instances of one and the same mental state, believing that p. Let us take the expression "the kind 'believing that p'" to refer to the kind whose members are all and only instances of believing that p. Let us take the expression "the kind 'believing'" to refer to the kind whose members are all and only instances of believing. Then Jones's instance of believing that p, and ours, are members of both of those kinds.

So much for the imperfect nominals "asserting" and "believing"; now for the perfect nominals. I said that "Smith's assertion" is ambiguous: it may refer to Smith's act of asserting something, or it may refer, instead, to what Smith asserted—that is, to the propo-

sition that is both the object and the content of his act of asserting. I said that I would throughout take it to refer to the latter.
"Jones's belief" is also ambiguous: it may refer to Jones's instance
of believing, or it may refer, instead, to what Jones believed—that
is, to the proposition that is both the object and the content of his
instance of believing. I will throughout take it to refer to the
latter.

And now: what are we to say about correctness in instances of
believing and in beliefs?

The kind 'asserting' fixes two ways in which its members can be
correct. The first is a consequence of (i) the fact that asserting is an
enterprise for which there is such a thing as carrying it out correctly
or incorrectly: it follows from that fact that an asserting can be an
internal-correct asserting that p or an internal-incorrect asserting
that p.

Not so the kind 'believing'. Believing is not an enterprise; therefore there is no such thing as carrying out the enterprise of believing internal-correctly or internal-incorrectly. So no instance of
believing is an internal-correct or internal-incorrect believing.

The kind 'asserting' fixes a second way in which its members can
be correct. This is a consequence of (ii) the fact that its members
have propositional contents. That, as I said, opens its members to
assessment of correctness or incorrectness of a different kind, turning on whether their propositional contents are true. It is because of
this fact that an asserting can be an external-correct asserting or an
external-incorrect asserting—it is an external-correct asserting just in
case its propositional content is true.

The members of the kind 'believing' also have propositional contents. (Unlike instances of the mental states feeling warm and feeling dizzy.) So its members too are open to assessment turning on
whether their propositional contents are true. And we can say: an
instance of believing is an external-correct believing just in case its
propositional content is true.

Since there is no such thing as believing internal-correctly or
internal-incorrectly, and since (as I take it) a believing can be a correct or incorrect believing *only* by way of being an external-correct
or external-incorrect believing, I will drop the modifier "external" for
believing. I will therefore say: a believing is a correct believing just
in case its propositional content is true.

We can be brief about the perfect nominals. I said that an asser-tion is a correct assertion just in case it is true; so also, a belief is a correct belief just in case it is true.[1]

Similarly for expectings and expectations, assumings and assumptions, and conjecturings and conjectures.

2.

Is 'being a correct believing' a favorable evaluative property? Well, is it a virtue in a believing? By way of reminder,

> (Virtues Analysis) For F to be a virtue in a K is for it to be the case that
> (i) K is a goodness-fixing kind, and
> (ii) a K is as good a K as a K can be only if it has F, and
> (iii) it is possible for there to be a K that lacks F, and
> (iv) it is not nomologically impossible for there to be a K that has F.

So let us ask: is the kind 'believing' a goodness-fixing kind? Its mem-bers include Smith's believing that p, and Jones's believing that q. Does what being a believing is itself set the standards that a believ-ing has to meet if it is to be good *qua* believing? What would count as a believing's being good *qua* believing?—what would mark a believing as a good specimen of the kind 'believing'?

Let us look at acts again. The kind 'performing Mozart's S' is a goodness-fixing kind. That is because there is an enterprise that con-sists in performing Mozart's S, and one can carry it out well or ill; a member of that kind is good *qua* member of that kind just in case the performer carries out the enterprise well—that is, performs Mozart's S well. The kind 'answering A's question' is a goodness-fix-ing kind. That is because there is an enterprise that consists in answering A's question, and one can carry it out well or ill; a mem-ber of that kind is good *qua* member of that kind just in case the answerer carries out the enterprise well—that is, answers A's ques-tion well. Similarly for the kind 'asserting that p'. More generally, an act-kind 'V-ing' is a goodness-fixing kind just in case there is such an enterprise as V-ing and one can carry it out well or ill; a member of

---

[1] For some further comments, see Addendum 2 on Correctness.

the kind is good *qua* member of the kind just in case the V-er carries out the enterprise well—that is, just in case he Vs well. (The act-
kind 'moving one's left thumb' is not a goodness-fixing kind, since
while there is such an enterprise as moving one's left thumb, there
is no such thing as carrying that enterprise out well or ill.)

Those considerations have no analogue for believing, for there is
no enterprise of believing, and a fortiori, there is no such thing as
carrying out, well, the enterprise of believing. (Nobody believes *well*
that it is raining out.)

So what is left that might mark a believing as good *qua* believing? Well, a person might believe that p correctly. Suppose Smith
believes that p, and suppose it is true that p. Then Smith's believing
that p is a correct believing. Does that fact mark Smith's believing
that p as good *qua* believing? No more, I say, than the fact that
Jones's asserting that p is an external-correct asserting marks it as
good *qua* asserting. Thus: not in the least.

To repeat: the kind 'asserting' is a goodness-fixing kind, but what
marks an asserting as good *qua* asserting is its being an internal-correct asserting—its being an external-correct asserting, if it is, is irrelevant to whether it is good *qua* asserting. And there is no more
reason to think that correctness in a believing marks it as good *qua*
believing than there is to think that external-correctness in an asserting marks it as good *qua* asserting.

Indeed, suppose you came to believe that p, and therefore
asserted that p. And suppose it turned out to have been the case that
p. It is not at all plausible to think that your believing turned out to
have been better *qua* believing than it otherwise would have been,
though your asserting did not turn out to have been better *qua*
asserting than it otherwise would have been.

Similarly for the perfect nominals. For a belief to be a correct
belief is just for it to be a true belief, and a true belief is not better
qua belief than a false one—as for an assertion to be a correct assertion is just for it to be a true assertion, and a true assertion is not better *qua* assertion than a false one.

I invite the conclusion that 'being a correct believing' and 'being
a correct belief' are not favorable evaluative properties.

3.

The fact that those two properties are not favorable evaluative properties has a bearing on another issue that has come in for discus-

sion in recent years, namely whether (as the idea is put) 'Belief is normative'.

There are several ways in which that idea has been interpreted. On one interpretation of it, it says (i) necessarily, if P is false, then one ought not believe P. On another, it says (ii) necessarily, a person who believes P does so correctly if and only if P is true.[2]

If (i) is true, then one might well feel inclined to report that fact in the words "Belief is normative," for directives are normative judgments. I postpone discussion of "One ought (ought not) believe P" until we reach the directives.

(ii), however, is another matter. In the first place, it is utterly trivial, since for a person who believes P to do so correctly just is for P to be true. Second, (ii) licenses our drawing the conclusion "Smith's believing P is a correct believing" from the premise that Smith believes P and P is true. But since 'being a correct believing' is not a favorable evaluative property, the conclusion (ii) licenses our drawing from that

---

[2] There are two stronger interpretations in the offing: they tell us what believing *is*. Let us take V_{mind}-ing here to be restricted to mental states whose propositional content is P. (Thus the V_{mind}-ings here include believing P, assuming P, conjecturing that P is true, and so on.) Then the first of the two stronger interpretations says:

(iii) believing P just is the V_{mind}-ing such that necessarily, if P is false, then one ought not V_{mind}.

The second of them says:

(iv) believing P just is the V_{mind}-ing such that necessarily, a person who V_{mind}s does so correctly if and only if P is true.

There are passages that suggest (iii) and passages that suggest (iv) in Nishi Shah, "How Truth Governs Belief," *Philosophical Review* 112, no. 4 (October 2003). I stress, however, that (iii) and (iv) are not the same.

As for (iii), I postpone discussion of "A ought (ought not) V_{mind}" until we reach the directives.

I should think that (iv) is true only if we take believing P to *include* the likes of expecting, assuming, and conjecturing. And what more do we have to include in believing P if we are to have included all 'the likes of' expecting, assuming, and conjecturing? I fancy that we have to include all V_{mind}-ings in which the V_{mind}-er commits himself to the truth of the proposition P that is the content of his V_{mind}-ing. If that is right, then it would be no wonder if (iv) were true!

I add that the fact that (iv) is true (assuming it is true) gives us no more reason to say "Belief is normative" than does the fact that (ii) is true.

A fifth idea connects correctness with reasons-for, and ascribes normativity to believings on ground of that connection. We will look at reasons-for in the following two chapters.

premise is not itself normative. There therefore is no good reason to say "Belief is normative" on the ground that (ii) is true.

Paul Horwich claims that "It is desirable to believe what is true and only what is true"; perhaps we can therefore take him to think that 'being a correct believing'—that is, 'being a true believing'—is, after all, a favorable evaluative property.[3] He considers the possibility that what makes his claim true is the fact that believing what is true pays, and believing what is false costs. But he says that while believing truly often pays, it is desirable to believe what is true even if doing so doesn't pay.

> Knowledge is valuable, as we often say, 'for its own sake'. . . . Without some such assumption, it would be hard to justify our pursuit of truth in fields of inquiry such as ancient history, metaphysics, and esoteric areas of mathematics—fields that may not be expected to have any pragmatic payoff. (351)

I can't bring myself to agree. Knowledge of some facts is valuable 'for its own sake': these are facts that are in one or another way interesting 'for their own sake'. But not all facts are. I meet you in the corridor on my way to my office and I say, "My left ankle started to itch last night at about 9:30." "Oh," you say, politely, "and then?" I say, "Well, then I scratched it, and the itch went away. I thought you might like to know." I doubt that you feel grateful to me for having added to your stock of true beliefs.

4.

Let us now look at some other mental states: trusting, admiring, fearing, disliking, and preferring. These are similar to believing in that they have objects; thus just as one believes a proposition, one trusts a person or institution, one admires a person or painting or proof, and so on. They differ from believing, however, in that they lack propositional contents.

The kind 'believing' is the kind whose members are all and only instances of believing; let us take the kind 'trusting' to be the kind whose members are all and only instances of trusting, and similarly for the kinds 'admiring', 'fearing', 'disliking', and 'preferring'.

---

[3] Paul Horwich, "The Value of Truth," *Nous* 40, no. 2 (June 2006).

The kind 'believing' is a correctness-fixing kind; are *these* kinds correctness-fixing? Well, is the following true: what being a trusting/admiring . . . *is* itself sets the standards that a trusting/admiring . . . has to meet if it is to be correct *qua* trusting/admiring . . .?

I take it to be at most rare to hear anyone describe a trusting/admiring . . . as a correct trusting/admiring. . . . However we do often say of a person that he was right to trust/admire . . . such and such, or right to prefer such and such to so and so. Or again, that a person rightly trusted/admired . . . such and such, or that he rightly preferred such and such to so and so.

How exactly does "right" differ from "correct"? The adjective "right" is like the adjective "correct" in being an attributive, and there therefore is no such property as rightness just as there is no such property as correctness. (For the analogous reason, there is no such property as wrongness.) Moreover, they are interchangeable in many contexts. The correct answer to a question is also the right answer to the question. The correct telephone number to use to telephone Jones is also the right telephone number to use to telephone Jones. The correct way to make risotto is also the right way to make risotto. But there are contexts in which they are not interchangeable. A performing of Mozart's S may be a correct performing of it but not a right performing of it. A correct belief is not a right belief.[4]

I bypass the question how exactly "right" differs from "correct". I think the following, anyway, is plausible enough: a person correctly trusts/admires . . . such and such, or correctly prefers such and such to so and so, if and only if he rightly trusts/admires . . . such and such, or rightly prefers such and such to so and so. Indeed, plausible enough to warrant our saying that there are correctness properties in the offing here—correctness properties which I will refer to as follows:

> being a correct trusting
> being a correct admiring
> being a correct fearing
> being a correct disliking
> being a correct preferring,

---

[4] I thank Peter Bach-y-Rita for the following happy example in which "wrong" and "incorrect" are not interchangeable. Suppose there are two camels out in the meadow, a tall one and a short one. I ask you to please bring me the tall one. You bring me the short one. I say, "You brought me the wrong camel!" I don't say, "You brought me the incorrect camel!"

where an instance of trusting has the first just in case the truster rightly trusts what he trusts, an instance of admiring has the second just in case the admirer rightly admires what he admires, and so on. Compare

being a correct believing:

an instance of believing has this property just in case the believer correctly—or we could say rightly—believes what he believes.

I stress that we are to take that analogy literally in the following respect. A believing is a correct believing just in case its propositional content is true. Thus a believing is not marked as a correct believing by the fact that the believer's other beliefs lend weight to, or even entail, the propositional content of his believing. Smith's believing P is not marked as a correct believing by the fact that it is rational in him to believe P. Whether a believing is a correct believing is an objective, not a subjective, matter. Similarly, Jones's trusting A is not marked as a correct trusting by the fact that it is rational in him to trust A. Suppose that A is in fact a villain. Jones's beliefs being what they are, it may be rational in Jones to trust A. But it is not the case that Jones is right to trust A—it is not the case that he rightly, that is, correctly, trusts A. Whether a trusting is a correct trusting is, like believing, an objective, not a subjective, matter.

Similarly for admiring and the others. Given Jones's beliefs about Hitler, it may be rational in him to admire Hitler, but it is not the case that he is right to admire Hitler. If Tiny Tim is a perfectly ordinary kitten (not a demon dressed in the flesh of a kitten), then it is not the case that anyone is right to be afraid of Tiny Tim. And so on.

Then it is surely a straightforward matter to say what the standards for correctness are that are set by the kinds 'trusting', 'admiring', ... For Jones's trusting A to be a correct trusting is for A to be worthy of, or, as I will mostly say, to *deserve*, Jones's trusting A. For Jones's admiring A to be a correct admiring is for A to be worthy of, or, as I will mostly say, to *deserve*, Jones's admiring A. And similarly for fearing, disliking, and preferring.[5]

---

[5] I have ignored in the text the fact that it may be that a trusting/admiring/. . . is not all or none. One may trust a person *qua* dentist but not *qua* investment advisor. One may admire a person *qua* Governor but not *qua* tennis player. These set analogous standards. For it to be the case that Jones is right to trust A *qua* dentist is for A to deserve Jones's trusting him *qua* dentist. And so on.

We will turn shortly to the question whether these correctness properties are favorable evaluative properties. But we should first take note of some correctness properties that can be possessed by some other mental states.

5.

Consider wanting. Wanting differs from trusting, admiring, fearing, disliking, and preferring, in the following respect: while some instances of wanting lack propositional contents, other instances have them. Smith can want Alfred's apple; let us call this object-wanting. Jones can want that Bert get into law school; let us call this propositional-wanting.[6]

It is an intuitively odd idea that there are two wholly independent kinds of wanting, object-wanting and propositional-wanting: they are surely connected in some way. But since we have no need to take a stand on how they connect, I bypass that question.

I take it to be at most rare to hear anyone describe a wanting as a correct wanting, just as it is at most rare to hear anyone describe a trusting/admiring . . . as a correct trusting/admiring. . . . However we do often say of a person that he was right to want this or that. Smith might rightly want Alfred's apple, and Jones might rightly want that Bert get into law school. So I take it that we can say that there are such correctness properties as

being a correct object-wanting

and

being a correct propositional-wanting.

In light of the fact that one can trust/admire/ . . . rightly, we might well wonder why those who say "Belief is normative" say this of believing in particular. For there is no better reason to say this of believing than there is to say it of trusting/admiring/. . . .

[6] Smith's wanting Alfred's apple is object-wanting, and Jones's wanting that Bert get into law school is propositional-wanting. What about Smith's wanting *an* apple? What that is is ambiguous. Quine said that "Smith wants a sloop" is ambiguous as between saying that there is some particular sloop that Smith wants (which is object-wanting), and saying that Smith just suffers from slooplessness—that is, Smith wants that he have a sloop (which is propositional-wanting).

What does possessing them come to? Suppose A wants an object O. Then we can say: for A's wanting O to be a correct object-wanting is for O to be worthy of, or, as I will mostly say, to deserve, A's wanting it. Again, suppose A wants that p. Let S be the state of affairs 'being the case that p'. Then we can say: for A's wanting that p to be a correct propositional-wanting is for S to deserve A's wanting that it obtain.

It will be propositional-wantings that figure in what follows, so I will abbreviate: unless otherwise noted, it will be propositional-wantings that I refer to by "wantings", and it will be the property 'being a correct propositional-wanting' that I have in mind by

> being a correct wanting.

In fact it will be a particular sub-class of propositional-wantings that figure in what follows, namely propositional-wantings whose contents are propositions to the effect that the wanter *do* this or that. Suppose Jones wants that he eat Alfred's apple. Let S be the state of affairs that consists in its being the case that Jones eats Alfred's apple. Then we can say: for Jones's wanting that he eat Alfred's apple to be a correct wanting is for S to deserve Jones's wanting that it obtain. More briefly put, for Jones's wanting that he eat Alfred's apple to be a correct wanting is for Jones's eating Alfred's apple to deserve Jones's wanting that it obtain. More generally,

> For A's wanting that he do a thing to be a correct wanting is for A's doing the thing to deserve A's wanting that it obtain.

Analogues of what holds of wanting hold also of hoping and regretting. Let S be the state of affairs that consists in its being the case that Bert gets into law school. For Jones's hoping that Bert will get into law school to be a correct hoping is for S to deserve Jones's hoping that it will obtain. Suppose Bert gets into law school, and that Jones later comes to regret that he did. For Jones's regretting that Bert got into law school to be a correct regretting is for S to deserve Jones's regretting that it did obtain. I take it to be plausible that Jones's earlier hoping was a correct hoping only if his later regretting was an incorrect regretting.

6.

In sum, just as there is such a property as being a correct believing, there are such properties as

> being a correct trusting
> being a correct admiring
> being a correct fearing
> being a correct disliking
> being a correct preferring
> being a correct wanting
> being a correct hoping
> being a correct regretting

I asked whether the property 'being a correct believing' is a favorable evaluative property, and suggested that we should agree that it is not. What about *these* properties? I suggest that we should say the same of them, for the kinds 'trusting', 'admiring', and so on, though correctness-fixing, are not goodness-fixing. You are very likely to be better off if your believings are correct believings than if they are not; that does not mean that a correct believing is better *qua* believing than an incorrect believing. Similarly, you are likely to be better off if your trustings are correct trustings than if they are not; that does not mean that a correct trusting is better *qua* trusting than an incorrect trusting. And similarly for admirings, fearings, and so on.

There is room to say that an ascription of 'being a correct trusting' to Smith's trusting Alfred *entails* a favorable evaluative judgment, for it entails that Alfred has 'deserves being trusted by Smith'—and 'deserves being trusted by Smith' is surely a favorable evaluative property. Again, an ascription of 'being a correct admiring' to Smith's admiring Bert entails that Bert has 'deserves being admired by Smith'—and 'deserves being admired by Smith' is surely a favorable evaluative property. I have no objection to that idea. It won't do for all of the properties on our list: 'deserves being feared by Smith' and 'deserves being disliked by Smith' are not on any view favorable evaluative properties. But it will presumably do for 'being a correct trusting', 'being a correct admiring', for example.

The important point, however, is that 'being a correct trusting' and 'being a correct admiring' are not themselves favorable evaluative properties. To ascribe them to a trusting and admiring is not to ascribe a favorable evaluative property to the trusting and admiring, for a trusting is not marked as a better trusting by its having a trustworthy object, and an admiring is not marked as a better admiring by its having an admirable object. Compare the fact that Jones's performing of Mozart's S is not a better performing than it would have been if the sonata had not been as good a piece of music as it is. (It can be the case that a performing of a great piece of music is dreadful *qua* performing, while a performing of a lesser piece is excellent *qua* performing.) And a map of Paris is not marked as a better map (as better *qua* map) than a map of Columbus, Ohio, by the fact that Paris is a more beautiful city.

7.

We have looked at a great many correctness properties in this and the preceding chapter. We focused on correctness-fixing act-kinds in the preceding chapter, and on correctness-fixing mental-state-kinds in this chapter. I said at the beginning of the preceding chapter that correctness properties differ from each other, and from goodness properties, in a variety of interesting ways, and that I would bring one out in particular, namely that while all goodness properties are favorable evaluative properties, some correctness properties are and some are not. All of the correctness-fixing act-kinds we looked at generate favorable evaluative properties; none of the correctness-fixing mental-state-kinds we looked at do.

It might pay to mention that just as there is such a thing as being a good-modified K, there is such a thing as being a correct-modified K. I have in mind the likes of the following:

> being the correct telephone number to use to telephone Jones
> being the correct title to use to address the judge in court
> being a correct form to use to file an application for a tax abatement
> being a grammatically correct sentence
> being a strategically correct chess move
> being a morally correct act.

I suggest that some of these are favorable evaluative properties and some are not. I leave it to the reader to say which are and which are not, and why.

What there aren't are correctness relations analogous to the betterness relations. "Correct" has no comparative, so nothing is more correct, or a more correct K, than anything else.

8.

Evaluative judgments are those in the making of which we ascribe evaluative properties and relations. We have by now looked at a great many favorable evaluative properties. The goodness properties are at the heart of the favorable evaluative properties. With them in hand, we were able to say what marks a property F as a virtue in a kind K, and thereby add the virtue/kind properties to our list of favorable evaluative properties. We were also able to add to our list some but not all correctness properties. We were also able to say of a great many relations that they are favorable evaluative relations— as, for example, 'being a better K' for all kinds K that are goodness-fixing kinds.

There are indefinitely many other favorable evaluative properties and relations. I have mentioned some others along the way, such as the relation being a better chess player than A by more than B is than C, and the relation being a sharper carving knife than A by more than B is than C. There are still others that we ascribe by use of the word "right"—in particular, many of those we would have ascribed if we had said "correct" instead of "right".

Also among the favorable evaluative properties are many of those we ascribe by use of the words "suitable", "fitting", "appropriate", "satisfactory", and "adequate". These words are attributives, like "correct" and "right", but they differ from "correct" and "right" in an interesting way: unlike "correct" and "right", they have comparatives. But we needn't make a special place for these properties since the ones that belong on our list are already on it. That is because they are virtues in a K. Thus suppose someone says of a toaster "That is adequate," meaning to ascribe to it: being an adequate toaster. Being an adequate toaster is a virtue in a toaster, since a toaster is not as good a toaster as a toaster can be unless it is an adequate toaster.

There are also unfavorable evaluative properties and relations, which I have for the most part ignored. These include what might be called badness properties, vices, and incorrectness properties. ("Vices"?! I will throughout use "vice" broadly, as I earlier said I would use "virtue". So used, it is true to say that aggressiveness is a vice in a seeing eye dog.[7])

There is an important class of unfavorable evaluative properties that I will call the defectiveness properties. "Defective" is yet another attributive adjective—a person can be a defective administrator and a nondefective teacher. The class includes not merely certain instances of 'being a defective K', but also certain instances of 'being a morally defective K' and 'being a physically defective K'. We will return to the defectiveness properties in chapter XII.

Meanwhile, I have been trying so far to do three things. First, to bring out how *very* rich in normativity our thinking is. Some of our evaluative thought is moral; vastly more is nonmoral.

Second, to bring out some of the ways in which our evaluative thinking works—works in general, whether what is in question is moral or nonmoral evaluation.

And third, to bring out that when we give up the single-minded fixation on morality that is so common in moral philosophy, we can see that something has gone badly wrong in us if we share the impression reported by Blackburn in the passage I quoted earlier, namely,

> The natural world is the world revealed by the senses, and described by the natural sciences: physics, chemistry, and notably biology, including evolutionary theory. However we think of it, ethics seems to fit badly into that world. Neither the senses nor the sciences seem to be good detectors of obligations, duties, or the order of value of things.

Anyway, something has gone badly wrong in us so far as the order of value of things is concerned—as, for example, whether one umbrella is a better umbrella than another, whether one carving knife is a better carving knife than another, and whether one answer to the question "Who won the battle of Shiloh?" is a better answer to it than another.

---

[7] The *Oxford English Dictionary*'s entry for "vice" supplies: "Of all the vices incidental to the horse, shying is one of the worst," and "The vice of the steam-engine lies in its inability to utilise heat of comparatively low grade."

What about obligations and duties? Or more generally, the (puta-tive) facts that we report on when we make directive judgments? In turning to the directives, we do not part company permanently with the evaluatives, for giving an account of the directives will require giving an account of how they connect with the evaluatives, I will suggest that the truth of the directives turns on the truth of certain particular evaluatives—which and how will emerge later.

VIII

Reasons-For
(Mental States)

1.

Which are the sentences we use to make directive judgments? Here are the three examples I gave at the outset: "A ought to be kind to his little brother," "B ought to move his rook," and "C ought to get a hair cut."

Those sentences contain "ought". Here are some that we use to make directive judgments that do not contain "ought": "A should move his rook," "B must take his blood pressure medication," and "C must turn up in court this morning, like it or not!" These differ in strength, from each other, and from those that contain "ought", and we will want to ask later about the source of that difference. However the literature focuses on those that contain "ought", and for the time being, I will too. And now we should ask: what makes them true when they are?

Moral philosophy took a turn to reasons for action in the 1950s.[1] In particular, many people came to think that what makes directives true, when they are, is facts about reasons for action. Thus many people say:

---

[1] To the best of my knowledge, the turn was caused by the appearance of books by Stephen Toulmin (*The Place of Reason in Ethics* [Cambridge: Cambridge University Press, 1953]) and Kurt Baier (*The Moral Point of View* [Ithaca, NY: Cornell University Press, 1958]). (To the best of my knowledge, there is nothing in the literature of ethics between 1903, when *Principia* appeared, and 1953, when Toulmin's book appeared, that leans in any serious way on the concept 'reasons for action'.) Thomas Nagel's *The Possibility of Altruism* (Oxford: Clarendon Press, 1970) made the turn seem even more attractive.

> (SLOGAN-I) What A ought to do is what there is most reason
> for A to do.

I call that "SLOGAN-I" because there is a second possibility in the offing, namely

> (SLOGAN-II) What A ought to do is what A has most reason
> to do.

How these differ is a question we will return to. In any case, many people nowadays say that what a person ought to do is fixed by the reasons he has, or there are, for acting in this or that way.

T. M. Scanlon has recently suggested that what makes evaluatives true, when they are, is reasons for action.[2] Anyone who accepts this view as well as the slogans thinks that *all* normative truths rest on truths about reasons for action.

Now I think that that turn to reasons for action was a bad idea. In the preceding chapters, I gave an account of many of the most familiar evaluatives, and reasons for action played no role in it; I will later give an account of the directives in which reasons for action play no role.

However, in light of the great popularity of those slogans, I stop to bring out why I recommend that we reject them.[3] I will suggest that the slogans have the matter upside down: directives do not rest on reasons for action, rather reasons for action rest on directives.

In any case, the question what it is for something to be a reason for action is an interesting one, which an account of normativity should surely speak to.

2.

What, then, is a reason for action? Scanlon says:

---

[2] He says: "being valuable is not a property that provides us with reasons. Rather, to call something valuable is to say that it has other properties that provide reasons for behaving in certain ways with regard to it." T. M. Scanlon, *What We Owe to Each Other* (Cambridge, MA: Harvard University Press, 1998), 96.

[3] I confess to thinking that people who are attracted by the view that evaluatives rest on truths about reasons for action are attracted by it because they regard evaluatives with suspicion, perhaps under the influence (conscious or not) of Expressivism.

I will take the idea of a reason as primitive. Any attempt to explain what it is to be a reason for something seems to me to lead back to the same idea: a consideration that counts in favor of it. 'Counts in favor how?' one might ask. 'By providing a reason for it' seems to be the only answer. So I will presuppose the idea of a reason, ...[4]

So on Scanlon's view, there is no such thing as an interesting analysis of what it is for X to be a reason for φ, whatever φ may be, whether φ is acting in a certain way or anything else that X might be a reason for. No interesting analysis, that is. Scanlon thinks that for X to be a reason for φ is for X to count in favor of φ, but that if you want to know how a reason counts in favor of what it is a reason for, the only available answer is the not at all helpful: "a reason counts in favor of what it is a reason for by providing a reason for it."

Now I am sure it is right to say that a reason counts in favor of what it is a reason for. But I fancy that we can say a lot more about how a reason counts in favor of what it is a reason for than Scanlon supposes.

3.

First, three preliminaries. These are nonsubstantive: we need to settle on them only in order to share a way of talking about reasons.

(i) The literature in ethics mostly focuses on reasons for acting, and their differences from reasons for believing. However, there are also reasons for trusting, admiring, hating, regretting, preferring, wanting, and so on.[5] I will assume that we should keep all of these in mind as we go—there must surely be something they all have in common.

(ii) But what *are* reasons for acting, believing, trusting, admiring, . . .? That is, of what ontological kind does X have to be for it to be

---

[4] Scanlon, *What We Owe to Each Other*, 17.

[5] Scanlon is among the few who take note of this fact. He says that believing, admiring, hating, etc. are attitudes (as opposed to mere feelings, such as hunger), and that they "can be characterized, with apparent but I think innocent circularity, as the class of 'judgment-sensitive attitudes.'" That is: if we are ideally rational, then we have the attitudes when we take ourselves to have sufficient reasons for them, and cease having them if we come to believe we did not or no longer do. Scanlon, *What We Owe to Each Other*, 20.

a reason for drinking milk, or for believing that A loves B, or for trusting C, . . .? I assume, and I hope you will agree, that a reason for doing any of those things is something one can reason *from*. One can't reason from an apple, or any other physical object; so physical objects aren't reasons for anything. The assumption leaves us with only two candidates, facts and propositions. Which should we opt for?

If we opt for the view that reasons for doing those things are propositions, then we have to add a constraint, for it is plain that reasons for doing those things are in shorter supply than propositions. Consider the proposition that drinking cyanide is good for people. Is that proposition a reason for you to drink some cyanide? Is there *any* reason for you to drink some cyanide? I take it we can assume that there isn't.

If propositions are reasons for doing those things, then it is anyway only true propositions that are. If the proposition that drinking cyanide is good for people were true, then it could be said to be a reason for you to drink some cyanide. But since it isn't true, it isn't a reason for you to do so.

On the other hand, we very often speak as if reasons-for were facts. Thus if I say that there is a reason for believing that drinking milk is good for a person, and you ask what that reason is, I might reply, "The fact that milk contains calcium." I think it very unlikely that I would reply, "The true proposition that milk contains calcium."

Now some people hold that facts just are true propositions. If they are right, then when I reply, "The fact that milk contains calcium," what I refer to *is* the true proposition that milk contains calcium. Other people hold that facts are not true propositions but are, instead, what make them true. We have no need to decide this question. We also have no need to decide the further question whether, if facts are not true propositions, it is facts or true propositions that are reasons-for. In light of common usage, let us stipulate that reasons-for are facts. There is nothing I will say that relies on our having chosen facts rather than true propositions as the things that are reasons-for.

It follows trivially from our stipulation that no apple is a reason for anything, though the fact that a certain apple is on a certain table might well be a reason for believing this or that, or for doing this or that.

It also follows trivially, and thus needs no argument of the kind that so often appears in the literature on reasons for action, that no desire is a reason for doing anything, nor is any other mental state. Though nothing of theoretical interest is thereby lost, for our stipulation leaves it open for argument whether the fact that A wants such and such, or the fact that B feels unhappy, or the fact that C loves D, is a reason for doing this or that.

By way of third preliminary, (iii), we should agree that the concept 'reason-for' differs from the concept 'reason-why'.

I take it that for X to be the reason why such and such is the case is for X to explain its being the case, and I will assume that this is right.

It follows straightway that (α) there being no reason for which a thing is behaving in a certain way is compatible with there being a reason why it is. Suppose a certain ship is sinking. The ship is obviously not sinking *for* any reason. However, we may presume that there is a reason *why* the ship is sinking. If its having been overloaded explains its sinking, then its having been overloaded is the reason why it is sinking.

Similarly for people. It may be that Smith is twiddling his thumbs, but not for any reason. (Perhaps he isn't even aware that he is twiddling them.) However, we may presume that there is a reason why he is doing so. If his feeling nervous explains his twiddling his thumbs, then that is the reason why he is doing so.

It also follows that (β) a person's having a reason for doing a thing is compatible with there being no reason why he does it. Smith may have a reason for doing a thing, and yet not do it; if so, he has a reason for doing it but, since he doesn't do it, there is no reason why he does it.

It also follows that (γ) a person may have a reason for doing a thing, and do it, but the reason he had for doing the thing is not the reason why he does it—what explains his doing it being something else entirely.

There are other differences too. I don't stop over them here any longer, since our topic throughout this and the following chapter will be reasons-for. However it will pay us to have taken note at the outset of the difference between those two concepts.

In sum, our preliminaries have been the following. (i) We are to keep in mind as we go that there are reasons for trusting, admiring, wanting, and so on, as well as reasons for acting and believing. (ii) Reasons-for are facts. (iii) Reasons-why are explanations.

4.

I turn now to some substantive suggestions. I suggest that we should accept the following general thesis:

(General Thesis) All reasons-for are reasons for believing.

We can be clearer. Unless otherwise noted, let X throughout range over facts, and ψ over propositions. Then the General Thesis says: for X to be a reason for φ is for X to be a reason for believing ψ, for ψ appropriate to φ.

And we can go deeper. For X to be a reason for believing ψ is for X to be evidence for, or to make probable, or, as I will mostly say, to lend weight to ψ. So we can take the General Thesis to say:

For X to be a reason for φ is for X to lend weight to ψ, for ψ appropriate to φ.

It should be noticed that if we accept the General Thesis, then we will have moved well beyond where Scanlon said that analysis had to stop. Thus we can of course say, with Scanlon, that for X to be a reason for φ is for X to count in favor of φ. But if the General Thesis is true, we can go on to say *how*: for X to be a reason for φ is for X to count in favor of φ by virtue of lending weight to ψ, for ψ appropriate to φ.

All of that was not only general but abstract, so let us look at some examples. I will proceed by focusing on a variety of locutions that we very often use in ascribing reasons-for. And I will restrict myself in this chapter to reasons for being in a mental state.

Let us begin in this section with sentences of the form

(1_{Vmind}) X is a reason for V_{mind}-ing,

where V_{mind}-ing is being in some or other mental state—thus, for example, believing that Bert is Alice's brother, trusting Smith, admiring Jones, or wanting that Jones get into law school.

However we need to stop for a moment in order to decide on an interpretation of (1_{Vmind}). Suppose someone says to you:

The fact that Charles says that Bert is Alice's brother is a reason for believing that Bert is Alice's brother.

I suppose he might mean that that fact is a reason for you in particular to believe that Bert is Alice's brother, leaving open whether it is
a reason for anyone else to believe that Bert is Alice's brother. But I
think that is unlikely. I think that people who say those words mean
that that fact is a reason for *just anyone* to believe that Bert is Alice's
brother. In any case, I will assume so. I will take it, quite generally,
that "X is a reason for V_{mind}-ing" means "X is a reason for just anyone to V_{mind}". And I will relabel: what we are concerned with in this
section are sentences of the form

$$(1_{Vmind}) \text{ X is a reason for just anyone to } V_{mind}.$$

The bearing of the General Thesis on these sentences is, by way
of first step:

For X to be a reason for just anyone to	V_{mind}	is for X to lend weight to	ψ,

for ψ appropriate to V_{mind}-ing.
   What is the ψ appropriate to V_{mind}-ing? I suggest that we should
say:

$$(1_{Vmind}\text{-analysis})$$

For X to be a reason for just anyone to	V_{mind}	is for X to lend weight to	ψ_{Vmind},

where ψ_{Vmind} is the proposition such that for a V_{mind}-ing to be a correct V_{mind}-ing is for ψ_{Vmind} to be true.
   Consider, for example, believing that Bert is Alice's brother. What
is the proposition such that for a believing that Bert is Alice's brother
to be a correct believing that Bert is Alice's brother is for it to be true?
Answer: the proposition that Bert is Alice's brother. So our analysis
yields:

For X to be a reason for just anyone to	believe that Bert is Alice's brother	is for X to lend weight to	the proposition that Bert is Alice's brother.

Consider trusting Smith. What is the proposition such that for a trusting of Smith to be a correct trusting of Smith is for it to be true? Answer: the proposition that Smith is worthy of, or deserves, being trusted—thus the proposition that Smith is trustworthy. So our analysis yields:

For X to be a reason for just anyone to	trust Smith	is for X to lend weight to	the proposition that Smith is trustworthy.

Analogously for admiring, fearing, disliking, preferring, and wanting, hoping, and regretting.

A consequence of this idea is that a fact X can be a reason for just anyone to V_{mind} only if the kind 'V_{mind}-ing' is a correctness-fixing kind. But that is surely as it should be. The kind 'feeling dizzy' is not a correctness-fixing kind, and there therefore is no such thing as feeling dizzy correctly, or for that matter, feeling dizzy incorrectly. (1_{Vmind}-analysis) therefore yields that nothing can be a reason for feeling dizzy—and rightly so.[6]

5.

In the preceding section, we looked at sentences of the form

$$(1_{Vmind}) \quad \text{X is a reason for just anyone to } V_{mind}.$$

Another set of locutions by the use of which we very often ascribe reasons-for are sentences of the form

---

[6] I suggest that what marks what Scanlon called 'judgment-sensitive attitudes' *as* 'judgment-sensitive'—see footnote 5 above—is the very fact that these are correctness-fixing mental state kinds.

(2_{Vmind}) X is a reason for A to V_{mind},

which contain references to particular people. I take these to be ambiguous, as between an objective and a subjective reading. Indeed, they wouldn't be worth stopping over if they weren't ambiguous in that way.

What I have in mind is this. I take it that sentences of the form (2_{Vmind}) have an interpretation that I will call an objective interpretation, according to which:

$(2_{Vmind}$-obj-analysis$)$

| For X to be a reason for A to | V_{mind} | is for X to lend weight to | ψ_{Vmind}, |

where ψ_{Vmind} is the proposition such that for a V_{mind}-ing to be a correct V_{mind}-ing is for ψ_{Vmind} to be true.

Thus, for example, for

(α) X is a reason for A to believe that Bert is Alice's brother,

objectively interpreted, to be true is for

(β) X lends weight to the proposition that Bert is Alice's brother

to be true.

However given our analysis of (1_{Vmind}), we know that for

(γ) X is a reason for just anyone to believe that Bert is Alice's brother

to be true is for (β) to be true. So (α) is equivalent to (γ)—and (α) is therefore of no independent interest. Similarly for all of the other V_{mind}-ings.

I am sure that (α) does have that objective interpretation: thus that we do sometimes take it that a fact is a reason for A to V_{mind} if and only if it is a reason for just anyone to V_{mind}. But I think that when we say instances of (2_{Vmind}), what we are asserting is typically something that neither entails nor is entailed by the proposition that X is a reason for just anyone to V_{mind}. What we are typically asserting is something on which A's own beliefs have a direct bearing.

For example, suppose it has never occurred to Alice that Bert might be her brother, but that we happen to know of a fact X—let it be a fact about their DNA—that lends weight to the proposition that he is her brother. We may say that X isn't a reason *for her* to believe that Bert is her brother, since she isn't aware of it.

Again, suppose Smith has offered you a partnership, and you will benefit from it if he is trustworthy—but only if he is trustworthy. You are not aware of any facts that count one way or the other about him. We, by contrast, know Smith well; and we know facts about him that count strongly in his favor. But we may say that those facts aren't, after all, reasons *for you* to trust Smith, since you aren't aware of them.

In a different kind of case, A is aware of a fact X, which is a reason for just anyone, and hence is (objectively interpreted) a reason for A, to trust B, or to believe that p, but A doesn't believe that it is. Then here too we may say that X isn't a reason *for A* to trust B, or believe that p. Suppose, for example, that today is Sunday, and that the fact that today is Sunday is a reason for just anyone to believe that the Cambridge Post Office is closed today; a fortiori, it is (objectively interpreted) a reason for Alfred to believe that the post office is closed today. But we may suppose that although Alfred is aware of the fact that today is Sunday, he doesn't believe that that fact is a reason for believing that the post office is closed today. Then we may say that the fact that today is Sunday isn't a reason *for him* to believe that the post office is closed today.

When we employ stress in that way ("*for you*", "*for her*", "*for A*", "*for him*"), we typically indicate that it is a subjective interpretation of (2_{Vmind}) that we have in mind.

Usage supplies more than one subjective interpretation of (2_{Vmind}), but I think that the following is the most common:

(2_{Vmind}-subj-analysis)

For X to be a reason for A to V_{mind}	is for the following to be the case: A believes about X that it is a fact, and that it is a reason for him to V_{mind} (objectively interpreted).

I stress that on this analysis: (2_{Vmind}), subjectively interpreted, neither entails nor is entailed by (2_{Vmind}), objectively interpreted. And also that: it is possible for X to be a reason for A to V_{mind}, both objectively and subjectively interpreted.

6.

I have taken it to be clear that reasons for V_{mind}-ing turn on correctness in V_{mind}-ing. In particular, then, they do not turn on what will or would be the consequences of a person's V_{mind}-ing. We should stop over that idea, however. There are people who say that we should distinguish among reasons for V_{mind}-ing between theoretical reasons for V_{mind}-ing, and pragmatic reasons for V_{mind}-ing, and that while the theoretical reasons turn on correctness in V_{mind}-ing, the pragmatic reasons turn on the consequences of V_{mind}-ing.

Those people do not have in mind that theoretical reasons are reasons, objectively interpreted, and pragmatic reasons are reasons, subjectively interpreted: it is among reasons, objectively interpreted, that they would have us distinguish between the theoretical and the practical. So from here on—indeed, for the rest of this chapter—it will everywhere be the objective interpretation that we are to attach to ascriptions of reasons for V_{mind}-ing. (I will occasionally add "objectively interpreted" only for stress.)

In a familiar kind of example, Bert offers to give Alfred, tomorrow, a million dollars if Alfred by then believes that the earth is flat. Suppose what he says is true, and let

> GIFT = the fact that Bert will give Alfred a million dollars
> tomorrow if Alfred by then believes that the earth is
> flat,

and

> FLAT = the proposition that the earth is flat.

GIFT plainly lends no weight to FLAT; the suggestion I made in the preceding section therefore yield that GIFT isn't a reason for Alfred to believe FLAT.

"Not so," says the friend of pragmatic reasons. "You've shown that GIFT isn't a theoretical reason for Alfred to believe FLAT. All the same, it's a pragmatic reason for Alfred to believe FLAT."

And what marks a fact as a pragmatic reason for a person to believe a proposition? Presumably something like this: "X is a pragmatic reason for A to believe P just in case X is a fact to the effect that A's believing P would cause something good." Let us ignore difficulties that issue from the appearance there of the word "good". And let us assume that Alfred's getting a million dollars tomorrow would be good. Then GIFT *is* a pragmatic reason for Alfred to believe FLAT since it is a fact to the effect that Alfred's believing FLAT would cause something good.

The friend of pragmatic reasons would have us agree that GIFT is therefore a reason for Alfred to believe FLAT.

What should we make of that idea? No doubt GIFT is a reason for Alfred to scurry about to try to find out if there is a way of getting himself to believe FLAT. (Would hypnosis work? If it would, then GIFT is presumably a reason for Alfred to get hypnotized.) But it is intuitively an odd idea that GIFT is a reason for Alfred to—simply—*believe* FLAT.

We might try the following quick way to block the idea: GIFT isn't a reason for Alfred to believe FLAT because it isn't a reason for him to believe that FLAT is *true*. The friend of pragmatic reasons replies: "I happily concede that GIFT isn't evidence for FLAT, doesn't make it probable, doesn't lend weight to it—as I said, it isn't a theoretical reason for Alfred to believe FLAT. But since it is a pragmatic reason for him to believe FLAT, it is a reason for him to believe FLAT, and a fortiori it is a reason for him to believe that FLAT is true." So we do have to go more slowly.[7]

Let us begin by taking note of the fact that if we accept the idea, then we must qualify something I said in the preceding section. I said there that a fact X is a reason for A to V$_{mind}$ if and only if it is a reason for just anyone to V$_{mind}$. (Remember that it is reasons, objectively interpreted, that we are concerned with here.) So in particular,

---

[7] There are other ways of blocking the idea than the one I go on to describe in the text. We might, for example, focus on the fact that the kind 'reasons for A to believe P' is a goodness-fixing kind, and therefore that its members are rank orderable—at least roughly—into better and worse. Suppose, then, that X is a theoretical reason for A to believe P, and Y is a pragmatic reason for A to believe P. What could be thought to mark one of those facts as a better reason for A to believe P than the other is? That is not a question that a friend of pragmatic reasons is going to find it easy to answer. But I think that the considerations I go on to describe in the text go more directly to the heart of the difficulty.

GIFT is a reason for Alfred to believe FLAT if and only if it is a reason for just anyone to believe FLAT. The friend of pragmatic reasons would tell us that that is of course true of theoretical reasons, but it is not true of pragmatic reasons, and therefore it is not true of reasons generally. Thus he would say: "X is a theoretical reason for A to V_{mind} if and only if it is a theoretical reason for just anyone to V_{mind}. But X can be a pragmatic reason for A to V_{mind} even if it is not a pragmatic reason for just anyone to V_{mind}. For example, GIFT is a pragmatic reason for Alfred to believe FLAT, but it isn't a pragmatic reason for just anyone to believe FLAT. It isn't a pragmatic reason for you or me to believe FLAT, since it isn't a fact to the effect that *your* or *my* believing FLAT would cause something good."

That X may be a pragmatic reason for A to V_{mind}, while not being a pragmatic reason for anyone else to V_{mind}, is of course due to the fact that what marks a fact as a pragmatic reason for a person to V_{mind} is what would be the consequences of *that person's* V_{mind}-ing. That should remind us of an area in which pragmatic reasons are entirely at home, namely action. Let "V_{act}-ing" be schematic for any act-kind. (Walking across Central Park, giving Bert a banana, and so on.) Then it is natural to take it that if X lends weight to the proposition that A's V_{act}-ing would cause something good, then X is a reason for A to V_{act}. And that of course means that the following is not only possible but very often the case: X is a reason for A to V_{act}, but not a reason for just anyone to V_{act}. For example, suppose A has disease D, and let X be the fact that his taking medicine M would cure him. It is natural to take it to follow that X is a reason for A to take medicine M. That is entirely compatible with X's being no reason at all for you or me to take medicine M.

Let us now notice something further about reasons for action. I take it that we can say: if X is a reason for A to V_{act}, then it can be the case that A will V_{act} for that reason. X might be a reason for A to V_{act}, and it not be the case that A V_{act}s for that reason: for example, A might have a better reason to refrain from V_{act}-ing. Still, if X is a reason for A to V_{act}, then it is possible that A will V_{act} for that reason.

Let X be a fact to the effect that A's V_{act}-ing will cause something good. Then, as I said, it is possible that A will V_{act} for that reason. I suggest that if he does, then his V_{act}-ing has a point or purpose, namely to cause that good thing. Alternatively put: if he does, then he V_{act}s in order to cause that good thing. So, for example, if A takes medicine M for the reason that it will cause him to be cured, then he takes M in order to cause himself to be cured. He takes M with the intention of bringing about that he is cured.

Let us now return to Alfred. We have been invited to agree that GIFT is a reason for Alfred to believe FLAT. Then it should be possible that Alfred will believe FLAT for that reason. So why not suppose he does believe FLAT for that reason? Then it should follow that the point or purpose of his believing FLAT is to get a million dollars. Alternatively put: he believes FLAT in order to get a million dollars, he believes FLAT with the intention of bringing about that he gets a million dollars. That can't be done, however. You can *do* something with the intention of bring about that you get a million dollars; it is not possible to believe something with the intention of bringing something about—or with *any* intention at all.

Believing P is not unique in that respect: it holds of all the V_{mind}-ings. You also can't trust B, admire C, fear D, dislike E, or want F with this or that intention—a fortiori, you can't be in these states with the intention of bringing something about. So it would be as puzzling how the fact that A's being in any of these states would cause something good could be a reason for A to be in the state.

Nor is it unique to mental states: it holds of all states. You can go to New York with an intention; you can't *be* in New York with an intention. You can get yourself to lose weight with an intention; you can't weigh so and so many pounds with an intention. Being in a state, any state, isn't a 'doing', and it therefore isn't something you can do with an intention. I add that this isn't a deep fact about states, it is right up there on the surface.[8]

So I suggest that it is a category mistake to say that GIFT is a reason for Alfred to believe FLAT, and similarly for all V_{mind}-ings. I have no objection to anyone's saying that GIFT is a pragmatic reason for Alfred to believe FLAT, so long as he goes on to say straightway that we are not to conclude from that that GIFT is a reason for Alfred to believe FLAT. As we are not to conclude that a thing is a duck from the fact that it is a decoy duck.

---

[8] I here differ from Shah and Velleman, who reject pragmatic reasons for believing on grounds that are unique to believing. See Shah, "How Truth Governs Belief", and Nishi Shah and J. David Velleman, "Doxastic Deliberation," *Philosophical Review* 114, no. 4 (2005).

7.

The objection I pointed to in the preceding section bears, not just on believings, but on V_{mind}-ings generally. However, we should stop for a moment to mention the fact that some people take trusting to be a special case. Thus while I am sure that no one thinks that regretting B conduces to B's becoming regrettable, or that preferring C to D conduces to C's becoming preferable to D, many people think that trusting a person conduces to his becoming trustworthy, and perhaps we should allow that *there* anyway, pragmatic reasons do have a role to play.

For example, Alice's son, Bert, is alas not trustworthy: he lies, he breaks promises when it suits him, and he steals small sums. A friend tells her that her trusting Bert would conduce to his becoming trustworthy. Suppose what the friend says is true, and let

> TRUST = the fact that Alice's trusting Bert would conduce to his becoming trustworthy.

TRUST lends no weight to the proposition that Bert is trustworthy, so it is not a theoretical reason for Alice to trust Bert. But it is a fact to the effect that Alice's trusting Bert would cause (or anyway conduce to the causing of) something good, namely Bert's becoming trustworthy. So a friend of pragmatic reasons would tell us that TRUST is a pragmatic reason, and therefore a reason, for Alice to trust Bert.

And perhaps some readers objected to my conclusion in the preceding section on precisely this ground.

But the difficulty remains. There just is no such thing as Alice's trusting Bert with the intention of conducing to his becoming trustworthy.

What is wanted, I think, is instead a diagnosis of why people are inclined to say that TRUST is a reason for Alice to trust Bert. The diagnosis, I think, is pretty clear. What people who say that trusting a person conduces to his becoming trustworthy have in mind is that acting trustfully toward a person conduces to his being trustworthy. Indeed, we often say "trust" when we mean "entrust"—we aren't always so fussy as to say, "I entrusted him with the money," we often say, rather, "I trusted him with the money". Now while I confess to private doubts about the matter, I suppose it is plausible to think that acting trustfully toward a person conduces to his being trustworthy; at any rate, many people think that there is such a fact. If there is, then it is surely a reason for Alice to act trustfully toward Bert. And here there is no difficulty of the kind I have been drawing attention to, for she *can* act trustfully toward Bert with the intention of conducing to his becoming trustworthy.

No doubt one's trusting a person conduces to one's acting trustfully toward him. But Alice can no more trust Bert with the intention of conducing to her acting trustfully toward him than she can trust Bert with the intention of conducing to his becoming trustworthy.

8.

To return to where we were. We looked at two kinds of locution that we very often use in ascribing reasons-for, namely sentences of the form

$$(1_{Vmind}) \text{ X is a reason for just anyone to } V_{mind},$$

and sentences of the form

$$(2_{Vmind}) \text{ X is a reason for A to } V_{mind}.$$

I suggested that we should accept the following analysis of sentences of the form (1_{Vmind}):

$(1_{Vmind}\text{-analysis})$

For X to be a reason for just anyone to	V_{mind}	is for X to lend weight to	ψ_{Vmind},

where ψ_{Vmind} is the proposition such that for a V_{mind}-ing to be a correct V_{mind}-ing is for ψ_{Vmind} to be true. I suggested that we should accept the following analysis of sentences of the form (2_{Vmind}), under their objective interpretation:

$(2_{Vmind}\text{-obj-analysis})$

For X ro be a reason for A to	V_{mind}	is for X to lend weight to	ψ_{Vmind},

where ψ_{Vmind} is the proposition such that for a V_{mind}-ing to be a correct V_{mind}-ing is for ψ_{Vmind} to be true. So interpreted, "X is a reason for A to V_{mind}" is equivalent to "X is a reason for just anyone to V_{mind}." And I suggested, last, that we should accept the following analysis of sentences of the form (2_{Vmind}), under their subjective interpretation:

$(2_{Vmind}$-subj-analysis)

For X to be a reason for A to	V_{mind}	is for the following to be the case: A believes about X that it is a fact, and that it is a reason for him to V_{mind} (objectively interpreted).

We should now take note of three other kinds of locution that we very often use in ascribing reasons-for. I will be brief about sentences of the forms

(3_{Vmind}) There is a reason for A to V_{mind}, namely X

and

(4_{Vmind}) A has a reason for V_{mind}-ing, namely X.

I think it intuitively plausible that (3_{Vmind}) means (2_{Vmind}), objectively interpreted, and that (4_{Vmind}) means (2_{Vmind}), subjectively interpreted. Readers with a good memory may remember that the two slogans I drew attention to at the beginning of this chapter differ in that one contains "what there is most reason for A to do" and the other contains "what A has most reason to do". We will focus on reasons for action in the following chapter, and we will then look more closely at the analogues for action of (3_{Vmind}) and (4_{Vmind}).

9.

I turn finally to sentences of the form

(5_{Vmind}) X is A's reason for V_{mind}-ing.

I suggest that we should say:

$(5_{Vmind}$-analysis)

For X to be A's V_{mind}-ing reason for	is for the following to be the case: (α) A believes about X that it is a fact, and that it is a reason for him to V_{mind} (objectively interpreted), and (β) A's having that compound belief is the reason why he V_{mind}s.

Suppose, for example, that Alfred believes that Bert is Alice's brother. What is his reason for believing that? Suppose it is the fact that Alice said that Bert is her brother. Let

X = the fact that Alice said that Bert is her brother.

The analysis yields that for X to be Alfred's reason for believing that Bert is Alice's brother is for the following to be the case: (α) Alfred believes about X that it is a fact, and that it is a reason for him to believe that Bert is Alice's brother, and (β) Alfred's having that compound belief is the reason why he believes that Bert is Alice's brother. That, I take it, is intuitively very plausible.

Similarly for the other V_{mind}-ings. Let

X = the fact that Alfred's friend Jones said that Smith is trustworthy.

What marks X as Alfred's reason for trusting Smith (if it is) is that (α) Alfred believes about X that it is a fact, and that it is a reason for him to believe that Smith is trustworthy, and (β) Alfred's having that compound belief is the reason why he trusts Smith.

Four things are worth drawing attention to. First, while $(5_{Vmind}$-analysis) requires for the truth of (5_{Vmind}) that A believes about X that it is a fact, and that X is a reason for him to V_{mind}, it does not require for the truth of (5_{Vmind}) that X really is a reason for him to V_{mind}. But that is as it should be. A person might reason badly—indeed, reason irrationally—from a fact that he has in hand. A fact that he has in hand may fail to be a reason for him to V_{mind}, and yet be *his* reason for V_{mind}-ing.

Second, according to $(5_{Vmind}$-analysis), (5_{Vmind}) is compatible with there being, and A's having, a lot of reasons for V_{mind}-ing, only one of which is his reason for V_{mind}-ing. That too is as it should be. The following is possible: A has a lot of reasons for (as it might be) believing that p, but only one of them—say X—is such that his having the compound belief about X that it is a fact, and that it is a reason for him to believe that p, is the reason why he believes that p.

Third, I leave open what exactly it is for clause (β) "A's having that compound belief is the reason why he $V_{mind}s$"—to be true. I assume that for it to be true is for the following to be true: A's having that compound belief explains A's V_{mind}-ing. But what is required for *that* to be true—more generally, what is required for it to be the case that X explains Y, where X and Y are any facts you like, whether mental or nonmental—is a familiar, longstanding problem, and I say nothing about it here.[9]

Finally, fourth, our stipulation at the outset that reasons-for are facts commits us to the possibility that a person may believe that there is a fact that is his reason for V_{mind}-ing, and yet be mistaken. Suppose Alfred believes that his pig can fly. We ask him what his reason for believing that is, and he replies, in all sincerity: "The fact that all pigs can fly. That's my reason for believing that my pig can." Well, there is no such fact. What should we say of Alfred?

We might try: there is a fact that is his reason for believing that his pig can fly, but he is mistaken as to which it is. Thus we might try: the fact that is his reason for believing that his pig can fly is the fact that he believes that all pigs can fly.

That won't do. There are cases in which a person believes that q, and his reason for believing that q is the fact that he believes that p. For example, Bert might believe that Whitefoot will win this afternoon's race, and when asked what his reason is, he might reply: "On consideration, I just found myself believing that Whitefoot will win all the afternoon races he is entered in, and the fact that I found myself believing that is my reason for believing that Whitefoot will win this afternoon's race." But cases of this kind are very rare, and Alfred's is not among them. Alfred did not reason to his conclusion that his pig can fly from the premise that he *believes* that all pigs can fly; he reasoned to his conclusion from the premise that all pigs *can* fly.

Then if he can offer us no other fact that is his reason for believing that his pig can fly—no other fact than the (putative) fact that all

---

[9] I draw attention here only to the interesting fact that it is the same word "reasons" that appears in both "reasons for" and "reasons why", and that cannot be mere happenstance—it, itself, calls for explanation.

pigs can fly—we would surely be right to conclude that his mistake is not as to which fact is his reason for believing that his pig can fly: his mistake is in thinking—falsely—that there is a fact that is his reason for believing that his pig can fly.

Opting for that conclusion doesn't commit us to saying that Alfred's believing that his pig can fly simply popped into existence, for no reason. We can distinguish. We can say that while there is no fact such that he believes about it that it is a fact, and that it is a reason for him to believe that his pig can fly, he believes that there is; and his believing that there is such a fact is *why* he believes that his pig can fly.

Analogously for the person who trusts Smith and, when asked for his reason, says "My reason is the fact that you told me he is trustworthy," where as a matter of fact, we did no such thing.

10.

As I said earlier, I take it to be clear that reasons for V_{mind}-ing turn on correctness in V_{mind}-ing.

But I should perhaps add that I have not been assuming that everybody believes that they do. Consider again, for example,

$(5_{Vmind}$-analysis)

| For X to be A's V_{mind}-ing reason for | is for the following to be the case: (α) A believes about X that it is a fact, and that it is a reason for him to V_{mind} (objectively interpreted), and (β) A's having that compound belief is the reason why he V_{mind}s. |

That does not tell us what A has to *believe* if he is to believe that X is his reason for V_{mind}-ing; it tells us only what would make it *true* that X is his reason for V_{mind}-ing.

IX

Reasons-For (Acts)

1.

Let us from here on take "V_{act}-ing" be schematic for acting in one or another way. Then what we will do is to attend to the following locutions:

(1_{Vact}) X is a reason for V_{act}-ing,
(2_{Vact}) X is a reason for A to V_{act},
(3_{Vact}) There is a reason for A to V_{act}, namely X,
(4_{Vact}) A has a reason for V_{act}-ing, namely X,

and

(5_{Vact}) X is A's reason for V_{act}-ing.

2.

I begin with two similarities between reasons for V_{act}-ing and reasons for V_{mind}-ing. First, I said in section 4 of the preceding chapter that I take it that "X is a reason for V_{mind}-ing" means "X is a reason for just anyone to V_{mind}." I take it, similarly, that "X is a reason for V_{act}-ing" means "X is a reason for just anyone to V_{act}". So I will relabel: what we are concerned with is sentences of the form

(1_{Vact}) X is a reason for just anyone to V_{act}.

Second, I take it that

(2_{Vact}) X is a reason for A to V_{act}

is ambiguous as between an objective and a subjective reading, just as "X is a reason for A to V_{mind}" is. And I take it that (1_{Vact}) entails (2_{Vact}) under the objective interpretation of (2_{Vact}). Thus I suppose that the fact that milk contains calcium is a reason for just anyone to drink milk; and I take it to follow that that fact is a reason (objectively interpreted) for A in particular to drink milk, whoever A may be.

But now the differences start to emerge. To begin with, a fact may be a reason for A in particular to do a thing (objectively interpreted) without being a reason for just anyone to do it. It is a requirement on an account of reasons for action that it accommodate that possibility.

So what are we to think makes (2_{Vact}) true, under its objective interpretation? One thing that is clear is that reasons for a person to V_{act} do not turn on correctness in V_{act}-ing. Let

> X = the fact that if I now play notes N on a piano, in way W, then I will be playing Mozart's S correctly.

That is no reason at all for me to now play notes N on a piano, in way W. I have no interest that would be served by my doing that, and nobody else has either.[1] (Anyway, what piano? I don't have a piano!)

The General Thesis says that all reasons-for are reasons for believing. For believing *what* in the case of reasons for action? For lending weight to *what*? I suggest:

(2_{Vact}-obj-analysis)

For X to be a reason for A to V_{act} (objectively interpreted)	is	for X to lend weight to the proposition that A should V_{act}.

That suggestion obviously calls for defense.

---

[1] Gideon Rosen made this important point in "Brandom on Modality, Normativity, and Intentionality", cited above in chapter VI. The Mozart example I gave is a variant on his. (He invited us to imagine that his daughter is discouraged because she has performed Mozart's S incorrectly, and will be cheered if he too performs it incorrectly.)

3.

Let us divide the likely objections to (2_{Vact}-obj-analysis) into two groups. I begin with those that are objections to a weaker thesis that is entailed by (2_{Vact}-obj-analysis), namely

(2_{Vact}-obj-iff)

X is a reason for A to V_{act} (objectively interpreted)	if and only if	X lends weight to the proposition that A should V_{act}.

I postpone until section 5 an objection to the idea that the two concepts are not merely coextensive, but, more strongly, that one is reducible to the other in the manner indicated in (2_{Vact}-obj-analysis).

What should we think of (2_{Vact}-obj-iff)? I suspect that one objection to it is likely to be this: the fact that A would enjoy V_{act}-ing may very well be a reason for A to V_{act}, but does not lend weight to the proposition that A *should* V_{act}.

I fancy that anyone who thinks this is thinking of "should" as imputing moral requirement. It certainly isn't plausible to think that the fact that we would enjoy doing a thing is a reason for believing that we are morally required to do it.

But "should" doesn't impute moral requirement. To say "You should do such and such" is to give *advice*, and not all advice is moral advice. I say "You should taste this wine," not thinking that morality requires you to; what I have in mind, which inclines me to say what I say, is nothing more than just that you'd like it. Or "You should read such and such novel, it's very witty." Or "You should take the route north of the lake when you go home, it's much prettier than the route south of the lake." Or "You should go see such and such movie, I loved it."

The judgment that A should V_{act} is the weakest of the directives. People often assert stronger directives in such contexts. "You ought to go see such and such movie" is common enough. "You must go see such and such movie" is rather more hectic, but not uncommon. (I have never heard anyone say "You must go see such and such movie, like it or not!" This is not unimaginable, though no one would say it on the ground that you would enjoy the movie. Presumably someone who says this to you thinks you'd learn some important lesson from it.) But "You should go see it" is anyway very

often said on the mere ground that you'd enjoy it. That is why it is
"should" that appears in (2_{Vact}-obj-analysis).

A different kind of concern might lie in the possibility that what
A would enjoy doing is something dreadful. Let

X = the fact that Alfred would enjoy breaking Bert's legs.

Then an objector may say that X is a reason for Alfred to break Bert's
legs, and yet that it doesn't lend weight to the proposition that Alfred
should break Bert's legs.

Should we agree? We have two other options.

(i) We can say: "No, X is no reason at all for Alfred to break Bert's
legs. So of course the fact that X lends no weight to the proposition
that A should break Bert's legs is no objection to (2_{Vact}-obj-iff)." I said
just above that the fact that A would enjoy V_{act}-ing may very well be
a reason for A to V_{act}; I refrained from saying that it is a reason for
A to V_{act}, whatever V_{act}-ing may be, precisely in order to leave room
for our preferring to say that in the case of some V_{act}-ings, on some
occasions, it isn't.

(ii) We can instead say: "Yes, X is a reason for Alfred to break
Bert's legs, but a *very* bad one. But then it is also the case that X
lends weight to the proposition that Alfred should break Bert's legs,
though *very* little." Some people so use "reason for" that nothing is
a reason for φ unless it is a good reason for φ . I can see no good
reason for joining them.

For my own part, I prefer (i) to (ii): breaking a person's legs
being what it is, the fact that Alfred would enjoy breaking Bert's
strikes me as no reason at all for him to proceed. We should, I am
sure, allow that some reasons for V_{act}-ing are bad reasons for V_{act}-
ing. (As also that some reasons for V_{mind}-ing are bad reasons for
V_{mind}-ing.) But the fact that Alfred would enjoy breaking Bert's legs
strikes me as less than a bad reason for him to proceed.

On the other hand, there are people who take the fact that one
would enjoy doing a thing as always providing *some* reason for one
to do the thing. Utilitarians, for example, hold this view. We should
remember about them, however, that they also say that the fact that
one would enjoy doing a thing always lends *some* weight to the
proposition that one should, in fact ought, to do the thing.

Let us therefore leave it open which of (i) and (ii) is preferable
to the other. What matters for present purposes is only that we

should reject the objector's view. I take it that you can't believe that X is a reason for Alfred to break Bert's legs without also believing that it lends *some* weight to the proposition that he should break them. As I take it that you can't believe that the fact that your friends would enjoy seeing such and such a movie is a reason for them to see it without also believing that it lends *some* weight to the proposition that they should see it.

4.

There is a currently popular view about reasons for action that *appears*, intuitively, to warrant a second objection to:

(2_{Vact}-obj-iff)

X is a reason for A to V_{act} (objectively interpreted)	if and only if	X lends weight to the proposition that A should V_{act}.

The view I have in mind is:

(Reasons Internalism)

X is a reason for A to V_{act} (objectively interpreted)	only if	X lends weight to the proposition that A's V_{act}-ing would satisfy a want of A's.

Why might Reasons Internalism be thought to warrant an objection to (2_{Vact}-obj-iff)? Well, suppose we accept Reasons Internalism. Then if we also accept (2_{Vact}-obj-iff), we are committed to accepting:

(Should Internalism)

X lends weight to the proposition that A should V_{act}	only if	X lends weight to the proposition that A's V_{act}-ing would satisfy a want of A's.

But Should Internalism is surely very implausible! For example, let

ROPE = the fact that Bert will drown unless Alfred throws him the rope that he has in hand.

It is very plausible to think that ROPE lends weight to the proposition that Alfred should throw Bert the rope. Does ROPE lend weight to the proposition that Alfred's throwing Bert the rope would satisfy a want of Alfred's? It might. It does if Bert's fate matters to Alfred. But it might be that Alfred couldn't care less about Bert's fate. Suppose that is true of Alfred. Then ROPE lends no weight to the proposition that Alfred's throwing Bert the rope would satisfy a want of Alfred's. In sum, it is plausible to think that ROPE lends weight to the proposition that Alfred should throw Bert the rope, but lends no weight to the proposition that Alfred's throwing Bert the rope would satisfy a want of Alfred's.

How should we respond to this objection?

Some people say that appearances notwithstanding, we should accept Should Internalism. Why so? Some people say we should accept Should Internalism because Reasons Internalism and $(2_{Vact}$-obj-iff) are both true.[2] Others give an independent reason for accepting Should Internalism: it is analogous to the reason many people give for accepting Reasons Internalism.[3] So let us take a closer look at Reasons Internalism.

We should notice at the outset that we already have in hand something that looks like a countercase to Reasons Internalism. For consider ROPE again. I said it is very plausible to think that ROPE lends weight to the proposition that Alfred should throw Bert the rope. Isn't it also plausible that ROPE is a reason for Alfred to throw Bert the rope, objectively interpreted? By hypothesis, however— since by hypothesis, Alfred couldn't care less about Bert's fate— ROPE lends no weight to the proposition that Alfred's throwing Bert the rope would satisfy a want of Alfred's.

---

[2] The people I have in mind here think $(2_{Vact}$-obj-iff) true because they accept something stronger than $(2_{Vact}$-obj-iff), namely one or other or both of the slogans that I set out at the beginning of the preceding chapter. (We will turn to them in section 5 below.) The people I have in mind include Philippa Foot; see her "Morality as a System of Hypothetical Imperatives," reprinted in her *Virtues and Vices* (Oxford: Basil Blackwell, 1978).

[3] I take Thomas Nagel to be, or anyway at one time to have been, among them. I quote a passage from him in footnote 4 below.

So *why* is it to be thought that we should accept Reasons Internalism? I think that what moves people to accept it is the following idea. You and I think that ROPE is a reason for Alfred to throw Bert the rope. But given that by hypothesis, Alfred couldn't care less about Bert's fate, it is surely unlikely that *Alfred* thinks that ROPE is a reason for him to throw Bert the rope.

More generally, the following is very plausible:

(Reasons-Belief Internalism)

A believes that: X is a reason for for him to V_{act} (objectively interpreted)	only if	A believes that: X lends weight to the proposition that his V_{act}-ing would satisfy a want of his.[4]

But if you can *believe* that X is a reason for you to V_{act} only if you *believe* that X lends weight to the proposition that your V_{act}-ing would satisfy a want of yours, surely we can conclude that X *is* a reason for you to V_{act} only if X *does* lend weight to the proposition that your V_{act}-ing would satisfy a want of yours. Hence: Reasons Internalism.

That "surely" and "hence" are unjustified. Not because Reasons-Belief Internalism is false. I should think it is true. Let

DEADLINE = the fact that today is April 15.

I believe that DEADLINE is a reason for me to get my tax return in. Do I believe that DEADLINE lends weight to the proposition that my getting my tax return in would satisfy a want of mine? Well, yes. Not that I want to pay my taxes. I have never wanted to pay my taxes. But I am always willing to pay them because I want to avoid the grief that comes of not paying them.

On the other hand, Reasons Internalism does not follow from Reasons-Belief Internalism. Consider ROPE again. ROPE, we are

---

[4] Here is Thomas Nagel in support of Should Internalism: "[Should] Internalism's appeal derives from the conviction that one cannot accept or assert sincerely any ethical proposition without accepting at least a prima facie motivation for action in accordance with it." See his *The Possibility of Altruism* (Princeton, NJ: Princeton University Press: 1970), 7.

supposing, lends no weight to the proposition that Alfred's throwing Bert the rope would satisfy a want of Alfred's. But on the assumption that he knows about ROPE that it is a fact, he knows that Bert's life is in danger and that he can easily save it. Then he *should* want to save it. It is a *failing* in him that he doesn't. So it is a *failing* in him that he doesn't have a want such that ROPE lends weight to the proposition that his throwing Bert the rope would satisfy it.

Then we should conclude, not that ROPE isn't a reason for Alfred to throw Bert the rope, but rather that it is a *failing* in that he doesn't believe it is.

In sum, Reasons-Belief Internalism does not warrant us in accepting Reasons Internalism.[5]

I know of no better reason for accepting Reasons Internalism.[6] In light of its intuitive implausibility, I therefore invite the conclusion that we should reject it.

But then if we reject Reasons Internalism, we need no longer worry about the fact that it appears, intuitively, to warrant an objection to

$(2_{Vact}\text{-obj-iff})$

X is a reason for A to V_{act} (objectively interpreted)	if and only if	X lends weight to the proposition that A should V_{act}.

5.

We looked in sections 3 and 4 at objections to $(2_{Vact}\text{-obj-iff})$. Let us now assume that $(2_{Vact}\text{-obj-iff})$ is acceptable, and look at an objection to the idea that one of the two concepts is reducible to the other in the manner indicated in the stronger thesis,

---

[5] And the analogous Should-Belief Internalism (see footnote 4 above) does not warrant us in accepting Should Internalism.

[6] A more complex argument for Reasons Internalism appears in a widely cited article by Bernard Williams, "Internal and External Reasons," reprinted in his *Moral Luck* (Cambridge: Cambridge University Press, 1981). I do not take space to discuss his argument in the text because of its complexity. My reasons for regarding it as unsatisfactory may be found in Addendum 3 on Reasons.

$(2_{V_{act}}\text{-obj-analysis})$

For X to be a reason for A to V_{act} (objectively interpreted)	is	for X to lend weight to the proposition that A should V_{act}.

I mentioned in footnote 2 in the preceding section that there are people who accept the weaker thesis, $(2_{V_{act}}\text{-obj-iff})$, because they accept one or other or both of the slogans that I set out at the beginning of the preceding chapter:

> (SLOGAN-I) What A ought to do is what there is most reason for A to do

and

> (SLOGAN-II) What A ought to do is what A has most reason to do.

On these views, for it to be the case that directives of the form "A ought to V_{act}" to be true is for ascriptions of reasons for action to be true. Friends of these views typically don't fix on the difference between "ought" and "should", and so don't say anything about weaker directives of the form "A should V_{act}." But I am sure they would say the same about them, namely one or other or both of:

> (SLOGAN-I*) What A should do is what there is most reason for A to do

and

> (SLOGAN-II*) What A should do is what A has most reason to do.

In short, they say that directive facts generally turn on facts about reasons for action.

I recommend the contrary view: facts about reasons for action turn on directive facts.

Let us therefore take a closer look at those slogans. At SLOGAN-I* and SLOGAN-II* in particular, since it is the weaker directives that we are concerned with in this chapter.

6.

I begin with a ground for saying that we should bypass SLOGAN-II*.

In section 2, I said that there is an ambiguity in

(2_{Vact}) X is a reason for A to V_{act}

as between an objective and a subjective interpretation, and I suggested that its objective interpretation is given by the following:

$(2_{Vact}$-obj-analysis)

For X to be a reason for A to V_{act} (objectively interpreted)	is	for X to lend weight to the proposition that A should V_{act}.

I think that usage supplies more than one subjective interpretation of (2_{Vact}), but I think that the following is the most common:

$(2_{Vact}$-subj-analysis)

For X to be a reason for A to V_{act} (subjectively interpreted)	is	for A to believe about X that it is a fact, and that it is a reason for him to V_{act} (objectively interpreted).

It is clear that on these analyses of them, (2_{Vact}), subjectively interpreted, neither entails nor is entailed by (2_{Vact}), objectively interpreted.

By analogy with reasons for V_{mind}-ing, I take it to be plausible to think that

(3_{Vact}) There is a reason for A to V_{act}, namely X

means (2_{Vact}), objectively interpreted. (See section 8 of the preceding chapter.) Does

(4_{Vact}) A has a reason for A to V_{act}, namely X

mean (2_{Vact}), subjectively interpreted? If so, then SLOGAN-I* and SLOGAN-II* are not trivially different rewordings of one and the same thesis: they express nontrivially different theses.

On Monday, Wednesday, and Friday, I think that (4_{Vact}) does mean (2_{Vact}), subjectively interpreted. Consider ROPE again. It is tempting to say that even if it is true that ROPE *is* a reason for Alfred to throw Bert the rope, Alfred doesn't *have* a reason for throwing Bert the rope—and that because he doesn't *believe* that ROPE is a reason for him to throw Bert the rope.

Not so on the other days of the week. Suppose Alan was driving to a restaurant to meet his friends. Let

> CHILD = the fact that there was a child in the path of Alan's car.

Suppose that Alan was aware of CHILD, but nevertheless did not stop his car because he didn't believe that the child's presence was a reason for him to do so. I feel inclined to say, not only that there *was* a reason for Alan to stop his car, namely CHILD, but also that Alan *had* a reason to stop his car, namely CHILD. Consider the court's likely reaction if Alan's lawyer addresses it as follows: "But look, Your Honor, my client had no reason to stop his car!—for he didn't believe that the child's presence was any reason for him to stop it."[7]

On the other hand, I see nothing to be gained by trying to force a decision about (4_{Vact}): what is in question here is a matter of usage, and I see no theoretical ground for insisting that (4_{Vact}) does, or that it does not, mean (2_{Vact}), subjectively interpreted.

So I will leave it open—and I will from here on therefore simply bypass (4_{Vact}).

But then we must also bypass

> (SLOGAN-II*) What A should do is what A has most reason to do.

For if we are leaving it an open question whether (4_{Vact}) means (2_{Vact}), subjectively interpreted, then we are leaving it an open question what SLOGAN-II* *says*.

It is worth pointing out also that if we are leaving it an open question whether (4_{Vact}) means (2_{Vact}), subjectively interpreted, then

---

[7] I thank David Kaplan for this example.

we are leaving it an open question whether SLOGAN-II* says that what A should do is what A believes he has most reason to do. That, however, can't be thought in the least degree plausible. If anything is clear, it is that what a person should do does not turn on what he believes he has most reason to do. (I will return to this point below.)

I add that analogous considerations suggest that friends of the turn to reasons for action would also do well to bypass SLOGAN II.

7.

That leaves us with

(SLOGAN-I*) What A should do is what there is most reason for A to do.

To accept it is to accept that directive facts turn on facts about reasons for action, objectively interpreted. I have recommended the contrary view: facts about reasons for action, objectively interpreted, turn on directive facts. Unless I explicitly say otherwise, it will from here on be reasons for action, objectively interpreted, that I will mean by "reasons for action".

If you think that directive facts turn on facts about reasons for action, what do you think that facts about reasons for action turn on? Let

APPLE = the fact that Alice promised Bob that she would giv him an apple.

APPLE is on any view a reason for Alice to give Bob an apple. What makes it be? On my view, what makes it be a reason for Alice to give Bob an apple is its lending weight to the proposition that Alice should give Bob an apple. What on your view makes it be a reason for Alice to give Bob an apple?

Perhaps something like this. In making her promise to Bob, Alice invited Bob to rely on getting an apple from her. Very well, but how does that help? In what way does that help explain why APPLE is a reason for Alice to give Bob an apple?

Note that it won't do to appeal to any concern that Alice may have for Bob's fate, for she might have no such concern, and it is reasons for action, objectively interpreted, that we are dealing with here. (Remember that ROPE is a reason for Alfred to throw Bert the rope, whatever Alfred's wants may be.)

Suppose that things have now changed: Alice has now kept her promise to Bob. Then APPLE isn't any longer a reason for Alice to give Bob an apple. Why not? What makes it have ceased to be a reason for Alice to give Bob an apple? On my view, what makes it have ceased to be a reason for Alice to give Bob an apple is its no longer lending weight to the proposition that Alice should give Bob an apple. What on your view makes it have ceased to be?

Again, let

HAT = the fact that Bill just put on a brown hat.

Is that a reason for Ann to catch the next plane to Chicago? Well, it certainly doesn't *sound* as if it is! Why not? What's missing?

Here are some possible background facts in virtue of each of which HAT would be a reason for Ann to catch the next plane to Chicago. (i) Ann and Bill had agreed that if Bill puts on a brown hat, then that will be a sign to Ann that a supply of the drug she needs to save her life has just been located in Chicago. (ii) Ann and Bill had agreed that if Bill puts on a brown hat, then that will be a sign to Ann that her missing child—who is being hunted for in Chicago— has been found there. (iii) Ann has promised Bill that if he puts on a brown hat, then she will go to Chicago straightway to take his place at the forthcoming meeting of Save the Whales, an organization they are both directors of. What do (i), (ii), and (iii) have in common such that if any one of them is the case, then HAT is a reason for Ann to catch the next plane to Chicago? On my view, if any one of them is the case, then HAT lends weight to the proposition that Ann should catch the next plane to Chicago. What on your view do (i), (ii), and (iii) have in common in virtue of which if any one of them is the case, then HAT is a reason for Ann to catch the next plane to Chicago?

Finally, the fact that Alan will die if he doesn't take some medicine M is a better reason for him to take it than the fact that he likes the taste of it. Why? On my view, the former fact lends more weight to the proposition that he should take it than the latter fact does. What is your answer to the question?

No doubt you can produce answers to each of these questions, but they are going to be a scatter. What makes those answers all *be* answers to the questions?

It would certainly be no surprise if friends of SLOGAN-I* turned my questions back to front. What makes a fact lend weight to the proposition that a person should do a thing if *not* its being a reason for the person to do the thing?

Good question! And I am sure that the popularity of the slogans lies chiefly in the very fact they supply a compact answer to the question what it comes to for it to be the case that a person should do a thing.

I said "chiefly" rather than "wholly" because there is another reason why the slogans have been popular. Many people think that if the slogans are right, then that would explain a fact about moral judgment that they think had been insufficiently appreciated, namely its link with action. Friends of the slogans say that their opponents view moral thinking as an effort to discover more or less interesting impersonal moral facts, which one may, or may not, then go on to give a place in one's life. They say that they, by contrast, make central to an understanding of moral thinking the fact that its *point* is to figure out how to act.

But if I have discovered that I should do a thing, then there is nothing impersonal in the fact that I have discovered: the fact I have discovered is a fact about *me*. And while I may, or may not, go on to give that discovery a place in my life, I should. That I should is, after all, exactly what I have discovered.

Have I misunderstood them? I am sure that friends of the slogans who take this line in support of their view have in mind that something more importantly personal is made room for when we recognize that finding out whether a person should do a thing requires finding out whether there is most reason for the person to do it. I am sure that they think that with this recognition comes recognition that what matters is what would issue in the person's acting in this or that way, namely the person's beliefs and wants.

More precisely, I suggest that what lies behind their taking this line is merely a conflation of reasons for action, objectively interpreted, and reasons for action, subjectively interpreted. If you think that the question whether a person should do a thing turns on whether there is most reason for him to do the thing, subjectively interpreted, then of course you are thinking that the question whether he should do the thing turns on personal facts about him, most importantly on what he believes are reasons for him to do the thing—and therefore, given

(Reasons-Belief Internalism)

A believes that: X is a reason for for him to V_{act} (objectively interpreted)	only if	A believes that: X lends weight to the proposition that his V_{act}-ing would satisfy a want of his,

on what his wants are, or anyway on what he believes would satisfy them.

But it is just a mistake to think that the question whether a person should do a thing turns on whether there is most reason for him to do it, subjectively interpreted.

What a person wants is always *relevant* to whether he should do a thing, and so of course also to whether there is reason for him to do it, objectively interpreted. But what the person wants is not dispositive. Other people's wants are always relevant too, and in some cases it is their wants that settle the matter.

I said at the beginning of the preceding chapter that I think the turn to reasons for action in the 1950s was a bad idea. I have two connected reasons for thinking so. First, it is altogether too easy to conflate reasons for action, objectively interpreted, with reasons for action, subjectively interpreted, and that conflation has made

(SLOGAN-I*) What A should do is what there is most reason for A to do

seem attractive in a way that is not warranted.

Second, if we fix firmly on reasons for action, objectively interpreted, then it is hard to see why that slogan should have seemed attractive at all. Intuitively, if Alice has not yet kept her promise to Bob, then the fact that she promised to give him an apple lends weight to the proposition that she should give him an apple. What makes that so? Why does "She promised" lend weight to "She should"? We might well think that the answer is to be found by attending to the fact that to promise to do a thing is to invite reliance on one's doing it, and trying to elicit what goes on in inviting reliance. The friend of SLOGAN-I* tells us that it won't be enough to elicit what goes on in inviting reliance: we can't conclude that "She invited reliance" lends weight to "She should" unless we have reached that conclusion *by* showing along the way that "She invited reliance" is a reason for her to do the thing she invited reliance on her doing. But why do we have to take that detour to the conclusion? It is no clearer what it comes to for a fact X to be a reason for A to do a thing than it is what it comes to for X to lend weight to the proposition that A should do it. Indeed, I have suggested that it is less clear.

In short, the slogans mislead badly: they give an impression of depth and explanatory power that they simply do not have.

8.

I said at the beginning of the preceding chapter that even if we reject that turn to reasons for action, the question what it is for something to be a reason for action is an interesting one, which an account of normativity should surely speak to. In this chapter, we attended to the following kinds of locutions that are often used to ascribe reasons for action:

(1_{Vact}) X is a reason for V_{act}-ing,
(2_{Vact}) X is a reason for A to V_{act},
(3_{Vact}) There is a reason for A to V_{act}, namely X,

and

(4_{Vact}) A has a reason for V_{act}-ing, namely X.

I suggested, most importantly, that (2_{Vact}) has both an objective and a subjective interpretation, and that (3_{Vact}) means (2_{Vact}), objectively interpreted. I said that it is tempting to think that (4_{Vact}) means (2_{Vact}), subjectively interpreted, but also tempting to think that it does not; I therefore suggested that we should bypass it.

But I have said nothing so far about

(5_{Vact}) X is A's reason for V_{act}-ing,

and we should now turn to it.

Let us begin by looking again at

(5_{Vmind}) X is A's reason for V_{mind}-ing.

I suggested that we should say:

$(5_{Vmind}$-analysis)

		is for the following to be the case:
For X to		(α) A believes about X that it is
be A's	V_{mind}-ing	a fact, and that it is a reason for him
reason		to V_{mind} (objectively interpreted), and
for		(β) A's having that compound belief
		is the reason why he V_{mind}s.

I suggest that we should say, analogously:

$(5_{Vact}$-analysis)

		is for the following to be the case:
For X to		(α) A believes about X that it is
be A's	V_{act}-ing	a fact, and that it is a reason for him
reason		to V_{act} (objectively interpreted), and
for		(β) A's having that compound belief
		is the reason why he is V_{act}-ing.[8]

There is a familiar kind of objection to that idea. A reason why is an explanation, so if we say that A's having the compound belief ascribed to him by (α) is the reason why A is V_{act}-ing, we are saying that his having that compound belief explains his V_{act}-ing. But didn't Hume teach us that a person's doing a thing is not explained merely by mentioning that he has this or that belief? Don't we have to mention a want as well as a belief?

Well, to begin with, if we were right to accept

(Reasons-Belief Internalism)

A believes that:		A believes that:
X is a reason for		X lends weight to
for him to V_{act}	only if	the proposition that
(objectively		his V_{act}-ing would satisfy
interpreted)		a want of his,

then given that A has the compound belief ascribed to him by (α), it follows that A believes that X lends weight to the proposition that

---

[8] These theses have a bearing on what I take to be the better of the two current conceptions of practical reasoning. See Addendum 4 on Reasoning.

his V_{act}-ing would satisfy a want of his. So a friend of (5_{Vact}-analysis) can say:

> (i) the fact that A has the compound belief ascribed to him by
>   (α)

explains A's V_{act}-ing by virtue of the fact that it entails

> (ii) the fact that A believes about X both that it is a fact, and
>   that X lends weight to the proposition that his V_{act}-ing
>   would satisfy a want of his,

where (ii) explains A's V_{act}-ing.

Does (ii) explain A's V_{act}-ing? After all, a person who offers (ii) as an explanation of A's V_{act}-ing mentions no particular want of A's. Indeed, we do well to take note of an ambiguity in

> (S) A believes that X lends weight to the proposition that his
> V_{act}-ing would satisfy a want of his.

A person who says (S) may mean that A has a want about which he believes that X lends weight to the proposition that his V_{act}-ing would satisfy it. Or the speaker may mean something weaker, namely: A believes that he has a want such that X lends weight to the proposition that his V_{act}-ing would satisfy it. On the weaker interpretation of (S), (S) is compatible with A's being mistaken from the ground up— thus that while A *believes* he has such a want, he doesn't.

On the other hand, there is no good reason to suppose it false to say that (ii) explains A's V_{act}-ing, even if (ii) mentions no particular want of A's, and even if A falsely believes he has a relevant want.

No doubt explaining A's V_{act}-ing by appeal to (ii) isn't very informative. If it is puzzling that A is V_{act}-ing, we may well want to know what want A has, or anyway why he believes he has a want, in virtue of which he is V_{act}-ing. But the fact that an explanation isn't very informative is entirely compatible with its being true.

In short, there are beliefs and beliefs, and some beliefs are beliefs about wants. Beliefs about wants of the kind I point to here should be enough to meet any requirement that Hume's followers are entitled to impose on us.

9.

Two final comments.

I said at the beginning of chapter VIII that given our stipulation that reasons-for are facts, no desire is a reason for anyone to do anything. I said, however, that nothing of theoretical interest is thereby lost, for our stipulation leaves it open that the fact that a person A wants such and such may be a reason for a person, A himself, or someone else, to do a thing.

It surely needs no argument that the fact that A wants such and such might be a reason for B to do a thing. But I have suggested that whether it is turns on whether it lends weight to the proposition that B should do the thing. And it might not. For example, suppose Smith wants Jones dead. I can't offhand imagine background facts in light of which the fact that Smith has that want lends weight to the proposition that we should arrange for Jones's death.

Similarly, it surely needs no argument that the fact that A wants such and such might be a reason for A to do a thing, as, for example, to satisfy his own want. But here too it might not be.

What is worth stopping over is the idea some people have that when people act—or anyway, when people act intentionally—they are acting for the reason that they want this or that.

It is, of course, entirely possible for the following to be true: the fact that A wants O is A's reason for V_{act}-ing. For let

X = the fact that A wants O.

It is entirely possible for the following to be true: (α) A believes about X that it is a fact, and that it is a reason for him to V_{act} (objectively interpreted), and (β) A's having that compound belief is the reason why he is V_{act}-ing. But such cases are in fact rare: people rarely do things for the reason that they want to. Consider people who drink milk. They typically do so for the reason that they enjoy drinking milk. Not so Alfred, let us suppose. For suppose Alfred is drinking some milk, and we ask him what his reason is for doing so, given we have never known him to like it. And suppose he laughs and says: "It's funny. I suddenly found that I had this craving for milk, and that's my reason for drinking it. See, there's this theory that when people have a sudden craving for things that they don't normally want to eat or drink, then that's because they have a nutritional deficiency that can only be cured if they eat or drink the things. Maybe it's a calcium deficiency in my case." *This*, we may say, is a case in which a person is doing a thing for the reason that he wants to—for in light of having heard of that theory, Alfred believes that his wanting to drink some milk is a reason for him to drink it, and that is why he is drinking it. But as I said, such cases are rare.

Finally, a brief comment on what is sometimes called 'means-end rationality'. It is often said that if a person adopts a certain goal for himself, then it follows that there is a reason for him to do what would conduce to his achieving it. That is plausible enough if what we have in mind is reasons for action, subjectively interpreted. But it is not at all plausible in the case of reasons for action, objectively interpreted. If Smith adopts the goal of bringing about Jones's death, then he may believe that the fact that Jones likes chocolates is a reason for him to offer Jones poisoned chocolates. But it isn't. Objectively interpreted, that is.

Let us now return to the directives.

X

On Some Views
about "Ought": Relativism,
Dilemmas, Means-Ends

1.

The literature on the directives focuses almost entirely on the word "ought", and this and chapter XI will do so too. I will focus on six ideas about "ought", three in this chapter, three in the following chapter. Five of them have been found attractive by philosophers. My conclusions about them will be negative, but certain lessons emerge from discussion of them that an account of "ought" has to accommodate, and I will lean on those lessons when I make positive suggestions in chapter XII. The sixth idea has not been much discussed, but I will suggest that we should accept it.

It is of interest that all six ideas can be seen as arguments for one and the same thesis. The thesis is itself, at first sight, intuitively very implausible. Let "V_{act}-1" be an abbreviation of a verb-phrase such that to say that A V_{act}-1s is to say that A acts in a certain way (as, for example, that A eats a banana), or that A refrains from acting in a certain way (as, for example, that A refrains from going to the grocery). Let "V_{act}-2" be another. The thesis, then, is that it can be that Smith says the words

(1) A ought to V_{act}-1,

and Jones says the words

(2) A ought to V_{act}-2,

and that A cannot both V_{act}-1 and V_{act}-2, *and* that neither Smith nor Jones misuses the words he says, *and* that both nevertheless speak truly.

I will call this the Consistency Thesis. Why would anyone want to accept it?

2.

Here is an argument for it. Suppose Alfred is playing chess, and it is his turn to move. He is in check, and can get out only by moving his queen. Knowing that, Smith whispers to us the words

(1a) Alfred ought to move his queen.[1]

In fact, a villain will blow up Chicago unless Alfred moves his bishop. Knowing that, Jones says the words

(2a) Alfred ought to move his bishop.

A Relativist now tells us that the words "A ought to V_{act}" mean "A's V_{act}-ing is prescribed by _____," and that a person who says those words is, for some body of rules, asserting that A's V_{act}-ing is prescribed by them. (Compare: the words "A is taller" mean "A is taller than _____," and a person who says those words is, for some

---

[1] On some views, it would be odd in Smith to say (1a): "why doesn't he say, 'Alfred must move his queen'?" For Smith's saying "ought" suggests that he thinks Alfred has another alternative, whereas in fact Alfred doesn't—after all, the game is over if Alfred moves any other piece. I chose this example for simplicity. And let us remember that if Alfred must move his queen, then it *follows* that he ought to.

We could have fixed on the following situation instead. Alice is playing chess, and it is her turn to move. It is mate in three if she doesn't move her queen. Smith whispers to us the words, "Alice ought to move her queen." Does this sound more plausible? Or are you inclined here too to think Smith should have said, "Alice must move her queen"? After all, while the game isn't over *now* if she moves any other piece, it shortly will be.

Here is yet another. Alan is playing chess, and it is his turn to move. He is in a bad position, and he is very likely to lose if he doesn't move his queen. Smith whispers to us the words, "Alan ought to move his queen." Does this sound more plausible? Or are you inclined here too to think Smith should have said, "Alan must move his queen"? After all, as I said, he is very likely to lose if he doesn't.

What will count for you as 'having no alternative' in such cases will turn on what matters to you, and how much.

In any case, I will focus on Alfred in the text, and comment on Alice and Alan in footnote 3 below.

thing, asserting that A is taller than it.) The body of rules might be the rules of chess, or of some other game. Or the rules of etiquette currently in force in the speaker's community. Or the current rules of English grammar. Or the rules for nominating a candidate for President of the Such and Such Club. Or the moral rules the speaker accepts.

So consider Smith. Smith says (1a), and is thereby, for some body of rules, asserting that Alfred's moving his queen is prescribed by them. We can suppose that the relevant body of rules is the rules of chess. Then the proposition that Smith is asserting is

(1a*) Alfred's moving his queen is prescribed by the rules of chess.

Smith is not misusing the words he says, and, given that Alfred is in check and can get out only by moving his queen, (1a*) is true, and Smith therefore speaks truly.

Consider Jones. Jones says (2a), and is thereby, for some body of rules, asserting that Alfred's moving his bishop is prescribed by them. We can suppose that the relevant body of rules is the moral rules that he, Jones, accepts. Then the proposition that Jones is asserting is

(2a*) Alfred's moving his bishop is prescribed by the moral rules that Jones accepts.

Jones is not misusing the words he says, and, given that a villain will blow up Chicago unless Alfred moves his bishop, we can suppose that Jones speaks truly—for we can suppose that Alfred's moving his bishop *is* prescribed by the moral rules that Jones accepts.

If we now add that Alfred cannot both move his queen and move his bishop, the Consistency Thesis follows straightway.[2]

---

[2] Gilbert Harman is among the Relativists: see his contribution to Gilbert Harman and Judith Thomson, *Moral Relativism and Moral Objectivity* (Oxford: Blackwell's, 1996).

Note that I speak throughout this and the following chapter, not of the meaning(s?) of the word "ought", but rather of the meaning(s?) of sentences of the form

(α) A ought to V_{act}.

What should we think of this argument?

I draw attention, first, to the intuitive implausibility of the following conclusion that the argument issues in: that there is no such thing as *the* proposition that A ought to V_{act}. (Just as there is no such thing as the proposition that A is taller.) The other side of that coin is that there is no such thing as *the* question whether A ought to V_{act}. (Just as there is no such thing as the question whether A is taller.) There is such a thing as the question whether Alfred ought to move his queen 'relative to' the rules of chess (answer: yes), and there is such a thing as the question whether Alfred ought to move his queen 'relative to' the moral rules that Jones accepts (answer: no), but there is no such thing as the question whether Alfred ought to move his queen. Similarly, there is no such thing as the question which one of the two Alfred ought to do, move his queen or move his bishop.

So the argument we are looking at had better be very powerful if we are to accept these consequences of accepting it.

Let us ask: how exactly do the rules of chess 'prescribe' Alfred's moving his queen? I said in chapter VI, section 5, that we can say

---

That is because of the variety of kinds of sentence in which "ought" appears. Consider, for example, sentences of the form

(β) It ought to be the case that p.

I take it that the meaningfulness of both kinds of sentence does not itself show that the word "ought" is ambiguous: it is compatible with the word's having a single meaning, the difference between the meanings of (α) and (β) being due to the difference between their structures.

But it might be asked why I focus on (α) rather than (β), for on some views, (β) is fundamental. Aaron Sloman, for example, says that (α) means

It ought to be the case that A V_{act}s,

and thus that (α) is a special case of (β). (See his "'Ought' and 'Better'", *Mind* 79, no. 315 [July 1970].) Linguists do so as well. I ignore this idea in the text since it seems to me that people who say sentences of the form (β) typically mean what they would have asserted if they had instead said

(β') He/she/they ought to see to it that p,

the person or group of people being fixed by the context, or

(β'') The world would be better if p,

the betterness relation fixed by the context. (I know of only one other possibility, which I will draw attention to in footnote 7 of the following chapter.) But (α) is plainly not a special case of (β'); quite to the contrary, (β') is a special case of (α). And to say that (α) is a special case of (β'') would be to opt for a version of Consequentialism—thus to make a substantive, normative assumption that the philosopher of language and the linguist have no business making.

that the rules of chess tell us what counts as a move in chess. Or what counts as a legal move in chess. Or what counts as a correct move in chess. Let us say they tell us what counts as a correct chess move. Then it is in the following sense that they prescribe Alfred's moving his queen: they tell us that his moving any piece other than his queen would be an incorrect chess move. Thus if when Smith says

(1a) Alfred ought to move his queen,

he is asserting the proposition

(1a*) Alfred's moving his queen is prescribed by the rules of chess,

then what he is asserting by saying (1a) is the proposition

(1a**) Alfred's moving any piece other than his queen would be an incorrect chess move.

However, as I also said in chapter VI, section 5: we cannot say that the rules of chess either are, or that they themselves license, directives. (We also know, from our discussion of correctness properties, that [1a**] does not license a directive.) It is entirely consistent to say that a certain move would be correct though you ought not make it, and that a certain move would be incorrect though you ought to make it.

But then the argument we are looking at won't do. For anyone who says (1a), meaning (1a*), thus (1a**), by it, misuses the words he says.[3]

---

[3] The rules of chess strategy are different from the rules of chess: the latter tell you how to play chess, the former how to play chess well—a chess move is strategically correct if and only if it is a move conducive to winning.

So consider Alice of footnote 1 above. It is Alice's turn to move, and it is mate in three if she doesn't move her queen. Suppose Smith therefore says, "Alice ought to move her queen." If what he means is that her moving her queen is prescribed by the rules of chess strategy—that is, her moving any piece other than her queen would be a strategically incorrect chess move—then he misuses the words he says.

Similarly for Alan of footnote 1 above.

Things are still worse for the Relativist in the case of Jones. We have been told that we can suppose that when Jones says

(2a) Alfred ought to move his bishop

he is asserting the proposition

(2a*) Alfred's moving his bishop is prescribed by the moral rules that Jones accepts.

And now let us ask: how exactly do the moral rules that Jones accepts 'prescribe' Alfred's moving his bishop? What do those moral rules *say*?

Indeed, what *are* they? You might have thought that a body of moral rules is a body of propositions to the effect that people ought to do this and ought to refrain from doing that. But if the Relativist is right, then there is no such thing as the proposition that, as it might be, one ought to give aid to the needy. (Compare the fact that there is no such thing as the proposition that Alfred is taller.) So if the moral rules that Jones accepts are propositions, then they are not propositions to the effect that people ought to do this and ought to refrain from doing that. But then what propositions are they?

Suppose Jones sits down in a cool hour, and tries to list for himself the moral rules that he accepts. If he says to himself along the way, "One ought to give to the needy," then according to the Relativist, he is asserting a proposition, namely the proposition that one's giving to the needy is prescribed by . . . well, by what body of rules? The moral rules that he accepts? So are the moral rules Jones accepts propositions to the effect that doing such and such is prescribed by the moral rules he accepts?

There is room for the Relativist to distinguish. He can say that while the rules of chess are propositions to the effect that such and such is a correct chess move, moral rules are not propositions at all. He can say that moral rules are commands or orders—"Do this!" and "Don't do that!" Then for giving to the needy to be prescribed by the moral rules that Jones accepts is for the commands that he accepts to include the command "Give to the needy!" (I leave aside the question what exactly his accepting a body of commands is to be thought to consist in.)

It is a curious idea. According to the Relativist, when Jones says

> (2a) Alfred ought to move his bishop,

he is, for some body of rules, asserting the proposition that Alfred's moving his bishop is prescribed by them; and we are to suppose that what he is asserting is the proposition

> (2a*) Alfred's moving his bishop is prescribed by the moral rules that Jones accepts.

If the moral rules that Jones accepts are commands, then the proposition he is asserting is

> (2a**) The commands Jones accepts include the command "Move your bishop, Alfred!"

Note that on this view, Jones isn't issuing or delivering the command, he is merely reporting about himself that he accepts it.

If the Relativist says that moral rules are commands, then perhaps he should say that when Jones says (2a), he *is* issuing or delivering a command—the command "Move your bishop, Alfred!"? (An Expressivist might say this.) Well, perhaps we could be bullied into agreeing that if Jones says "You ought to move your bishop" to Alfred, then he is commanding Alfred to move his bishop; but whom is Jones commanding, and to do what, if he says (2a) to us? No matter. This view is in any case not open to the Relativist. According to the Relativist, a person who says "A ought to V" *is* asserting a proposition; according to the Relativist, Smith and Jones may both be speaking truly.

The path down which we are led by Relativism is so unattractive that it may well strike us as puzzling that anyone opts for it. Why have so many people been tempted by Relativism? I take it that there are two reasons why.

The first reason is something quite general. Many philosophers regard it as very plausible to think that a person who says "A ought to V_{act}" asserts a proposition, but hopelessly unclear what proposition that might *be* if Relativism isn't true. A lot of good criticism of alternatives on offer is typically offered by Relativists to support this motivation.

The second reason is particular, and more interesting. People do say the likes of

(1a) Alfred ought to move his queen

when watching a chess player who is in a situation like Alfred's. They don't first look around to see who else besides the players may be affected by Alfred's moving his queen, and if so in what ways. They think themselves entirely warranted in saying (1a) by the fact of what is going on in the game, and the rules of chess.

It is not from philosophy that people learn to do this; doing it comes to us all very naturally. If someone has a weak grip on the rules of etiquette governing table-setting, and asks us where to put the forks, it is very natural to say, "You ought to put them on the left of the plates," as if the rules of etiquette settle the matter by themselves. These behaviors on our parts call for explanation, and Relativism supplies one.

But another, simpler and more mundane, explanation is available. When we say, "Alfred ought to move his queen," we are *assuming* that there is no reason lying in the world around Alfred for believing that he ought not move his queen—as there would be if, for example, harm would come of his moving it, or if he had committed himself to not moving it. We are also *assuming* that Alfred wants to win the game. We normally make these two assumptions when watching chess players, and we are normally right to make them. If we weren't making them, we wouldn't say, "Alfred ought to move his queen". At any rate, we would take a closer look at Alfred's circumstances and wants and weigh one thing against another before saying those words.

Indeed, this is a markedly better explanation than Relativism of our saying what we say. That it is emerges when we notice what happens if, after we have said, "Alfred ought to move his queen," someone draws our attention to the fact that villains will blow up Chicago unless Alfred moves his bishop. We don't say, "Well, all the same, Alfred ought to move his queen," on the ground that Alfred's moving his queen is prescribed by the rules of chess. What we say is, rather, "I was mistaken. I thought Alfred ought to move his queen, but that was wrong." That is certainly what we may expect Smith to say when he learns of the facts that led Jones to say "Alfred ought to move his bishop."

In sum, there is no good reason to think this a successful argument for the Consistency Thesis.

3.

A second argument for the thesis issues from a different kind of consideration, namely attention to what have been called moral dilemmas.

Here is an example of the kind typically offered us. Last week, Alice promised Bert that she would give Bert an alpha-pill today if it turns out that he needs one. Bert relied on that promise. Bert now finds that he does need an alpha-pill, and it will be disastrous for him if Alice breaks her promise to him. Fortunately, Alice has an alpha-pill. Knowing that, Smith says the words

(1b) Alice ought to give Bert an alpha-pill.

Last week, Alice promised Charles that she would give Charles an alpha-pill today if it turns out that he needs one. Charles relied on that promise. Charles now finds that he does need an alpha-pill, and it will be disastrous for him if Alice breaks her promise to him. Fortunately, Alice has an alpha-pill. Knowing that, Jones says the words

(2b) Alice ought to give Charles an alpha-pill.

I now add the further fact that you were no doubt expecting: Alice discovers that she has only one alpha-pill, and will not be able to get another until tomorrow, by which time it will be too late for both Bert and Charles.

Now by hypothesis, Alice has only one alpha-pill, and so cannot both give one to Bert, and give one to Charles. It is certainly plausible to think that neither Smith nor Jones misuses the words he says. If it can be the case that both Smith and Jones speak truly, then we have in hand a conclusive argument for the Consistency Thesis.

Can we suppose that both Smith and Jones *do* speak truly? Suppose that Bert and Charles will suffer equally from lack of an alpha-pill. Suppose that no more harm or good will come for others if Alice gives her one pill to one of them than will come for others if she gives it to the other of them. In case you feel the need of it, we can assume also that Alice made both promises concurrently—

she made her promises by letter, and put both letters in the mail together. In short, we can suppose that there is no better reason for Alice to keep the one promise than there is for her to keep the other. It doesn't, of course, follow from that that both Smith and Jones *do* speak truly. But on some views, they both do speak truly. I will call a person who says they do the Dilemmist.

It is an intuitively very implausible idea that they both speak truly. Intuitively, what Alice ought to do is to flip a coin, and give the winner her one pill.

Moreover, the consequences of accepting the idea that they both speak truly are intuitively implausible. I mention only one here. (I mention a second in a footnote.[4]) Suppose that Alice is now clear

---

[4] The second is that it is intuitively plausible to think that we should accept the following general principle: if A ought to V_{act}-1, and A ought to V_{act}-2, then A ought to both V_{act}-1 and V_{act}-2. Bernard Williams calls this the *agglomeration principle.* (For the reference, see footnote 5 below.) If we accept that Alice ought to give Bert the pill, and that Alice ought to give Charles the pill, then if we also accept the agglomeration principle, we are committed to the conclusion that Alice ought to both give Bert the pill and give Charles the pill. That conclusion is nigh on weird.

Dilemmists do tend to reject the conclusion that Alice ought to both give Bert the pill and give Charles the pill: after all, Alice can't do both! Williams therefore invites us to reject the agglomeration principle. We should (he says) agree that Alice ought to give the pill to Bert, and that she ought to give it to Charles, and *each* of these things she can do. But (he says) we should not conclude that Alice ought to give the pill to Bert and to give it to Charles, for she cannot do *both* of these things.

Now it is not in the least clear to me why anyone who balks at the idea that Alice ought to do both, given that she can't do both, doesn't also balk at the idea that Alice ought to do each, given that she can't do both. More generally, an agglomeration principle is as plausible for "each" as it is for "and". It is certainly plausible to think that if you ought to answer each of the two questions on your exam, then you ought to answer both.

Williams says that there are countercases to analogues of the agglomeration principle "in the general field of evaluation", as, for example, where what is at stake is whether a course of action is desirable, advisable, sensible, or prudent. He says that there are cases in which it is desirable for a person to V_{act}-1 and desirable for the person to V_{act}-2, but not desirable for him to do both. Are there? If it is not desirable for him to do both, then it is not the case that it is desirable that he V_{act}-1 and desirable that he V_{act}-2. What is desirable is at most that he either V_{act}-1 and not V_{act}-2, or V_{act}-2 and not V_{act}-1. Or so I think. If there is some strong reason for thinking otherwise, I can't imagine what it might be.

My impression, then, is that there is no independent ground for rejecting the agglomeration principle. The sole reasons for rejecting it are, on the one hand the idea that 'ought' implies 'can', and on the other hand such reason as there is for

about her situation—in particular, about what will happen to each of Bert and Charles if she fails to keep her promises to them. And suppose that she asks for advice: she asks, "Which ought I do?—give Bert the pill, or give Charles the pill?" The Dilemmist replies, "Well, you ought to give Bert the pill, and you ought to give Charles the pill." Alice may be expected to reply: "I can't do both! So which ought I do?" The Dilemmist can merely repeat: "No 'which' about it! You ought to give Bert the pill, and you ought to give Charles the pill." (Most of us would instead reply: "Well, don't do either until you flip a coin.")

So why should we agree with the Dilemmist? Bernard Williams is the father of Dilemmism, and I will focus on his account of the matter.[5] He begins by pointing to the fact that whichever promise Alice keeps, she will feel regret at not having been able to keep the other. She will also feel the need to make it up to the one she broke her promise to.

So far so good. Decency requires her to feel these things, and indeed to act on them. Thus whichever person Alice gives the pill to, decency requires her to regret not having been able to give it to the other, and to feel the need to make it up to him. And indeed to act on these feelings—to make such amends to him as are possible. Alice quite certainly may not give the pill to one of the two and then simply walk off, washing her hands of what she thereby causes the other.

But Williams goes on to say more. He says that to suppose that since Alice cannot keep both promises, and thus cannot do what Smith says she ought to and also do what Jones says she ought to, one of their assertions must be false, is to fail to do justice to the fact of regret. He says that to "eliminate from the scene the *ought* that is not acted upon" (175) is to ignore the fact that the *ought* that is not

---

accepting the Dilemmist's claim that Alice ought to give the pill to Bert and that she ought to give the pill to Charles. How good a reason the latter is is a matter I turn to shortly.

[5] See Bernard Williams, "Ethical Consistency," *Proceedings of the Aristotelian Society*, supplementary vol. 39 (1965). Reprinted in his *Problems of the Self* (Cambridge, England: Cambridge University Press, 1973). Page references are to the reprinted version.

See also Ruth Marcus, "Moral Dilemmas and Consistency," *Journal of Philosophy* 77, no. 3 (1980).

acted on has consequences. His idea is that in order to understand why Alice should feel regret, and try to make amends to the one to whom she does not give the pill, we have to suppose that it was true that she ought to give him the pill.

I will return to that idea shortly.

But let us first take note of the fact that Dilemmists actually come in two species. The Hard Dilemmist says what I said the Dilemmist says in reply to Alice's question "Which ought I do?" namely that she ought to give the pill to Bert and that she ought to give the pill to Charles—period. Williams seems to be a Hard Dilemmist. He allows that there is a further question that Alice may ask, namely which it would be best for her to do. But he seems to wish us to agree that so far as what Alice *ought* to do is concerned, there is nothing more to be said than that Alice ought to give the pill to Bert, and that Alice ought to give the pill to Charles.

Soft Dilemmists grant that that is not a happy outcome, so they offer a palliative. They recommend that we accept that "A ought to V_{act}" is ambiguous. No doubt (they say) it has a meaning under which Alice ought to give the pill to Bert, and ought to give the pill to Charles. That is a meaning of "A ought to V_{act}" under which there is no question which *one* of the two Alice ought to do. But (they say) "A ought to V_{act}" has another meaning—they often call it the 'all things considered' meaning of "A ought to V_{act}"—under which there *is* a question which one of the two Alice ought to do. For "Alice ought to give the pill to Bert, and Alice ought to give the pill to Charles" is compatible with "Alice ought$_{\text{all-things-considered}}$ to give the pill to Bert and not to Charles" and compatible also with "Alice ought$_{\text{all-things-considered}}$ to give the pill to Charles and not to Bert."

That description of this further meaning of "A ought to V_{act}"—namely that it is its 'all things considered' meaning—is unfortunate, since it is not as if the Hard Dilemmist hasn't considered all things. He has. And what he concludes, having considered all things, is that Alice ought to give the pill to Bert, and that she ought to give it to Charles.

So what is there for the Soft Dilemmist to take this further meaning of "A ought to V_{act}" to be?

Interestingly enough, Williams himself supplies an answer. I said above that Williams seems to be a Hard Dilemmist. But only until we reach the last two pages of his article. Here he turns out to be a Soft Dilemmist. He tells us that we should contrast the *ought* that occurs in statements of moral principle, and in the sorts of moral judgements about particular situations that we have been considering, with the *ought* that occurs in the deliberative question 'what ought I to do?' and in answers to this question, given by myself or another. (184)

Thus "A ought to V_{act}" is ambiguous, as between what might better, because more carefully, be expressed by "A $ought_{moral}$ to V_{act}" and "A $ought_{deliberative}$ to V_{act}". And it turns out now that Williams's view is more complex than we thought. He holds that Smith and Jones spoke truly if the propositions they asserted were that Alice $ought_{moral}$ to give the pill to Bert, and that Alice $ought_{moral}$ to give the pill to Charles. But he also holds that there is a further question, namely which one of the two she $ought_{deliberative}$ to give the pill to; and he holds that "Alice $ought_{moral}$ to give the pill to Bert, and Alice $ought_{moral}$ to give the pill to Charles" is compatible with "Alice $ought_{deliberative}$ to give the pill to Bert and not to Charles" and compatible also with "Alice $ought_{deliberative}$ to give the pill to Charles and not to Bert."[6]

Should we agree? I begin with "A $ought_{deliberative}$ to V_{act}." What exactly does *that* mean? The passage I just quoted says that "$ought_{deliberative}$" is what a speaker means when he asks "What ought I to do?" and when he himself, or somebody else, answers this question. We should ask: then why isn't "A $ought_{deliberative}$ to V_{act}" *the* meaning of "A ought to V_{act}"? Why should we think that it is only one of the two meanings of "A ought to V_{act}"?

We may expect Williams to reply: because "A ought to V_{act}" has another meaning, namely "A $ought_{moral}$ to V_{act}." But why should we think "A ought to V_{act}" does have this other meaning? The pressure Williams brings to bear on us to agree that it does issues *wholly* from

---

[6] It should be stressed that a Soft Dilemmist might say that while there is such a question as the question which one of the two Alice $ought_{deliberative}$ to give the pill to, there may be no answer to that question. Thus he might say that things having been as we have assumed they were, it is indeterminate which of the two Alice $ought_{deliberative}$ to give the pill to. And he might add that what Alice therefore $ought_{deliberative}$ to do is to flip a coin, and then give the pill to the winner.

But whether or not he takes that line, his view is that there is no indeterminacy in respect of what Alice $ought_{moral}$ to do. Alice quite determinately $ought_{moral}$ to give the pill to Bert, and quite determinately $ought_{moral}$ to give the pill to Charles.

Williams's point about regret. On the one hand, he gives us no account of what "A ought$_{moral}$ to V$_{act}$" means. On the other hand, he takes it to be clear that in order to understand why Alice should feel regret, and try to make amends to the one to whom she does not give the pill, we have to suppose that it was true that she (in a sense) ought to give him the pill.

But there is no good reason to accept that idea. It issues *wholly* from an unfortunate phenomenon that I mentioned earlier, namely ignoring the richness of our stock of normative concepts. There just is no need for us to accommodate the requirement that Alice feel regret by saying both "Alice ought to give the pill to Bert" and "Alice ought to give the pill to Charles."

For when Alice promised each that she would give him a pill, she gave them rights against her to be given a pill. Suppose she will give the one pill she has to Bert. Then she will infringe a right of Charles's, and will therefore owe amends to Charles. Therefore. That is, we need not explain why Alice will owe amends to Charles by saying that she ought to give a pill to Charles. We adequately explain why she will owe amends to Charles by pointing to the fact that she gave Charles a right against her to be given a pill, and will infringe that right if she does not give him one. Charles's having that right against Alice itself *includes* its being the case that if Alice infringes that right, then Alice will owe him amends.

That is a crucial fact about rights. They are important to us not merely because X's having a right against A that A will V$_{act}$ is a reason for believing that A ought to V$_{act}$—a reason that is not outweighed by the mere fact that it will be somewhat better for others if A does not V$_{act}$—but also because X's having the right against A includes A's being required to do what he can to see to it that if he fails to V$_{act}$, then X does not suffer from that failure. In short, it is not an "*ought* that is not acted upon" that has the consequences; it is a right that is infringed that has them.[7]

---

[7] I chose the example we have been looking at on Williams's own recommendation. He wished to have it be clear that the regret he is focusing on is not mere 'natural distress' at causing a harm. He says that there may be such cases. But he says that there are cases in which the regret "must surely arise *via* a moral thought— "an *ought* that is not acted upon"—as for example where the harm was caused by the breaking of a promise. (175) But to add that a promise was broken is precisely to add that a right was infringed.

I invite the conclusion that Williams has not made his case, and that the argument we have been looking at does not succeed.

4.

Here is a third argument for the Consistency Thesis. Suppose Alan concludes that it would be best for him to be in Denver this evening, and therefore forms the intention of getting there by 7 PM. There is one and only one way in which he can get there by then, namely catching the 3 PM plane. Knowing that, Smith says

(1c) Alan ought to catch the 3 PM plane.

Jones, however, knows that villains will blow up Chicago if Alan catches the 3 PM plane, so he says

(2c) Alan ought to refrain from catching the 3 PM plane.

Alan obviously cannot both catch the 3 PM plane and refrain from catching the 3 PM plane. Moreover, neither Smith nor Jones misuses the words he says, and both speak truly. The Consistency Thesis follows straightway.

Should we accept the claim that neither Smith nor Jones misuses the words he says, and both speak truly? A Relativist would offer us a ground for accepting it, but let us look at a different ground for doing so.

A friend of this different ground for accepting it draws our attention to the following passage in Kant's *Groundwork*:

> All imperatives are expressed by an "*ought*". . . . All *imperatives* command either *hypothetically* or *categorically*. Hypothetical imperatives declare a possible action to be practically necessary as a means to the attainment of something else that one wills (or that one may will). A categorical imperative would be one which represented an action as objectively necessary in itself apart from its relation to a further end.[8]

I discuss this matter at length in *The Realm of Rights* (Cambridge, MA: Harvard University Press, 1990).

[8] *Groundwork of the Metaphysic of Morals*, ch. 2.

In short, "A ought to V_{act}" has two meanings: "A ought$_{hypothetical}$ to V_{act}" and "A ought$_{categorical}$ to V_{act}." "A ought$_{hypothetical}$ to V_{act}" means

> A's V_{act}-ing is practically necessary as a means to his attaining something he intends to attain,

and "A ought$_{categorical}$ to V_{act}" means

> A's V_{act}-ing is objectively necessary in itself.

The friend of the argument then says: if when Smith says (1c), he is asserting the proposition that Alan ought$_{hypothetical}$ to catch the 3 PM plane, then he does not misuse the words he says, and he speaks truly, and if when Jones says (2c), he is asserting the proposition that Alan ought$_{categorical}$ to refrain from catching the 3 PM plane, then he does not misuse the words he says, and he too speaks truly.

It is a very puzzling idea. I leave aside "A ought$_{categorical}$ to V_{act}"; what is puzzling is the idea that "A ought to V_{act}" has, among its meanings, "A ought$_{hypothetical}$ to V_{act}," so defined. Suppose Ann intends to kill Bert. Suppose also that the only means she has of killing Bert is poisoning his coffee. Then it is true that her poisoning Bert's coffee is practically necessary as a means to her attaining something she intends to attain. Then it is true that she ought$_{hypothetical}$ to poison Bert's coffee. Does it follow that the words "Ann ought to poison Bert's coffee" have a meaning under which you would be speaking truly if you said them? Intuitively, she ought not poison Bert's coffee. Period. Intuitively, anyone who says "She ought to" either misuses the words he says or speaks falsely.

I stress that it won't do to say, "Well, anyway, *if* she intends to kill him, then she ought to poison his coffee." Intuitively, that is false, since she does intend to kill him, and it is, all the same, intuitively not true—in any sense of the words—that she ought to poison his coffee. We might well add that she also ought not intend to kill him.

So why has this idea seemed attractive to so many people? There seem to me to be two reasons.

First, an idea about rationality. By hypothesis, Alan intends to get to Denver by 7 PM. It is plausible to think that if he *believes* that there is one and only one way in which he can get there by then, namely catching the 3 PM plane, then it would be irrational in him not to intend to catch the 3 PM plane.[9] Thus, quite generally,

> (α) A intends to V_{act}-2, and believes that he can V_{act}-2 by and only by V_{act}-1-ing

entails

> (β) It would be irrational in A not to intend to V_{act}-1.

But (so this idea goes on) it is also plausible to think that (β) entails

> (γ) A ought to intend to V_{act}-1,

and thereby entails

> (δ) A ought to V_{act}-1.

Unfortunately that doesn't itself get us to the conclusion that Alan ought to catch the 3 PM plane, for while we had been supposing that Alan *can* get to Denver by 7 PM by and only by catching the 3 PM plane, we hadn't been supposing that Alan *believes* this. We had assumed that it is practically necessary for Alan to catch the 3 PM plane, but not that he is aware that it is. Still, it might be thought that that doesn't matter. It might be said that, given that his believing it is practically necessary for him to catch the 3 PM plane makes it irrational in him not to intend to, its *being* practically necessary for him to catch the 3 PM plane itself makes it the case that he ought to intend to.

There is certainly room for resistance to that last step, but let us bypass it, for there is a deeper difficulty lying in the prior step from

---

[9] On some views, something stronger can be said: if he believes that there is one and only one way in which he can get there by then, namely catching the 3 PM plane, then he *does* intend to catch the 3 PM plane. This view issues from the idea that intending an end *includes* intending what you believe to be the means to it. I bypass this stronger claim, not just because it is dubious, but also because there is no hope at all of getting from there to the conclusion that "Alan ought to catch the 3 PM plane." For it is surely plain, on any view, that the fact that Alan intends to catch the 3 PM plane does not warrant the conclusion that he ought to, in any sense of "He ought to". The rationale I describe in the text relies, not on Alan's intending to catch the 3 PM plane, but on its being irrational in him not to.

(β) to (γ). By hypothesis, Ann intends to kill Bert. Suppose that it is not merely true that she can kill Bert by and only by poisoning his coffee, but that she believes it is true. It is plausible to think that entails

> (β′) It would be irrational in Ann not to intend to poison Bert's coffee.

It is not in the least plausible to think that (β′) entails

> (γ′) Ann ought to intend to poison Bert's coffee.

That it would be irrational in a villain not to intend to do what he believes will serve his villainous purpose simply does not warrant the conclusion that he ought to intend to do it.

It will perhaps be clear from the objection I have just pointed to that I assume that the conception of rationality in play here is what is sometimes called "means-ends rationality" (or "Humean rationality"). According to that conception of rationality, rationality requires acting in a way that one believes will enable one to accomplish one's goal, and has nothing to say about either one's choice of a goal, or about the means required for accomplishing it other than that they are required for accomplishing it. So understood, rationality requires Ann's intending to poison Bert's coffee; so understood, it is irrational in her not to intend to.

Some philosophers—typically moral philosophers—opt for a different conception of rationality, which is richer and rosier. We might call this the thick conception of rationality. Being thick rational requires that both one's ends and means meet certain moral standards. A philosopher who opts for a thick conception of rationality might deny that it is irrational in Ann not to intend to poison Bert's coffee.

A number of questions then arise. Do we really understand what thick rationality is to be thought to consist in? If we do, are means-ends rationality and thick rationality really two different concepts 'rationality', or instead two competing conceptions of one and the same concept 'rationality'? If they are two competing conceptions of one and the same concept 'rationality', which is the correct conception of it? Fortunately we can bypass these questions. For whatever their answers are, it is means-ends rationality alone that can be appealed to in support of the idea that this third argument for the Consistency Thesis is a good argument for it. For

> (α) A intends to V_{act}-2, and believes that he can V_{act}-2 by and only by V_{act}-1-ing

entails

> (β) It would be irrational in A not to intend to V_{act}-1

only if that "irrational" is to be understood as "means-ends irrational". But so understood, (β′) does not entail (γ′).

I asked earlier why the idea we are looking at has seemed attractive to so many people, and I said that there seem to me to be two reasons. The first was an idea about rationality. The second is the fact that people do say the likes of

> (1c) Alan ought to catch the 3 PM plane

when confronted by a situation such as Alan is in. They don't first look around to see who else besides Alan may be affected by Alan's catching the 3 PM plane, and if so in what ways. They think themselves entirely warranted in saying (1c) by how things are with Alan. And it is not from philosophy that people learn to do this; doing it comes to us all very naturally. This behavior on our parts calls for explanation, and the idea that "A ought to V_{act}" has "A ought$_{hypothetical}$ to V_{act}" among its meanings supplies one.

But we have met this phenomenon before. Compare Alfred of section 2 above, about whom we readily say, "He ought to move his queen." Here, as there, a simpler and more mundane explanation of the phenomenon is available: we normally *assume* that there is no reason lying in the world around Alan for believing that he ought not catch the 3 PM plane, and we are normally right to do so. If we weren't making that assumption, we wouldn't say, "Alan ought to catch the 3 PM plane." At any rate, we would take a closer look at Alan's circumstances and weigh one thing against another before saying those words.

And here again, this is a markedly better explanation of the phenomenon than the idea that "A ought to V_{act}" has "A ought$_{hypothetical}$ to V_{act}" among its meanings. That it is emerges when we notice what happens if, after we have said "Alan ought to catch the 3 PM plane," someone draws our attention to the fact that villains will blow up Chicago if Alan catches the 3 PM plane. We don't say, "Well, all the same, Alan ought to catch the 3 PM plane," on the ground that his catching that plane is practically necessary as a means to his attaining something he intends to attain, namely getting to Denver by 7 PM. What we say is, rather, "I was mistaken. I thought Alan ought to catch the 3 PM plane, but that was wrong." That is certainly what we may expect Smith to say when he learns of the fact that led Jones to say, "Alan ought to refrain from catching the 3 PM plane."

In sum, I suggest that we should reject this argument for the Consistency Thesis.

5.

We have now looked at three arguments for the Consistency Thesis, and I have suggested that none of them succeed. Nevertheless, as I said at the outset, certain lessons emerge from attention to them that an account of the locution "A ought to V_{act}" has to accommodate, and that I will lean on when I make some positive suggestions about it later.

Two are of particular importance. Attention to the first and third arguments brings home that the truth of what people are saying when they say sentences of the form "A ought to V_{act}" turns on more than just what those of A's immediate circumstances are that provoked their saying the sentences. Alfred is in check, and can get out only by moving his queen; that provokes our saying, "He ought to move his queen." Alan intends to get to Denver by 7 PM; that provokes our saying, "He ought to catch the 3 PM plane." But the reason why we are provoked to say these things does not lie wholly in Alfred's and Alan's immediate circumstances. It lies also in assumptions we are making make about the rest of the world. We are typically right to make those assumptions. But we all the same do make them, and whether we speak truly turns on whether those assumptions are correct.

Attention to the second argument brings home the importance of remembering that our normative thinking is not limited to ascriptions of the concept 'ought'. If we expect too much of that concept, we lose track of what lies at the heart of it.

We will return to both of these matters. Let us first look at three more arguments for the thesis.

XI

On Some Views about "Ought": Belief, Outcomes, Epistemic Ought

1.

By way of reminder, we are looking at arguments for the Consistency Thesis. Let "V_{act}-1" and "V_{act}-2" be abbreviations of verb phrases. The thesis says that it can be that Smith says the words

(1) A ought to V_{act}-1,

and Jones says the words

(2) A ought to V_{act}-2,

and that A cannot both V_{act}-1 and V_{act}-2, *and* that neither Smith nor Jones misuses the words he says, *and* that both nevertheless speak truly.

Here is a fourth argument for the thesis. Suppose Alfred's child has just started to show symptoms of what Alfred recognizes is a dread disease that children are susceptible to—it is currently called Disease. Alfred believes that the only hospital in the area equipped to cure Disease is Traditional Hospital, which is north of town. Knowing all this, Smith says to us the words

(1d) Alfred ought to take his child to Traditional.

In fact, however, the only hospital in the area equipped to cure Disease is Modern Hospital, which is south of town. Knowing this, Jones says to us the words

(2d) Alfred ought to take his child to Modern.

There isn't time for Alfred to get to both hospitals. A friend of this fourth argument says that it can be that neither Smith nor Jones misuses the words he says, and that both speak truly. The Consistency Thesis follows straightway.

Why should we accept the claim that it can be that neither Smith nor Jones misuses the words he says, and that both speak truly? The friend of the argument says we should agree that "A ought to V_{act}" is ambiguous: it has both a subjective and an objective meaning. He says they differ in the following way: saying "A ought to V_{act}," meaning "A ought$_{subjective}$ to V_{act}," is asserting a proposition whose truth turns on what A believes about what the world is like, whereas saying "A ought to V_{act}," meaning "A ought$_{objective}$ to V_{act}," is asserting a proposition whose truth turns on what the world is really like. Then in particular, if when Smith says (1d) he is asserting the proposition

(1d*) Alfred ought$_{subjective}$ to take his child to Traditional,

then he is not misusing the words he says, and he does speak truly. And if when Jones says (2d) he is asserting the proposition

(2d*) Alfred ought$_{objective}$ to take his child to Modern,

then he is not misusing the words he says, and he too speaks truly.

Should we agree? Given that, by hypothesis, the only hospital in the area equipped to cure Disease is Modern, it is intuitively odd to think that a person might be speaking truly if he said (1d). Intuitively, if anyone says (1d), he either misuses the words he says, or he speaks falsely. Given that the only hospital in the area equipped to cure Disease is Modern, Smith ought not take his child to Traditional. Period. So it is intuitively odd to think that "A ought to V_{act}" has "A ought$_{subjective}$ to V_{act}" among its meanings.

There is a familiar idea that issues in the conclusion that "A ought to V_{act}" means *only* "A ought$_{subjective}$ to V_{act}." The idea I have in mind is that what a person ought to do is fixed by what he would be at fault for not doing. Thus:

(Ought-Fault Thesis) A ought to V_{act} if and only if A would be at fault if he did not V_{act}.

Many people think that idea very plausible. Many people also think it plausible that whether a person would be at fault if he did not V_{act} turns on what he believes at the time of acting—not on what the world is and will in fact be like if he V_{act}s, but on what he believes the world is and will in fact be like if he V_{act}s. If they are right, then "A ought to V_{act}" means only "A $ought_{subjective}$ to V_{act}."

Let us call the view that "A ought to V_{act}" has only a subjective meaning Subjectivism.[1]

We should certainly reject it. Suppose I am Alfred's child's doctor. Alfred, feeling nervous, telephones me to say that his child shows symptoms of Disease, and to ask me whether he ought to take it to Traditional. If Subjectivism is true, and I know that it is, then I know that I can't answer Alfred's question whether he ought to take the child to Traditional unless he tells me what he believes about Traditional. For even if *I* know that Modern is the only hospital in the area equipped to cure Disease, what matters to whether he ought to take his child to Traditional is not what is the case, but what he believes is the case.

If Subjectivism is true, then—quite generally—if anyone asks you whether he ought to do a thing, you display ignorance of the meanings of the words he uses if you don't, by way of reply, say the likes of, "Why ask me? Are you having trouble figuring out what your own beliefs are?" That is just silly.

It might be said that if I know that Modern is the only hospital in the area equipped to cure Disease, then I $ought_{subjective}$ to tell Alfred that it is, and thus that I ought to tell Alfred that it is. And then, if Alfred believes me, it will become true that he $ought_{subjective}$, and hence ought, to take his child to Modern. "Become true"? So that although it wasn't the case that he ought to take his child to Modern, I will have made it the case that he ought to? And if I lie, and tell Alfred that the only cure for Disease is to keep the child at home

---

[1] According to the Subjectivist, the truth or falsity of what you assert if you say "A ought to V_{act}" turns on what A's beliefs are. A first cousin of that idea is the idea that the truth or falsity of what you assert if you say "A ought to V_{act}" turns on what A's intention in V_{act}-ing would be if A were to V_{act}. I know of no one who claims that "A ought to V_{act}" is ambiguous in the following way: one meaning under which intentions are conclusive, a second under which intentions are irrelevant. Those who think intentions conclusive anywhere think them conclusive everywhere. It is for that reason that I do not include an argument from intentions for the Consistency Thesis.

and pray, and Alfred believes me, then I will have made it the case that he ought, instead, to keep his child at home and pray?

Subjectivism does not issue in wildly implausible outcomes only where what is in question is first and second person exchanges: the same holds of exchanges about third parties. Suppose Bert tells me he has heard that some children in town have recently showed symptoms of Disease, and asks me whether I know what their parents ought to do by way of getting treatment for them. (He himself has no children, and doesn't know any of the parents: he is merely curious.) I happen to know that Modern is the only hospital in the area that is equipped to cure Disease. If Subjectivism is true, it would, all the same, be called for that I reply "Who knows? Maybe some of the parents ought to take their child to Modern, but maybe others ought not—we'd have to find out what each of them believes if we were to find out what each of them ought to do." It needs no saying that that can't be right.

So, as I said, we should certainly reject Subjectivism.

Should we therefore take "A ought to V_{act}" to have an objective as well as a subjective meaning? Those meanings don't sit well together. If you are tempted to think that "A ought to V_{act}" is sufficiently closely linked to fault to warrant saying that it has a subjective meaning, why would you think that "A ought to V_{act}" *also* has an objective meaning?

And there is in any case good reason to reject the idea that "A ought to V_{act}" is ambiguous in that way. I said that if Subjectivism is true, then if anyone asks you whether he ought to do a thing, you display ignorance of the meanings of the words he uses if you don't, by way of reply, say the likes of, "Why ask me? Are you having trouble figuring out what your own beliefs are?" And I said that that is just silly. If "A ought to V_{act}" is ambiguous in the way indicated, then if anyone asks you whether he ought to do a thing, you display ignorance of the meanings of the words he uses if you don't, by way of reply, say the likes of, "Well which do you want to know? Whether you ought$_{subjective}$ to do the thing? Or whether you ought$_{objective}$ to do the thing." This is just as silly. If anyone asks you whether he ought to do a thing, then what he *plainly* wants to know is whether he ought$_{objective}$ to do the thing. Similarly, I add, if anyone asks you whether some third party ought to do a thing.

Similarly when a person reports that a third party ought to do this or that. Knowing what he knew, Smith said the words

(1d) Alfred ought to take his child to Traditional.

But when he learns what Jones knew, which led Jones to say

(2d) Alfred ought to take his child to Modern,

Smith may be expected to say, "Oops! I was mistaken—I thought Alfred ought to take his child to Traditional, but that was wrong."

This means that we must also reject

(Ought-Fault Thesis) A ought to V_{act} if and only if A would be at fault if he did not V_{act}.

Alfred ought to take his child to Modern, and yet, given his beliefs, he would not be at fault if he did not take his child to Modern. Again, given his beliefs, Alfred would be at fault if he did not take his child to Traditional, and yet it is not the case that he ought to take his child to Traditional. Quite generally, it can be true that a person ought to do a thing, but would not be at fault if he did not do it: and it can be true that a person would be at fault if he did not do a thing, though it is not the case that he ought to do it.

"Ought" does have an intimate link with "fault". But the nature of the link is not quite as simple as it is at first sight intuitively plausible to think it is. We will have a closer look at it later.

Meanwhile, "A ought to V_{act}" is not ambiguous in the way in which friends of this fourth argument take it to be.

2.

A friend of the fourth argument says that "A ought to V_{act}" has a subjective and an objective meaning, which differ in the following way: saying "A ought to V_{act}," meaning "A $ought_{subjective}$ to V_{act}," is asserting a proposition whose truth turns on what A believes about what the world is like, whereas saying "A ought to V_{act}," meaning "A $ought_{objective}$ to V_{act}," is asserting a proposition whose truth turns on what the world is really like. I hope it is agreed that "A ought to V_{act}" does not have a subjective meaning, so characterized.

That leaves us with the idea that it has an objective meaning, so characterized, and indeed with the possibility that its objective meaning is its only meaning. But there lurks here the possibility of a much more interesting fifth argument for the Consistency Thesis.

Suppose Alice is a doctor, whose patient

has a minor but unpleasant skin condition on his leg. There is only one drug that is capable of curing the skin condition completely. In 95% of cases it does so without any deleterious side effects but in 5% of cases it leads to the loss of the affected limb. But there is no way of knowing which group any given patient falls into.[2]

Knowing all that, Smith says the words

> (1e) Alice ought to refrain from giving her patient the drug,

for he thinks that a .95 probability of cure of an unpleasant skin condition is not worth buying at the cost of a .05 probability of losing a leg. I stress: Smith does not just think that *Alice* thinks that a .95 probability of cure of an unpleasant skin condition is not worth buying at the cost of a .05 probability of losing a leg. He may or may not have a view about what Alice thinks. What we are to suppose is that he thinks that (whatever Alice's views may be) a .95 probability of cure of an unpleasant skin condition just isn't worth buying at the cost of a .05 probability of losing a leg—and it is for *that* reason that he says (1e).

As a matter of fact, Alice thinks so too, and she therefore does not give her patient the drug.

As things later turn out, however, a fail-safe test for whether a patient falls into the 95% or the 5% group is developed, and it reveals that Alice's patient is in the 95% group. Thus it reveals that Alice's giving her patient the drug would have caused him no harm and would, instead, have cured his skin condition. Knowing this, Jones says the words

> (2e) It was then the case that Alice ought to give her patient the drug.

---

[2] I take this example—with emendations—from Frank Jackson and Michael Smith, "Absolutist Moral Theories and Uncertainty," *Journal of Philosophy* 3, no. 6 (June 2006). My emendations consist in this: Jackson and Smith tell the reader not merely that those are facts about Alice and her patient, but also that she knows that they are. I leave aside Alice's beliefs, and a fortiori, what she knows: what interests the friend of the fifth argument is the facts I listed, not that Alice knows they are facts. For the conclusion Jackson and Smith themselves draw from their example, see footnote 4 below.

It was not then possible for Alice both to refrain from giving her patient the drug and to give him the drug. A friend of this fifth argument says that it can be that neither Smith nor Jones misuses the words he says, and that both speak truly. The Consistency Thesis follows straightway.

Why should we accept the claim that it can be that neither Smith nor Jones misuses the words he says, and that both speak truly? The friend of the argument says we should agree that "A ought to V_{act}" is ambiguous: it has a meaning that we might express as "A ought$_{objective\text{-}expectation}$ to V_{act}," and another meaning that we might express as "A ought$_{outcome}$ to V_{act}." Here I must go a little slower in saying how I take a friend of this argument to want us to understand these expressions. Let us call him, for a reason that I am sure you can already foresee, the Double Objectivist.

Let it be the case that A's V_{act}-ing might cause a battery of outcomes: O_1, O_2, O_3, and so on. Then the Double Objectivist says that saying "A ought to V_{act}," meaning "A ought$_{objective\text{-}expectation}$ to V_{act}," is asserting a proposition whose truth turns on the probabilities of the Os, and on their values. Note that the Double Objectivist does not say that the truth of that proposition turns on what A *believes* those probabilities and values are: he says that it turns, rather, on what the probabilities and values actually are—hence it is an objective and not a subjective proposition.

The Double Objectivist might offer us in addition a particular account of what marks a possible outcome as having this or that value. He might say that their values consist in their degrees of goodness or badness. (Thus he might be opting for an objective 'expected utility' variant on Consequentialism.) Or he might offer a different account of what their values consist in. What matters for his purposes as a friend of the argument is only that on his view, the truth of the proposition that A ought$_{objective\text{-}expectation}$ to V_{act} turns on what is more or less likely to happen if A V_{act}s. And we can be sure that he would say that, on the assumption that when Smith says (1e) he is asserting the proposition

(1e*) Alice ought$_{objective\text{-}expectation}$ to refrain from giving her patient the drug,

Smith is not misusing the words he says, and does speak truly.

The Double Objectivist then says that saying "A ought to V_{act}," meaning "A ought$_{outcome}$ to V_{act}," is also asserting an objective, not a subjective, proposition. But the truth of this proposition turns on the values of the outcomes that A's V_{act}-ing will in fact cause if he V_{act}s. The probabilities of the possible outcomes of his acting are irrelevant.

Here too the Double Objectivist might offer us in addition a particular account of what marks outcomes as having this or that value. He might say that their values consist in their degrees of goodness or badness. (Thus he might be opting for Consequentialism.) Or he might offer a different account of what their values consist in. What matters for his purposes as a friend of the argument is only that on his view, the truth of the proposition that A ought$_{outcome}$ to V_{act} turns on what will happen if A V_{act}s. Now as it turned out, Alice's patient would have suffered no harm and been cured of his unpleasant skin condition if she had given him the drug. So we can be sure that the Double Objectivist would say that, on the assumption that when Jones says (2e) he is asserting the proposition

> (2e*) It was then the case that Alice ought$_{outcome}$ to give her patient the drug,

Jones is not misusing the words he says, and does speak truly.[3]

So this is why I called a friend of the argument the Double Objectivist: he thinks that "A ought to V_{act}" has two objective meanings.[4]

Should we agree? I leave aside the Double Objectivist's reliance on the concept 'value', and focus first on the assumption he makes

---

[3] Jackson and Smith say, "We will rightly say, looking back, something like 'The right decision was made at the time, but we can now see that it would have been best to have prescribed the drug.' But if it would have been best, there must be some good sense in which it ought to have been done" ("Absolutist Moral Theories and Uncertainty," 269).

[4] The conclusion that Jackson and Smith themselves draw from their example is also that "A ought to V_{act}" has two meanings. One is an objective meaning, which is the one I express as "A ought$_{outcome}$ to V_{act}." But I take them to have in mind that the other is a subjective meaning, which I expressed in the preceding section as "A ought$_{subjective}$ to V_{act}". I attribute that view to them because they say that what is relevant to whether a person ought to do a thing in this second sense is the person's *own* "epistemic situation". (In fact I take them to have been motivated by thoughts of fault, for they say that the reason why it is a person's own epistemic situation that

about probabilities, namely that there is an objective question whether it is very probable, or .n probable, that such and such will happen. Thus that you might think it very probable, or .n probable, that such and such will happen, and be mistaken. For example, you might think it probable that Bert will come to our party tonight and be mistaken because you are not aware of facts that make it probable that he won't—as it might be, the fact that he has just fallen ill. Again, you might think it .5 probable that a certain coin will come up heads when tossed, and be mistaken because you are not aware of the fact that the coin is loaded. It is because of the Double Objectivist's making this assumption that the fifth argument differs importantly from the fourth.

Moreover, I join him in making it. There is a conception of probability according to which probabilities are subjective: on this conception, there is no such thing as *the* probability now that O will come about, there is only the probability now that O will come about relative to the information I now have, and the probability now that O will come about relative to the information you now have, and so on for each of us. That is not the conception of probability that we make use of in ordinary life. I may tell you that you are mistaken in thinking it probable that Bert will come to our party tonight, not on the ground that I think you have miscalculated the probability that the information you have lends to his coming, but rather on the ground that I have information that you lack. And this is not an odd performance on my part: we say such things around the clock.

The conception of probability that I take it we make use of in ordinary life is one under which probabilities *are* 'relative to evidence', but the evidence they are relative to is information that is *available* at the time. Available to human beings, for what God knows is irrelevant to assessments of probability. This means that there is room for a change of mind. We might think that the information available makes it very probable that O will come about, and decide later that more information was available than we had thought—perhaps we have by now become aware of facts that we

---

matters is that it is the person's own epistemic situation "which determines the question of an agent's responsibility for an action.") The conclusion the Double Objectivist draws from Jackson and Smith's example is therefore importantly different from the conclusion that they themselves draw from it.

think we could easily have become aware of then—in light of which we can now see that it wasn't really probable that O would come about. It means that there is also room for unsettleable disputes as to whether the facts we later become aware of were then available to us. But on the one hand, vagueness of this kind does seem to be present in the conception of probability that we make use of in ordinary life. And on the other hand, it is very often the case that no such difficulties arise. For example, it might be clear that as of the time at which Alice had to decide whether to give her patient the drug, the available information made it .95 probable that her doing so would cure his skin condition and cause him no harm, and .05 probable that her doing do would cause him to lose a leg.

So I suggest that we should join the Double Objectivist in thinking that there is a conception of probability—the one we make use of in ordinary life—under which there is an objective question whether it is very probable, or .n probable, that such and such will happen.

I suggest, in addition, that we should join the Double Objectivist in thinking that "A ought to V_{act}" has a meaning under which the truth of the proposition that A ought to V_{act} (so interpreted) turns on probabilities (so understood). Whether we should join him in thinking that this meaning is "A ought$_{objective-expectation}$ to V_{act}"—relying as that does on the concept 'value'—is another matter, which I postpone discussion of.

But we should reject his view that "A ought to V_{act}" has "A ought$_{outcome}$ to V_{act}" among its meanings.

For suppose Bert knows that Alex loves dangerous enterprises, so he makes Alex the following offer: if Alex will play Russian Roulette on himself with a fair gun—with a bullet in one of the gun's ten chambers—and survives it, then Bert will pay Alex a thousand dollars. Alex delightedly accepts the offer and fires the gun on himself. Lo, he survives, and Bert pays him a thousand dollars. Then Alex's firing the gun on himself caused no one a harm, and indeed, he profited from firing it. I take it to follow that if you say

(α) It was then the case that Alex ought$_{outcome}$ to fire the gun on himself,

then you speak truly. Does

(β) It was then the case that Alex ought to fire the gun on himself

have (α) among its meanings? So that if Jones says (β), meaning (α) by it, then he not only speaks truly, he does not misuse the words he says?

I take it to be a *datum* that the answer is no.[5] (β) does not have such a meaning: anyone who says (β) either misuses the words he says or speaks falsely. For what was then the case is that Alex ought not fire the gun on himself. Period.

But that it is a datum leaves us with the good question why it is. *Why* was it the case that Alex ought not fire the gun on himself? One answer that we cannot rely on wholly is this: Alex was going to be grossly at fault if he fired the gun on himself. I don't for a moment deny that Alex was going to be grossly at fault if he fired the gun on himself: doing so was going to be (among other failings) grossly imprudent. And I also don't deny that the fact that Alex was going

---

[5] I here reject a view that I have argued for in several places over the years, namely that "A ought to V_{act}" means "A $ought_{outcome}$ to V_{act}." I argued for that view largely because (i) I assumed that probabilities had to be understood subjectively, and thus that we had to choose between saying that "A ought to V_{act}" means "A $ought_{outcome}$ to V_{act}", and saying that "A ought to V_{act}" means "A $ought_{subjective}$ to V_{act}" (contrast Jackson and Smith, who say that "A ought to V_{act}" means both), and (ii) it seemed to me plain that "A ought to V_{act}" does not mean "A $ought_{subjective}$ to V_{act}," because saying that "A ought to V_{act}" means "A $ought_{subjective}$ to V_{act}" commits one to the objectionable conclusion that Alfred of the preceding section ought to take his child to Traditional.

Opting for the idea that "A ought to V_{act}" means "A $ought_{outcome}$ to V_{act}" commits one to the objectionable conclusion that it was the case that Alex ought to fire the gun on himself: but I thought this conclusion less objectionable, and thought it had to be swallowed, like it or not.

I interpret chapter 3 of Jonathan Bennett's *The Act Itself* (Oxford: Oxford University Press, 1995) as suggesting that, for the purposes of ethics, we should understand probabilities objectively in the manner I described in the text above: doing so suggests a third possible meaning of "A ought to V_{act}". "A $ought_{objective-expectation}$ to V_{act}" is a version of it: I will later recommend that we opt for a different version of it. What matters here is just that with a third possibility available to us, we are not forced to choose between saying that "A ought to V_{act}" means "A $ought_{outcome}$ to V_{act}", and saying that "A ought to V_{act}" means "A $ought_{subjective}$ to V_{act}": we can say that it means neither—and we can therefore reject both the objectionable conclusion that Alfred ought to take his child to Traditional, and the objectionable conclusion that it was the case that Alex ought to fire the gun on himself.

to be grossly at fault if he fired the gun on himself is *somehow* involved in what made it the case that he ought not fire the gun on himself. But, as I said, we cannot rely wholly on that fact about fault, for it will be remembered that we have rejected the idea that the fact that a person would be at fault if he did a thing itself shows that he ought not do it.

What is surely to the point is that in firing the gun on himself, Alex was going to be imposing a one in ten chance of death on himself for the sake of the pleasure of engaging in a dangerous enterprise and a thousand dollars. He could not have known at the time that he would survive the enterprise. What he could then have known is at most the probability of his surviving. I stress: he could not have known that he would survive even if our world is determined. Even if our world is determined, God alone could have known all of the facts about the gun that were going to determine that the barrel would stop spinning when there was no bullet under the firing pin.

Jonathan Bennett says that "a wrong action must be one which a well-enough-informed bystander could in principle have advised against. . . ."[6] Advised against at the time of the agent's deciding whether to act, which means that the adviser's advice would have had to rest on probabilities. And why must a wrong action be one which a well-enough-informed bystander could in principle have advised against? Bennett says that "an agent who has acted wrongly should have at least a theoretical chance of learning from the wrongness of his action, seeing how he could have done better and may do better in future."

What I suggest is that whether or not we think of it as required that an agent have a theoretical chance of learning how to do better, we should accept the general principle that we ought to do a thing only if a human being can know that we ought to. There is no way in which we can plausibly think that a person ought to have done a thing, or ought to have refrained from doing it, unless we think a human being could have known at the time that the person ought to. And that means that what matters to whether a person ought to do a thing at a time is not what will happen if he does, but rather what is more or less likely to happen if he does—objectively interpreted.

---

[6] Bennett, *The Act Itself*.

In sum, we should reject the idea that "A ought to V_{act}" has "A ought$_{outcome}$ to V_{act}" among its meanings.

3.

We have now looked at five arguments for the Consistency Thesis. There are others, but I have discussed only the ones that seem to me to be most interesting. They usually appear independently in metaethical writings, but I think it helpful to see them together. Each issues from a different pressure, a different difficulty we face in trying to understand what it comes to for it to be the case that a person ought to do a thing. The extent of this range of difficulties must be unique in philosophy. There is no other important concept—not 'knowledge' or 'causality' or 'perception'—that is under pressure from so many different directions. That, I suggest, is partly because we use the word "ought" in so many different kinds of context and on so many different kinds of ground, which encourages hasty ascriptions of ambiguity, and partly because we overlook the richness of our stock of normative concepts, which inclines us to think of the concept 'ought' as having to do more work than it actually does.

In the following chapter, I will make a suggestion as to what is at its heart. More precisely, about what is at the heart of the *normative* concept 'ought'. That qualifier is necessary since there is a nonnormative concept 'ought' that is very familiar and interestingly different.

What I have in mind is what emerges on consideration of a sixth argument for the Consistency Thesis. Suppose it is 1:30 PM, and we ask Smith whether we can expect Alan to be at home at 2 PM. Smith knows that Alan regularly goes for a walk at 2 PM, and plans to do so as usual today, so he says to us:

(1f) Alan ought to go for a walk at 2 PM.

However, Alan had promised Jones that he would mow his lawn at 2 PM, and Jones therefore says to us, in some annoyance:

(2f) Alan ought to mow my lawn at 2 PM.

Alan cannot both go for a walk at 2 PM and mow Jones's lawn at 2 PM. A friend of this sixth argument says that it can be that neither

Smith nor Jones misuses the words he says, and that both speak truly. The Consistency Thesis follows straightway.

The friend of this sixth argument says that "A ought to V_{act}" is ambiguous, as between a normative meaning and a nonnormative meaning. And he is surely right.

The normative meaning, expressible as "A $ought_{normative}$ to V_{act}," is, *very* roughly: A is called on, or required to V_{act}. People who say sentences of the form "A ought to V_{act}" make directive judgments if and only if what they mean is that A $ought_{normative}$ to V_{act}: and it is what makes those propositions true that will occupy us in the following chapter.

What is less than clear is how to characterize the nonnormative meaning of "A ought to V_{act}." We can suppose that Smith meant (1f) nonnormatively. Anyone who says, "The sun ought to come out soon," can also be presumed to mean what he says nonnormatively. Similarly for many sentences of the more general form "A ought to V." Anyone who says, "That stain ought to come out if you use Clorox on it," "The car keys ought to be on the hall table," and "This piece of string ought to be long enough to tie your package with," may be presumed not to mean that the sun, the stain, the car keys, the piece of string are called on, or required, to do or be those things. Presumably what they mean is

---

[7] Similarly for many sentences of the form "It ought to be the case that p". In footnote 2 of the preceding chapter, I discussed the idea that we should take it that

(β) It ought to be the case that p

is fundamental: thus that "A ought to V_{act}" means "It ought to be the case that A $V_{act}s$," and therefore is just a special case of (β). I objected that people who say sentences of the form (β) typically mean what they would have asserted if they had instead said

(β') He/she/they ought to see to it that p,

the person or group of people being fixed by the context, or

(β″) The world would be better if p,

the betterness relation fixed by the context. I then said, in parentheses, that I know of only one other possibility, which I would draw attention to in this footnote. What I had in mind is that a person who says (β) might mean what he would have asserted if he had instead said

(β‴) It $ought_{epistemic}$ to be the case that p.

I think this relatively rare. Still, a person might say "It ought to be the case that we'll win if we bet on Bert to finish first," adding by way of reason for saying so, "after all, he's in better shape than the other runners": such a person may be presumed to mean that it $ought_{epistemic}$ to be the case that we'll win if we bet on Bert to finish first.

something nonnormative.[7] The *Oxford English Dictionary* (OED) calls these "epistemic uses" of "ought", and I will follow it in doing so—thus I will express this meaning of "A ought to V" as "A ought$_{epistemic}$ to V.

I stop, though, to forestall a confusion that that usage might cause. It is often said that sentences of the form "A ought to believe that p" are 'epistemic ought-sentences', and that anyone who says them makes an 'epistemic ought judgment'. That is not the usage I follow here. I take it that a person who says "A ought to believe that p" might mean that A ought$_{normative}$ to believe that p, and thus be making a normative judgment about A. But such a person might instead mean that A ought$_{epistemic}$ to believe that p, and thus be making a nonnormative judgment about A. Suppose that Bert has invented a procedure that he has found capable of causing a person to believe that pigs can fly—insert electrodes in the person's brain in positions X, Y, and Z: turn on the current, and leave on for five minutes. Bert uses the procedure on Charles. Five minutes after having turned on the current, Bert says, confidently, "By now, Charles ought to believe that pigs can fly." We may presume that he is not making a normative judgment about Charles, thus that he isn't asserting that Charles is called on, or required, to believe that pigs can fly. Rather, he is making a nonnormative judgment about Charles—a judgment in the relevant respect like the judgment that Smith makes about Alan in saying (1f).[8]

The epistemic use of "ought" is so very common that it is surprising that—to the best of my knowledge—there is nothing in the literature of epistemology that addresses it.[9]

An obvious idea is that for it to be the case that A ought$_{epistemic}$ to V is for it to be the case that it is probable that A Vs. Thus that if you ask me where the car keys are, and I say "They ought to be on the hall table," meaning "They ought$_{epistemic}$ to be on the hall table," then what I assert is true just in case it is probable that the car keys are on the hall table.

---

[8] I thank Johanna Goth for drawing my attention to examples of this kind.

[9] Ralph Wedgwood discusses this use of "A ought to V" briefly in "The Meaning of 'Ought'," *Oxford Studies in Metaethics*, vol. 1 (Oxford: Clarendon Press, 2006), suggesting that it can be fitted into an account of 'ought-sentences' that takes them to be of the form "It ought to be the case that p."

But that idea faces difficulties. First, it is very implausible to think that this ambiguity of "A ought to V" is a mere happenstance ambiguity, like the ambiguity of "bank" and "bat". It is plausible to think, rather, that there must be a link between those two meanings of "A ought to V." (Compare the two meanings of "healthy", namely "being in good health" and "being conducive to good health".) But it is hard to see how the two meanings of "A ought to V" could be linked, if one is "A ought$_{normative}$ to V" and the other is "It is probable that A Vs." I hope it is clear that we cannot say, for example, that it is probable that A Vs if and only if we ought$_{normative}$ to believe that A Vs. We are not called for, or required, to believe that p wherever it is true that p, much less wherever it is so much as probable that p.

Moreover, this ambiguity is not local to "ought". The same holds of "should". Among the OED's examples of the epistemic use of "ought" is one that is also an example of the epistemic use of "should": "He should be able to catch the tide just as it was nearing high water. Allowing it to swing him north-west until it fulled, he ought to be a third of the way across by the time it slackened." Indeed, it also holds of "must"—think how often we say the likes of "There *must* be some beer left! I bought a dozen cans!" So something general is surely at work here.

A second, and related, difficulty is that it would remain to be explained why people who wish to assert that it is probable that the car keys are on the hall table sometimes choose to do so by saying "They ought to be on the hall table." (Or that they should or must be there.) Why say "ought" (or "should" or "must")? Why not just say "It is probable that they are on the hall table"?

Here is a third difficulty: the analysans is too strong. Consider Rasputin. He was hard to kill. First his assassins poisoned him, then they shot him, then they finally drowned him. Let us imagine that we were there. Let us suppose that the assassins fed him pastries dosed with a powerful, fast-acting poison, and then left him alone for a while, telling him they would be back in half an hour. Half an hour later, one of the assassins said to the others, confidently, "He ought to be dead by now." The others agreed, and they went to look. Rasputin opened his eyes and glared at them. "He ought to be dead by now!" they said, astonished. It might be thought that when they first said the words, they meant that it was then probable that he was dead. Not so when they second said the words. By the time they second said the words, they knew perfectly well that he wasn't dead.

I stress that events like their second saying of the words are very common. Five minutes after having turned on the current, the inventor Bert said, confidently, "By now, Charles ought to believe that pigs can fly." So he removed the electrodes, and asked Charles whether he does. "Certainly not!" says Charles. "How odd," says Bert. "Charles ought to believe that pigs can fly." It might be thought that when Bert first said the words, he meant that it was then probable that Charles believed that pigs can fly. Not so when he second said the words. By the time he second said the words, he knew perfectly well that Charles didn't. Less recondite, and much more familiar: "The 2 o'clock train ought to have arrived by now," Dora says at 2:30, gazing in dismay at the still empty track. Indeed, when you tell me that the car keys aren't on the hall table, I may believe you, and yet say, puzzled, "Well, they ought to be there!—I'm certain that I left them there."

But I think that this third difficulty is easily dealt with, for what it calls for is simply that we distinguish: if I say "The car keys ought to be on the hall table," then I assert different propositions, according as my state of knowledge is different. If (i) I don't know that the car keys are, or that they aren't, on the hall table, then if I say "They ought to be on the hall table," what I mean is that it is probable that they are there. If (ii) I know that they aren't there, then if I say "They ought to be on the hall table," what I mean is that it *was* probable that they would be there. (I bypass the remaining possibility, in which I know that they are there. If I know that they are there, then I don't say "They ought to be on the hall table" at all: I say "They *are* on the hall table.")

That leaves us with the first and second difficulties, however. With no great confidence, I suggest that we may be able to overcome them if we make a further revision, a revision that is surely called for anyway. Consider Alice of the preceding section. Knowing that it is .95 probable that the drug would cure her patient's skin condition and cause him no harm, she might say to us "It ought to cure him and cause him no harm." (Of course, responsible doctor as she is, she will add that it would be mad to count on that, and so she won't.) But what if she had known that it was only .55

probable that the drug would cure him and cause him no harm? Then I doubt that she would say, "It ought to cure him and cause him no harm." I fancy that we do not say "A ought to V" unless we think it either (i) is, or (ii) was, *very* probable that A Vs.

But then perhaps we now have the beginnings of a way of coming to understand why we often say "ought" in such cases. The proposition

(α) It is very probable that A will V

entails the proposition

(β) There is good reason for believing that A will V.

Is (β) a normative proposition? I should think it is. (Compare the proposition that there are good umbrellas in the world.) No matter whether or not it is, for in any case, (β) is true only if there is at least one fact F such that

(γ) F is a good reason for believing that A will V

is true of it, and (γ) is on any view normative—though it is normative in that asserting it is making an evaluative rather than a directive judgment. (Asserting that DRY is a good umbrella is making an evaluative rather than a directive judgment.)

More strongly, we think that (α) is true only where we think that (β) is true and believe about some fact F that it is a good reason for believing that A will V. It seems to me possible, then, that where we think that (α) is true, we express that thought by saying "A should/ought/must V," whose use is primarily normative, when we want to stress that the reason we have in mind is a good reason for believing that A will V—using "should", "ought", or "must" according as we think the reason we have in mind is the better. The judgment we make is not a directive: but we use the words we use in expressing directive judgments in order to stress the evaluative (thus normative) judgment that issued in our making it.

As I said, however, I have no great confidence in this suggestion, so I leave the question what to make of the epistemic use of "ought" to the reader. What I will rely on is only our having an intuitive grasp of the difference between "A ought$_{normative}$ to V" and "A ought$_{epistemic}$ to V."

4.

It will be the directives that concern us from here on, so I will from here on mean "A ought$_{normative}$ to V" by "A ought to V."

XII

Directives

1.

Let us take it for the time being that a directive is a judgment to the effect that a thing A ought to V. (Thus I ignore "should" and "must" for the time being.)

The first point to notice about the directives is that they include judgments that are not about people. A toaster ought to toast toastables—bread, bagels, frozen waffles, and the like; I'll just say bread, for short. A valve of a certain kind ought to blow when the pressure in the pipe it is installed in reaches so and so many degrees. A seeing eye dog ought to stop its master at street corners. The pancreas ought to secrete digestive enzymes. I don't mean that a toaster, a valve of that kind, a seeing eye dog, a pancreas is likely to do these things, though that may (or may not) be true. I mean rather that they are called on, or required to. My judgments about them are normative, not epistemic. I suggest that it is precisely by virtue of what we learn when we attend to directives that are about nonhuman things that we can best understand all of the directives, and thus those that are about people as well.

2.

Let us begin with artifacts. Toasters, for example. I said: a toaster ought to toast bread. So let A be a toaster. Then the following is true:

(1) A ought to toast bread.

What makes it true?

Well, by hypothesis,

(α) A is a toaster.

The kind 'toaster', it will be remembered, is a goodness-fixing kind. More important for present purposes, there is such a property as being a defective toaster. What would mark a toaster as a defective toaster? Obviously: its not toasting bread. Another possibility: its being unsafe to use to toast bread. (As, for example, if it would electrocute the user.) Another: its taking a half an hour to toast a single slice of bread. Another: its being too fragile to survive a year's normal use to toast bread. These are defects in a toaster.

What fixes that they are? Toasters are manufactured to be used by people to toast bread. If a toaster comes off the assembly line and is unable to toast bread, or cannot be used by people to toast bread safely and efficiently, or is incapable of surviving a year's normal use to toast bread, then it is not capable of doing what toasters are manufactured to do. It is *therefore* a defective toaster. So we can say

(β) If a toaster doesn't toast bread, then it is a defective toaster.[1]

I now suggest that we can say: the truth of (α) and (β) is what makes (1) true. A *ought* to toast bread since A is a toaster, and a toaster that doesn't toast bread is a defective toaster.

To forestall an objection, I should add that the words I wrote in writing (β) have to be understood as an abbreviation. A toaster is a defective toaster if it doesn't toast bread, but not in just any circumstances. A toaster is marked as defective when it fails to toast bread only if it has been plugged in, the bread was inserted in the slots, the bar was depressed, and you aren't sitting in the bathtub while doing all of that. A toaster is marked as defective when it fails to toast bread only if it fails to toast bread in suitable circumstances—

---

[1] I assume that there in fact are toasters that don't toast bread, and therefore are defective toasters. What if there weren't? I invite a strong reading of (β)—and of its analogues in what follows—so that it not turn out to be true by falsity of antecedent, namely: If a toaster doesn't, or weren't to, toast bread, then it is, or would be, a defective toaster. None of the examples we will look at will raise a difficulty on this score, so, for brevity, I omit the counterfactuals.

that is, circumstances such that toasters are manufactured to toast bread in them.

But then the words I wrote in writing (1) also have to be understood as an abbreviation. The same abbreviation. It is only when it is in those circumstances that a toaster ought to toast bread. I won't try to spell out what exactly all those suitable circumstances are; I leave them to intuition. And I will for the most part help myself to similar abbreviations in what follows.

A generalization suggests itself. Let us say that a kind K is a directive-generating kind—a directive kind, for short—just in case there is such a property as being a defective K. Then let us say:

> (Directive Thesis) For it to be the case that A ought to V is for it to be the case that there is a directive kind K such that: A is a K, and if a K doesn't V, then it is a defective K.

Let us look at some other examples. Seeing eye dogs are not artifacts: they are not manufactured to do things, they are instead trained to do things—in particular, to serve as eyes for the blind. Suppose A is a seeing eye dog. Then

> (2) A ought to stop its master at street corners

is true. What makes (2) true? There is such a property as being a defective seeing eye dog, so the kind seeing eye dog is a directive kind; and A is a member of it, and if a member doesn't stop its master at street corners, then it is a defective member.

The kinds toaster and seeing eye dog are function-kinds. That is, there is a function associated with each of those two kinds which is such that it is a member's failing to carry out that function, or carrying it out badly, that *marks* it as a defective member of the kind. The function in the case of the kind toaster is to toast bread; the function in the case of the kind seeing eye dog is to serve as eyes for the blind. Among the functions of the pancreas is to secrete digestive enzymes, and an instance that fails to do that, or does it badly, is thereby marked as a defective instance. It is a disputed issue in the philosophy of biology just what it is that gives the pancreas and other human organs the functions they do have, that is, whether it is evolution, or the role they currently play in the bodily economy, or both; and I leave aside the question what should be said about that issue. Whatever explains why the pancreas has the function it does, it nevertheless does have the function of secreting digestive enzymes. So if A is your pancreas, then A is a member of a function-kind, and therefore of a directive kind, such that if a member doesn't secrete digestive enzymes, then it is a defective member; and

(3) A ought to secrete digestive enzymes

is therefore true.

But we should notice that the directive kinds are not limited to the function-kinds. Beefsteak tomatoes are bred to be big and fat at maturity, and if a particular beefsteak tomato turns out to be little at maturity—perhaps because of some freak in the weather—then it is a defective beefsteak tomato. But being big and fat at maturity isn't a function of a beefsteak tomato—it is just a feature such that if a beefsteak tomato lacks the feature, then it is a defective beefsteak tomato. So though the kind beefsteak tomato isn't a function-kind, it is all the same a directive kind; and we can say that if A is a beefsteak tomato, then

(4) A ought to be a big, fat tomato at maturity

is also true.

By contrast, there are no such properties as being a defective pebble and being a defective piece of wood; therefore the kinds pebble and piece of wood are not directive kinds. That leaves room for the possibility that a given pebble or piece of wood ought to do such and such, for it leaves open the possibility that the thing is a member of *some* directive kind K such that if a K doesn't do the such and such, then it is a defective K. But as we might put it: there is nothing that the thing ought to do *qua*, or in virtue of, being a pebble or piece of wood.

That points to what I take to be an attractive feature of the Directive Thesis, namely that it explicitly commits us to accepting that what a thing ought to do is what it ought to do *qua* being of this or that kind. Alternatively put: it is not true of A that it ought to V unless A is of a kind such that everything of that kind ought to V—where it is the fact that everything of that kind ought to V that makes it the case that A ought to. No directive falls from the heavens on A alone. That is no surprise, of course, since if it is to be true that A ought to V, then there has to be something that makes it true, and that something had better be a generalization.

We get at that conclusion from another direction if we accept that it is avoidance of defect that is at the heart of the concept 'ought', for it will be remembered that "defective" is an attributive adjective— nothing is simply defective, a thing can be at most a defective K, for some K.

So far, so plausible, I hope.

3.

Alas, it won't do. Imagine that a pet shop advertises a new kind of dog, called Quiet Dogs, for sale in particular to people who live in small apartments: they are terriers that have been operated on early to cut their vocal cords, so that they are unable to bark. If the operation fails in the case of a particular Quiet Dog, so that it isn't unable to bark, then the result is a defective Quiet Dog. (You can return it, and get your money back.) Let us suppose that Fido is a Quiet Dog, and suppose that

> (Directive Thesis) For it to be the case that A ought to V is for it
> to be the case that there is a directive kind K such that:
> A is a K, and if a K doesn't V, then it is a defective K

is true. Then

> (5) Fido ought to be unable to bark

is true. That is because the kind Quiet Dog is a directive kind, and Fido is a Quiet Dog, and if a Quiet Dog isn't unable to bark, then it is a defective Quiet Dog.

But we should notice that the kind terrier is also a directive kind: it is a physical norm for terriers that they be able to bark—thus if a terrier isn't able to bark then it is a physically defective terrier, and thus a defective terrier.[2] (What the operation on a Quiet Dog does,

---

[2] In an early draft of this material, I had written that a dog that is unable to bark is a defective dog. At a conference at which I presented the material, a participant drew my attention to Basenjis, a breed of dog in which it is natural and normal to be unable to bark. (Basenjis apparently produce a queer kind of yodel instead of a

if it succeeds, is to *make* it be defective terrier.) Now since Fido is a Quiet Dog, it is also a terrier. If it isn't able to bark, it is a defective terrier. So

> (6) Fido ought to be able to bark

is also true. It is obvious that (5) and (6) can't both be true.

A way of revising the Directive Thesis all but suggests itself. Let us say:

> (Improved Directive Thesis) For it to be the case that A ought to V is for it to be the case that there is a directive kind K such that:
>
> (α) A is a K, and
> (β) if a K doesn't V, then it is a defective K, and
> (γ) there is no directive kind K+ such that K is a sub-kind of K+, and such that if a K+ does V, then it is a defective K+.

(I take K to be a sub-kind of K+ just in case necessarily, every K is a K+.) So revised, the thesis doesn't yield that (5) is true. There is a directive kind K such that Fido is a K, and if a K isn't unable to bark, then it is a defective K. We can suppose that there is only one such K, namely the kind Quiet Dog. But that kind is a sub-kind of the directive kind terrier, and if a terrier is unable to bark then it is a defective terrier. And so revised, the thesis does yield that (6) is true. For the kind terrier is a directive kind, and if a terrier isn't able to bark then it is a defective terrier—and we can suppose that there is no directive kind K+ of which the kind terrier is a sub-kind such that if a K+ is able to bark then it is a defective K+. I take it to be an attractive fact about our thesis that it does not yield (5) and does yield (6).

Moreover, revising the thesis in this way makes no trouble for

> (1) A ought to toast bread,

---

bark.) It follows that it is not a physical norm for dogs that they be able to bark; that is a physical norm only for breeds in which it is natural and normal to be able to. Terriers, for example.

given that A is a toaster. For the kind toaster is a directive kind, and if a toaster does not toast bread, then it is a defective toaster; and we can suppose that there is no directive kind K+ of which the kind toaster is a sub-kind such that if a K+ does toast bread then it is a defective K+. Similarly for (2), (3), and (4).

4.

We should stop to take note of a question that might well arise here. I said I take it to be an attractive fact about our thesis that it does not yield (5) and does not yield (6). That is, it is intuitively plausible that what fixes what Fido ought to do is not its being a member of the sub-kind Quiet Dog, but its being a member of the super-kind terrier. Alternatively put: the super-kind terrier 'trumps' its sub-kind Quiet Dog.

Indeed, we might rewrite our thesis more briefly as follows:

(Abbreviated Improved Directive Thesis) For it to be the case that A ought to V is for it to be the case that there is a directive kind K such that:
(α) A is a K, and
(β) if a K doesn't V, then it is a defective K, and
(γ) K is not trumped by any directive super-kind.

It might well be asked, however, why we should think that true. Why not instead suppose that what fixes what Fido ought to do is not what issues from the fact that Fido is a member of the super-kind terrier, but rather what issues from the fact that Fido is a member of the sub-kind Quiet Dog?

That a directive super-kind K+ trumps a directive sub-kind K in that way is intuitively plausible quite generally. When we reason about what a thing ought to do, we look for generalizations, and we take what issues from the more general to have more weight than what issues from the less general if what issues from the more general conflicts with what issues from the less general.

Why so? Appeal to the concept 'defect' supplies a justification. Consider Fido. The fact that Fido is a Quiet Dog guarantees that it is in some way defective. (For if it is able to bark, then it is a defective Quiet Dog, whereas if it is unable to bark, then it is a defective terrier.) Not so the fact that Fido is a terrier. (It is entirely possible to be a terrier without being in some way defective.) *That* is why what fixes what Fido ought to do is not the fact that it is a Quiet Dog but instead the fact that it is a terrier.

5.

I suggest that the

> (Improved Directive Thesis) For it to be the case that A ought
> to V is for it to be the case that there is a directive
> kind K such that:
> (α) A is a K, and
> (β) if a K doesn't V, then it is a defective K, and
> (γ) there is no directive kind K+ such that K is a sub-
> kind of K+, and such that if a K+ does V, then it is a
> defective K+

is true if A is a toaster, a seeing eye dog, a gland, a beefsteak tomato, a Quiet Dog. But human beings make trouble for it.

I said just above that it is a physical norm for terriers that they be able to bark, and therefore that if a terrier is unable to bark, then it is a physically defective terrier, and therefore a defective terrier. That is why the thesis yields that a Quiet Dog, indeed, any terrier, ought to be able to bark.

It is a mental norm for terriers that they be able to learn simple commands. Therefore if a terrier is unable to learn simple commands, then it is a mentally defective terrier, and therefore a defective terrier. So the thesis yields—as it surely should—that a Quiet Dog, indeed, any terrier, ought to be able to learn simple commands.

Can we say that being a defective terrier just is being either a physically or mentally defective terrier? Presumably we can. Whether or not we can, we can anyway say that if a terrier is either a physically or mentally defective terrier, then it is a defective terrier.

Toasters lead much narrower lives than terriers—their failings are all physical. Thus being a defective toaster just is being a physically defective toaster. Similarly for glands and beefsteak tomatoes.

But human beings are another matter. It is a physical norm for the species that a member be capable of seeing, and another that a member have two legs. So we should be able to conclude that a human being ought to be capable of seeing, and ought to have two legs. Well, since these are physical norms for the species, we can say that a human being who is not capable of seeing, or who has only one leg, is a physically defective human being. But we surely cannot conclude from the fact that he/she is a physically defective human being that he/she is a defective human being.

Again, it is a mental norm for the species that a member be capable of reasoning. So we should be able to conclude that a human being ought to be capable of reasoning. Well, since this is a mental norm for the species, we can say that a human being who is not capable of reasoning is a mentally defective human being. But we surely cannot conclude from the fact that he/she is a mentally defective human being that he/she is a defective human being.

Or so I believe. Toasters lead narrower lives than terriers, and terriers lead narrower lives than human beings do—they aren't capable of the injustice (among other possibilities) that marks a human being as a defective human being. But then the thesis does not yield that a human being ought to be capable of seeing and ought to have two legs, and ought to be capable of reasoning. So how *are* those conclusions to be reached?

I think that the simplest and most perspicuous way to respond to this difficulty is this. Restrict the replacements for "A" in the Improved Directive Thesis to names of the likes of toasters and terriers. For human beings, distinguish among the replacements for "V", and opt for a further thesis, namely:

> (HB/Norm Thesis) If A is a human being, and V-ing is a physical or mental norm for the species, then for it to be the case that A ought to V is for it to be the case that a human being is a physically or mentally defective human being if he does not V.

I take it that it is for biologists to tell us what are the physical and mental norms for the species, just as it is for dog breeders to tell us what are the physical and mental norms for the various breeds of dog.

6.

A more interesting set of replacements for "V-ing" are V_{act}-ings. Let A be a human being. Under what conditions is it true that A ought to V_{act}? Consider an example we met in the preceding chapter. We supposed that Alfred's child has just started to show symptoms of what Alfred recognizes is a dread disease that children are susceptible to. Alfred believes that the only hospital in the area equipped to cure it is Traditional Hospital, but we know better: we know that the only hospital in the area equipped to cure it is Modern Hospital. So we say

(7) Alfred ought to take his child to Modern.

What makes that true?

It is plain enough that we cannot say: for (7) to be true is for it to be the case that a human being is a physically or mentally defective human being if he/she does not take his/her child to Modern.

We also cannot say: for (7) to be true is for it to be the case that a human being is a defective human being if he/she does not take his/her child to Modern. We cannot even say that for (7) to be true is for it to be the case that *Alfred* is a defective human being if he does not take his child to Modern. For if Alfred is entirely fault-free in believing that the only hospital in the area equipped to cure the disease is Traditional, then he is without fault if he does not take his child to Modern. And if he is without fault if he does not take his child to Modern, we obviously cannot say that he is a defective human being if he does not take his child to Modern. Yet he ought to take it to Modern.

Does this mean that we must give up the idea that the concept 'defect' lies at the heart of the concept 'ought'? The answer, I suggest, is no. We must just be more careful about the connection between those concepts. I suggest that we should opt for:

> (HB-V_{act} Thesis) If A is a human being, then for it to be the case that A ought to V_{act} is for it to be the case that if A knows at the time what will probably happen if he V_{act}s and what will probably happen if he does not, then he is a defective human being if he does not.[3]

---

[3] I invite a strong reading of the analysans here, namely "if A knows, or knew, at the time what will, or would, probably happen if he V_{act}-ed and what will, or would, probably happen if he did not, then he is, or would be, a defective human being if he did not." For brevity, I omit the counterfactuals. (Compare footnote 1 above.)

Consider (7). Suppose that what will probably happen if Alfred takes his child to Modern is that his child will live, and no one will be harmed. Suppose that what will probably happen if Alfred does not take his child to Modern is that his child will die. Suppose, finally, that Alfred knows those facts about probability. Then he is a defective human being if he does not take his child to Modern. The thesis therefore yields that he ought to.

Perhaps it isn't *probable* that his child will live if he takes it to Modern? Perhaps there is only a small chance that it will live if he takes it to Modern, and hardly any chance that it will live if he doesn't? If he knows this, then here too, he is defective if he doesn't— and therefore he ought to.

In what way is he defective if, knowing the probabilities, he doesn't take his child to Modern? Well, that depends on why he doesn't. If he doesn't because he hates his child, then he is malicious. If he doesn't because he doesn't care what happens to his child, then he is callous. If he doesn't because it snowed this morning, and he doesn't want to bother shoveling the driveway, then he is both callous and lazy. If he doesn't because he is his child's heir, then he is both callous and greedy. There are other possibilities too. Consider

(8) Alice ought to give Bert an apple.

Suppose that if she does, she will probably be keeping her promise to Bert and causing no one a harm. Suppose that if she doesn't, she will probably be breaking her promise to Bert, and causing him a harm. Suppose, finally, that Alice knows these facts about probability. Then she is a defective human being if she doesn't. What is her defect? Injustice. If she refrains because she wants to cause him a harm, then maliciousness as well. If she refrains because she doesn't care, then callousness instead of maliciousness. Perhaps also greed.

The defects I have mentioned so far might be called 'other-regarding'. There are self-regarding defects too. Consider another example we met in the preceding chapter. We supposed that Bert knows that Alex loves dangerous enterprises, and therefore makes Alex the following offer: if Alex will play Russian Roulette on himself with a fair gun—with a bullet in one of the gun's ten chambers— and survives it, then Bert will pay Alex a thousand dollars. Then it is plain that

(9) Alex ought to refrain from firing the gun on himself

is true. Why? It is plain that Alex will be grossly at fault if he fires
the gun on himself, but I said that we cannot take that fact to
explain what makes (9) true, for we have rejected the idea that the
fact that a person would be at fault if he did a thing itself shows that
he ought not do it. (By hypothesis, Alfred believes that Traditional
is the only hospital in the area equipped to cure disease, so he is at
fault if he takes his child to Modern. All the same, he ought to take
it to Modern.) What is special about Alex is not just that he will be
at fault if he fires the gun on himself, but that what makes him *be*
at fault if he does so is his knowing what will probably happen if
he does and if he doesn't. The thesis yields that he ought not fire
the gun, not simply because he will be at fault if he does so, but
rather because it is his knowing what those probabilities are that
makes him be at fault if he does so. What is the fault? Gross imprudence. Recklessness. If I knowingly buy a very risky stock, then—
my financial condition being what it is—perhaps recklessness is
over-strong, perhaps my defect is only imprudence. Or perhaps—my
financial condition being what it is—it is no defect in me to buy that
stock, in which case, the thesis yields, as it should, that it is not true
that I ought not buy it.

The ways of being defective that I have mentioned so far are
malicious, callous, lazy, greedy, unjust, reckless, and imprudent.
Here are some others: ruthless, cruel, sanctimonious, jealous, rude,
weak-willed, unscrupulous, vengeful, petty, intemperate, cowardly,
irresolute, misanthropic, irresponsible, lacking in self-respect, and
lacking in generosity.[4] They plainly overlap. For my own part, I
think they can all be seen as more or less grave ways of being
either unjust, or lacking in generosity, or both—provided that we
grant (as I think it plain that we should) that one can be unjust, or
lacking in generosity, or both, in respect of oneself as well as in
respect of others. But I leave the question whether that is right to
moral theory.

---

[4] Aristotle is translated as having said: "the man who shuns every pleasure, as
boors do, becomes in a way insensible" (*Nicomachean Ethics*, Book II, ch. 2).
Perhaps that "insensible" is best understood as: apathetic, cold, impassive.

7.

There is another matter I leave to moral theory. Opting for

> (HB/V_{act} Thesis) If A is a human being, then for it to be the case that A ought to V_{act} is for it to be the case that if A knows at the time what will probably happen if he V_{act}s and what will probably happen if he does not, then he is a defective human being if he does not

is clearly opting for an account according to which what A *in fact* believes does not fix that he ought to V_{act}. And, I have suggested, rightly so. The fact that Alfred believes that Traditional is the only hospital in the area equipped to cure his child does not warrant the conclusion that he ought to take it to Traditional. Indeed, that fact lends no weight at all to the conclusion that he ought to take it to Traditional.

Similarly for the intentions with which A would *in fact* V_{act} if he did. If Alfred has not yet been told otherwise, and would take his child to Traditional with the good intention of getting it cured, that lends no weight to the conclusion that he ought to take it to Traditional. If he hates his child, and would take it to Modern with the bad intention of causing its death while giving the false impression that he wants it cured and believes Modern the only hospital that can cure it, then that lends no weight to the conclusion that he ought to refrain from taking it to Modern.

There is a distinction that some philosophers have thought morally significant, namely that between on the one hand, what an agent intends to bring about by V_{act}-ing, and on the other hand, what an agent merely foresees that he will bring about by V_{act}-ing but does not intend to bring about by V_{act}-ing. Here is a pair of examples commonly offered in support of that view. Suppose Villain Country has unjustly attacked us, and we are in process of defending ourselves against it. In the first example, our Bomber Command has learned of the position of a munitions factory, and has ordered Captain Alan to bomb it. Bomber Command knows that there are civilians living near the factory, and that however carefully Alan is able to drop his bombs, his dropping the bombs will cause their deaths. Nevertheless, the philosophers I refer to say that it is morally permissible for Alan to drop his bombs. Alternatively put:

(10) It is not the case that Alan ought not drop his bombs.

In the second example, Bomber Command has learned that the citizens of Villain Country will want the war stopped if they learn that their cities can be successfully bombed, and will begin to take steps toward getting their government to end the war. So Bomber Command orders Captain Arthur to drop bombs on a city. The philosophers I refer to say that it is not morally permissible for Arthur to drop his bombs—thus,

(11) Arthur ought not drop his bombs.

What could justify that difference? The philosophers I refer to say the following. Alan may drop his bombs since he would be intending to destroy the factory, not intending to cause the civilian deaths but merely foreseeing that he will cause them. Arthur may not drop his bombs since he would be intending to cause the civilian deaths as a means to getting the citizens to begin to take steps toward getting their government to end the war.

Can that be right? We do well to begin by asking: how do you know what Alan's and Arthur's intentions would be? They might be anything! Suppose Alan believes that destroying the factory would do Villain Country's war effort no real harm, but that killing the civilians would get Villain citizens to begin to take steps toward getting their government to end the war—so that killing the civilians is what he intends, merely foreseeing that the factory will be destroyed. Suppose Arthur believes that the city he is ordered to drop bombs on contains several major munitions factories, and destroying those factories is what he would be intending in dropping his bombs, merely foreseeing the civilian deaths. Are we to say that if we learn this, we thereby learn that we were mistaken, thus that it is Alan who ought not drop his bombs whereas Arthur may drop his? That will hardly do.

There is a more general point in the offing. I drew attention earlier to the fact that it is a silly idea that if A asks us whether it is morally permissible for him to V_{act}, then we should reply, "We can't tell unless you first tell us what you believe will happen if you V_{act}." It is equally silly to suppose that if A asks us whether it is morally permissible for him to V_{act}, then we should reply, "We can't tell unless you first tell us what you would be intending, as opposed to merely foreseeing, if you V_{act}-ed."[5]

That means that anyone who wants to justify the claim that Alan may drop his bombs whereas Arthur may not must find grounds for it lying, not in subjective facts about their intentions and beliefs, but rather in objective facts about the circumstances in which they would be acting. More particularly, I suggest, in objective facts about what would probably happen if they acted in those circumstances, and probably happen if they did not, and in whether they would be marked as defective if they knew about those facts and nevertheless proceeded. I leave the question how that is to be done to moral theorists.[6]

8.

However there is a different point about intentions that we should stop over briefly. Opting for

> (HB/V_{act} Thesis) If A is a human being, then for it to be the case that A ought to V_{act} is for it to be the case that if A knows at the time what will probably happen if he V_{act}s and what will probably happen if he does not, then he is a defective human being if he does not

is opting for an account according to which the intentions with which A would in fact V_{act}, if he did, are irrelevant to the question whether he ought or ought not V_{act}. For example, suppose Alice's child is ill, and can be cured only if given an alpha-pill. Then other things being equal,

> (12) Alice ought to give her child an alpha-pill

---

[5] I have argued at greater length elsewhere that we should reject the idea that the intending/foreseeing distinction makes the moral difference it is here called on to make, for example, in "Physician-Assisted Suicide: Two Arguments," *Ethics* 109 (April 1999). An exceedingly good discussion of the idea may be found in Jonathan Bennett's *The Act Itself*, ch. 11.

[6] I add only that the examples I gave are grossly underdescribed, which is common in much of this literature, and which is at least *a* source of the difficulty.

is true. It is true even if Alice believes that giving her child an alpha-pill would kill it, and, hating the child, would give it an alpha-pill (if she did) in order to kill it.

I am sure that some readers will have felt discomfort (at a minimum!) at the fact that the thesis commits us to that conclusion. And I suspect that they may not feel adequately relieved if I point to the fact that we can say (i) that she will be at fault if she gives her child an alpha-pill with that intention, and (ii) that her doing it with that intention will mark her as a defective person, and (iii) that her doing it with that intention will be a morally bad act. (Consequentialists also point to such facts when their readers object to Consequentialism's also yielding that [12] is true even if Alice's intention in acting would be to kill her child.)

So it may pay to draw attention to the fact (iv) that the truth of (12) is entirely compatible with the truth of

> (13) Alice ought not give her child an alpha-pill in order to kill it.

Suppose V_{act}-1-ing and V_{act}-2-ing are two distinct act-kinds. Let us ask what the conditions are under which the following is true:

A ought not V_{act}-1 in order to V_{act}-2.

One thing that would plainly make it true is its being the case that A ought not V_{act}-1. (If you ought not do a thing, then a fortiori, you ought not do it in order to bring such and such about.) I suggest that there is one other thing that would make it true, namely its being the case that A ought not V_{act}-2. (If you ought not bring such and such and such about, then you ought not try to.) In sum, I suggest that we should accept:

> For it to be the case that A ought not V_{act}-1 in order to V_{act}-2 is for the following to be the case: either A ought not V_{act}-1, or A ought not V_{act}-2.

We were supposing that (12) is true. But we may certainly also suppose that Alice ought not kill her child. It follows that (13) is true.

Are there also truths of the form:

A ought to V_{act}-1 in order to V_{act}-2?

Alice ought not give her child an alpha-pill in order to kill it. Ought she give her child an alpha-pill in order to cure it? I don't myself feel inclined to say so. I don't myself think it matters much to what she ought to do for what V_{act}-2-ing it is such that she gives her child an alpha-pill in order to V_{act}-2, so long as it is not the case that she ought not V_{act}-2. (Though it might well matter to our assessment of how good a mother she is.) But others may think otherwise, and I therefore leave it open.

9.

Let us now turn to V_{mind}-ings. I begin with the conditions under which A ought to believe a proposition P—thus, for example, the conditions under which it would be true to say:

> (14) Alice ought to believe that an alpha-pill would cure her child.

We should stop first, however, to take note of an argument that many people have taken seriously, an argument to the effect that the likes of (14) are never true. The argument proceeds as follows. First premise: it cannot be true to say that a person ought to V unless the person can V at will. Second premise: it is not possible for a person to believe a thing at will. Conclusion: it cannot be true of any person that he ought to believe a thing. So (14) and its ilk are all false.

I say that many people have taken that argument seriously, though many of them have argued that it should be rejected, thus that one or the other of the premises is false. But the argument is not really worth taking seriously, since its first premise is so obviously false.

For (i) believing a thing is being in a certain state, and one can't be in a state—*any* state—at will. Trusting a person is being in a mental state. So is preferring X to Y. Being in Chicago is being in a physical state. So also is weighing so and so many pounds. One can't be in any of these states at will. That is not a deep point, it is right up at the surface. Being in a state isn't something that is done, and a fortiori one can't do it at will.

Yet (ii) there are states such that it is very often true to say of a person that he ought to be in this one or that. It may be true that A ought to trust B. It may be true that A ought to prefer X to Y. Suppose that A has promised to be in Chicago today, and that people have been counting on his being there today. I run across A in Harvard Square today, and I say, in some surprise, "You ought to be in Chicago today!" What I say may be true. Again, a doctor may say of a child "Given its age, that child ought to weigh more than 37 pounds," and be speaking truly when he does.[7]

And (iii) there is no reason at all to think that believings are unique among states in that it is not possible for a person to say the likes of (14) and be speaking truly when he does.

It may be objected that "A ought to be in Chicago today" is true only if A could at will have done something that would have caused him to be in Chicago today. (In that he could at will have caught a plane or train.) And it might therefore be suggested that a weaker pair of premises will suffice for the conclusion. Weaker first premise: it cannot be true to say that a person ought to V unless the person could, at will, have caused himself to V. Weaker second premise: it is not possible for a person to, at will, cause himself to believe a thing. Conclusion: it cannot be true of any person that he ought to believe a thing.

I leave open whether it is right to think that "A ought to be in Chicago today" is true only if A could, at will, have caused himself to be in Chicago today. (We must in any case allow that even if A could, at will, have done something yesterday that would have caused him to be in Chicago today, he may by now have left it too late: there may be nothing at all that he could, at will, do now that would cause him to be in Chicago today—compatibly with its being the case that he ought to be there today.) But it is in any case wrong to think that "A ought to trust B" is true only if A could, at will, have caused himself to trust B. And wrong to think that "A ought to prefer X to Y" is true only if A could, at will, have caused himself to prefer X to Y. And wrong to think that "That child ought to weigh more than 37 pounds" is true only if the child could, at will, have caused itself to weigh more.

So let us ignore this argument, and turn to the question what might make it true that a person ought to believe a thing.

---

[7] Remember, moreover, that a toaster ought to toast bread, and that a valve of a certain kind ought to blow when the pressure in the pipe it is installed in reaches so and so many degrees.

10.

Under what conditions might it be true that A ought to believe a proposition P? It is a popular idea that for that to be true is for it to be the case that the total body of evidence that A has in hand for P supports it.[8] Let us call this idea Subjectivism about Belief. Why should we accept it? The reason we are given is that if the total body of evidence that A has in hand for P supports it, then it would be irrational in A to not believe P.

Subjectivism about Belief is plainly a first cousin of the idea we called Subjectivism in the preceding chapter. The source of Subjectivism was

> (Ought-Fault Thesis) A ought to V_{act} if and only if A would be at fault if he did not V_{act};

the source of Subjectivism about Belief is the analogous thesis

> A ought to believe P if and only if A would be at fault if he did not believe P—

the fault here being irrationality.

And it plainly faces the same objection. People for whom it is important to find out whether P is true often ask us "Ought I believe P?" If Subjectivism about Belief were true, then it would be called for that we reply that they'll have to tell us what their evidence is, because what they ought to believe turns on the evidence they already have. That's a silly idea. What they want to know is not whether the evidence they have in hand supports P; what they want to know is whether P is true.

On the other hand, it won't do to say that a person ought to believe P if P is true. It just so happens that there are three maple leaves now on my doormat—it can't for a moment be thought that everyone ought to believe that there are.

Something in one or another way important, involving A, has to be at stake if it is to be true that A *ought* to believe P. An idea that

---

[8] Richard Feldman recommends that we opt for a view of this kind in "The Ethics of Belief," *Philosophy and Phenomenological Research* 60 (2000): 667–95. But Feldman imposes a condition: one ought to believe a proposition that one's evidence supports *if* one is going to have any doxastic attitude toward it at all.

suggests itself is that the 'something important' has to consist in there being something that A ought to do. Thus that its being the case that A ought to *believe* something rests in some way on its being the case that A ought to *do* something.

Suppose, for example, that the following proposition is true:

> (P) Alice's child will probably live if she gives it some medicine M, and die if she doesn't.

Something important is certainly at stake here! Other things being equal—and let us for simplicity suppose that they are—Alice ought to give her child some M. (Why so? Well, if she knows that P is true, then she is defective if she doesn't give her child some M.)

So here if anywhere we have a case in which a person ought to believe a thing, for if anyone ought to believe a thing, Alice ought to believe P. But why, exactly? Here is a suggestion: Alice ought to believe P because the fact that P is true is among the facts that jointly make it the case that she ought to give her child some M.

I think we take it that if A ought to V_{act}, then he ought to believe that he ought to V_{act}. Moreover, not just any reasons for believing it will do: A ought to believe it for the right reasons. He ought to believe not only that he ought to V_{act}, but also all those propositions such that it is their being true that makes it the case that he ought to V_{act}, and therefore explains why he ought to. In short, when we ought to do a thing, we ought to be clear that and why we ought to.

It might not be Alice's fault that she does not believe P. Just as it might not be her fault that she does not give her child some M. (As it might not be Alfred's fault that he does not take his child to Modern.) Again, it might be that Alice does believe both that she ought to give her child some M, and the reason why she ought to, and nevertheless does not give it some M. For example, she might not care what happens to her child. Again, it might be that Alice will give her child some M, not believing P, but rather believing that M is a poison, and wanting the child to die. These possibilities are compatible with its being the case both that she ought to give her child some M, and ought to believe P—and (as the suggestion says) ought to believe P because its being true is among the facts that make it the case that she ought to give her child some M.

Not all cases are as melodramatic as that one. Anne and I are standing at the window, gazing at the heavens, which look gray. Anne knows I have heard a weather report, and she asks me, "Ought I believe it will snow this afternoon?" Since I think she plans to go out, I take it that she wants to know whether it will snow because she wants to know whether she ought to wear her boots. And since the weather report I heard said snow this afternoon, and since the fact of snow this afternoon is among the facts that would make it the case that she ought to wear her boots, I say yes, she ought to believe it will snow.

Of course it might turn out that Anne has no intention of going out. Then it is not the case that she ought to wear her boots. Is there anything else she ought to do such that the fact of snow this afternoon would contribute to making it the case that she ought to do it? No, it turns out. Then I see no reason to think that she *ought* to believe it will snow. As I see no reason to think that she ought to believe that there are three maple leaves now on my doormat.

More generally, then:

> (HB/Belief Thesis) If A is a human being, then for it to be the case that A ought to believe P is for it to be the case that (α) P is true, and (β) there is something that A ought to do such that the fact that P is true is among the facts that make it the case that A ought to do it.

11.

If that thesis is acceptable, then the other V_{mind}-ings fall into place neatly.

What might make

(15) Alfred ought to trust Bert

true? What's Bert to Alfred that Alfred ought to trust him? What *turns on* Alfred's trusting Bert?

Suppose we say, as is independently plausible, that for (15) to be true is for

(16) Alfred ought to believe that Bert is trustworthy

to be true. I don't say that trusting a person is believing the person trustworthy. We can leave the question whether it is aside. Whether or not it is, what makes it the case that you ought to trust a person (if you ought to) is whatever it is that makes it the case that you ought to believe that the person is trustworthy.

Now the HB/Belief Thesis tells us that for (16) to be true is for the following to be the case:

> (α) Bert is trustworthy, and (β) there is something that Alfred ought to do such that the fact that Bert is trustworthy is among the facts that make it the case that Alfred ought to do it.

Then we can conclude that for (15) to be true is also for that to be the case. And now we know what has to turn on Alfred's trusting Bert for it to be true that he ought to trust him: there has to be something that Alfred ought to do such that Bert's being trustworthy is among the facts that make it the case that Alfred ought to do it.

Thus suppose that Bert is Alfred's financial adviser, and has recommended to him that he buy stock in Such and Such Company. Alfred tells us this, and asks us, "Ought I trust Bert?" We ourselves have no independent source of information about Such and Such Company, but we know a lot about Bert. In particular, we know that Bert is trustworthy. So we think that the fact that Bert is trustworthy is among the facts that make it the case that Alfred ought to act as Bert recommends; and we therefore reply, "Yes, you ought to trust him."

In sum, if we say

> For it to be the case that A ought to trust B is for it to be the case that A ought to believe that B is trustworthy,

then we indirectly capture what has to turn on A's trusting B for it to be true that he ought to trust him, for the HB/Belief Thesis directly captures what has to turn on A's believing that B is trustworthy for it to be true that he ought to believe that B is trustworthy.

Analogously for its being the case that A ought to admire C, fear D, dislike E, prefer F to G, and so on.

A generalization is available. I take it we can say that a person ought to V_{mind} only if there is such a thing as a V_{mind}-ing's being a correct V_{mind}-ing. It might be true that Alfred ought to trust Bert; it can't be true that Alfred ought to feel warm.[9] Then if we help ourselves to a device that I made use of in chapter VIII, we can generalize as follows. Let ψ_{Vmind} be the proposition such that for a V_{mind}-ing to be a correct V_{mind}-ing is for it to be true. (Thus the proposition that B is trustworthy is the proposition such that for a trusting of B to be a correct trusting of B is for it to be true. The proposition that C is admirable is the proposition such that for an admiring of C to be a correct admiring of C is for it to be true. And so on.) Then we can say:

(HB/V_{mind} Thesis) For it to be the case that A ought to V_{mind} is for it to be the case that A ought to believe ψ_{Vmind}.

Anyone who wants to know what would make it true that A ought to believe ψ_{mind} is invited to consult HB/Belief Thesis.

12.

What we have reached is a battery of theses governing directive judgments, some about people, some about things that are not people. There are any number of directives of kinds other than those we have attended to, but I believe that none of them raise radically different issues.

A matter that calls for attention, however, is this. I said at the beginning of this chapter that we should take it for the time being that a directive is a judgment to the effect that a thing A ought to V. Thus we have ignored "should" and "must". Let us turn to them now.

My own impression is that

A should V
A ought to V
A must V
A must V, like it or not

differ only in the gravity of the defect that is in the offing if A fails to V. I say "You should give Bert an apple" if I think that if you know

---

[9] Notice that if Alfred was shivering, and we have given him brandy and wrapped him in blankets, we might say the words, "Alfred ought to feel warm by now." But if we do, the judgment we make is not normative.

what will probably happen if you do and will probably happen if you don't, then it is only a minor defect in you if you don't. Perhaps it would be ungenerous in you to not give him an apple. He isn't *starving*; he'd merely like to have one of your apples, and you have lots of extras that you neither need nor want. If he is starving, then something stronger is in order: you ought to give him one. If no one else is in a position to help him, then you must. If the apples are his, and you stole them from him, then you must, like it or not!—here the defect in the offing if you don't is not mere ungenerosity, it is gross injustice.

It might pay to mention that this scale is present even where the defects in the offing are not traditionally viewed as moral defects. Alfred should pay a little more into his retirement fund. If Alan doesn't pay anything at all into a retirement fund, then he ought to—perhaps, indeed, he must. Like it or not, Andrew must stop gambling. The defects in the offing here are minor to major imprudence.

Those differences were due to differences in probable outcomes. A similar difference accompanies differences in the probability of the same outcome. The more probable it is that you will unjustifiably cause a harm if you do a thing, the more grave the defect if you wittingly do it, and therefore the more likely we are to shift from "should not" to "ought not" to "must not".

I stress, however, that the concept 'defect' lies at the heart of the concepts 'should' and 'must' just as (as I said) it lies at the heart of the concept 'ought'.

Call that view the Directive Constraint. I briefly summarize three reasons for regarding it as attractive.

First, it gives expression to the fundamental fact about the directives, namely that they are true of a thing A only by virtue of A's being a member of a kind, and that the kinds K that generate directives governing their members just are those for which there are such properties as being a defective K. Toaster. Beefsteak tomato. Terrier. Human being. Not so pebble and piece of wood. If A isn't a member of any directive-generating kind, then no matter what else is or may be true of A—no matter how it does or may behave, in what circumstances—it isn't, for any K, a defective K, and *that* is why no directives are true of it.

Second, both the Consequentialist and the friend of the Directive Constraint reduce directives to evaluatives, but the evaluatives they rely on are different: the Consequentialist relies on the property goodness (or the relation better world than), whereas the friend of the Directive Constraint relies on the properties being a defective K, for this and that K. This gives the friend of the Directive Constraint an advantage of great importance. It is very commonly said that Consequentialism yields objectionable directives: on the one hand, it demands too much of us, and on the other hand, and even more important, it allows for the possibility that what is demanded of us is flatly unjust. The Directive Constraint yields no such outcomes. It does not demand that we do something unless we would be defective human beings if we wittingly failed to do it. This does not demand saintliness, and it positively rules out injustice.

Third, in that it does not demand saintliness, the Directive Constraint *seems* to me to be preferable to those theories about what a person ought to do that are nowadays called virtue theories. I stress "seems to me", however, since it is not altogether clear to me what those theories do demand of us. The received summary of what they require is this: what a person ought to do is what a virtuous person would do. But how demanding is that prescription? Is a person virtuous for simply not being vicious? Or is more required? Perhaps the Directive Constraint can be thought of as, rather, a vice theory: what a person ought to is to avoid the vices.

However, that is as I think it should be. What true directives about us require is only decency. Of course, it isn't nothing to do what decency requires, and it's a sad business how often people fall below it. Moreover, decency may require a lot of us on occasion. But it typically doesn't. "He did what he ought" is very rarely high praise.

We should remember too that if the directives don't require anything exciting of us, and set us no ideals, there is no reason why they should. Normativity is not restricted to the directives. There is plenty of room in normativity for evaluative judgments in the making of which we praise people whose conduct is not merely decent but splendid.

ADDENDUM 1

"Red" and "Good"

1.

Peter Geach said that "red" is a predicative adjective whereas "big" and "good" are attributives. I think he was right about all three, but some people would object that while he was right about "big" and "good", he was not right about "red". For our purposes, it matters only that Geach was right about "big" and "good": thus for our purposes, it does not matter what is said about "red". But I think it pays to make a case for his having been right about "red".

Geach said that what marks "red" as predicative is this: if K_1 and K_2 are kinds, then the conjunction of the propositions

A is a red K_1

and

A is a K_2

entails the proposition

A is a red K_2.

For example, the conjunction of

A is a red car

and

233

> A is a Mercedes

entails

> A is a red Mercedes.

But it has been objected that that won't do. Here is an example I was given recently: the conjunction of the propositions

> A is a red wine

and

> A is a liquid

does not entail the proposition

> A is a red liquid.

Well, it isn't convincing. Some red wines are very dark red liquids, but a very dark red liquid *is* a red liquid. So let us shift to "white", since what holds of "red" should also hold of "white". The conjunction of the propositions

> A is a white wine

and

> A is a liquid

surely doesn't entail the proposition

> A is a white liquid.

A white wine isn't a white liquid! ("White" is certainly vague, but it doesn't stretch *that* far.) A white wine is a yellow liquid.

But this is a bad argument: it rests on an obvious equivocation. The expression "white wine" has two meanings, which I will call its conventional meaning and its literal meaning. People who say the words "A is a white wine" are likely to mean "white wine" conventionally. When they do, the proposition they assert is true only if A is a yellow liquid—it being a yellow liquid that results when the skins of the grapes are removed before fermentation.

However "white wine" also has a literal meaning. People who are so far benighted as to say "A is a white wine," meaning "white wine" literally, are asserting a proposition that is true only if A is a white liquid. Since no wine is a white liquid, the proposition they assert is false.

We can make clear that we mean "white wine" literally by use of emphasis. Thus if we say to the benighted person "No wine is a *white* wine!" the proposition we are asserting is very likely to be that no wine is literally a white wine.[1]

"Yellow wine" also has a literal meaning. Thus if we say to the benighted person "All white wines are *yellow* wines," meaning "white wine" conventionally and "yellow wine" literally, then the proposition we assert is true.

To return to the argument. The conjunction of the proposition that is asserted by one who says "A is a white wine," meaning "white wine" conventionally, and the proposition that A is a liquid, does not entail the proposition that A is a white liquid. There is no reason why it should. But if a person who says "A is a white K_1" means "white K_1" literally, then the conjunction of the proposition he asserts, and the proposition that A is a K_2, does entail the proposition that A is a *white* K_2—for wines as for any other kinds.

"White wine" is not the only expression that has a conventional as well as a literal meaning. Compare "white people". They aren't *white* people. (No man is a *white* man unless he has been dead for quite a while.) Black people ("blacks") typically aren't *black* people. People who have red hair typically have *orange* hair. It is not clear what the sources of these conventions are. "White wine", "white people", "black people", and so on, aren't metaphors, like "purple prose" and "black mood": wines and people do have colors, unlike bits of prose and moods. They seem, rather, to be exaggerations that for one or another reason have become conventional. But I leave this open.

---

[1] Wittgenstein pointed out the interesting fact that no piece of glass or portion of a liquid is both white and transparent. So for a wine to be a *white* wine, it would have to look like milk. None do, of course.

2.

I said in chapter I that there is no such property as goodness. And I said that people who say the words "A is good" are not all asserting one and the same proposition, namely the proposition that is true just in case A has the property goodness: there being no such property as goodness, there is no such proposition. Rather, people who say the words "A is good" are asserting different propositions—such as that A is a good toaster, that A is a good tennis player, and that A is good at doing crossword puzzles. We know which proposition the speaker is asserting only if we know something about the context in which he is speaking. This view is often described as the view that the word "good" is *context sensitive*.

In recent years, many philosophers have been saying of a great many expressions in ordinary use that they are context sensitive. Cappelen and Lepore (henceforth C&L) claim that they are mistaken.[2] C&L say that some expressions really are context sensitive. For example, the personal pronouns "I", "you", "she", and "it". Also the demonstratives "this" and "that", and the adverbs "here", "now", and "yesterday", and the tenses ("is", "was", "will be"). People who say the words "I am hungry" are not all asserting one and the same proposition: each is asserting a proposition about himself. People who say the words "A was hungry yesterday" are not all asserting one and the same proposition: each is asserting a proposition the truth-value of which turns on which day it is on which they say the words. People who say "A is happy" are not all asserting one and the same proposition: each is asserting a proposition the truth-value of which (again) turns on which day it is on which they say the words. But C&L say that many of the other expressions philosophers say are context sensitive aren't. "Good" is not among the examples C&L discuss, but they would certainly say that "good" is not context sensitive.

They supply three tests for context sensitivity. I will take space to describe only the first, since it is very plausible to think that if an expression fails even just this first test, then the expression is not context sensitive.

---

[2] Herman Cappelen and Ernie Lepore, *Insensitive Semantics* (Malden, MA: Blackwell Publishing, 2005). From here on, page numbers are of pages in that volume.

According to the test, an expression is context sensitive only if its presence in a sentence 'typically blocks disquotational indirect reports'. What they have in mind emerges in examples. The personal pronoun "I" passes the test in that if Smith says the words "I am always hungry at midnight," then we speak falsely if we later report what he asserted by saying the words "Smith asserted that I am always hungry at midnight".[3] So also does the adverb "yesterday" pass the test, for if Smith says on Wednesday the words "A was hungry yesterday," then we speak falsely if we later, as it might be, on Thursday, report what he asserted by saying the words "Smith asserted that A was hungry yesterday".

By contrast, C&L would say, "good" fails this test since its presence in a sentence does not block such indirect reports. If Smith says the words "A is always good," then we speak truly if we at any later time report what he asserted by saying the words "Smith asserted that A is always good". It doesn't matter in what context Smith said "A is always good." It also doesn't matter in what context we are when we say the words "Smith asserted that A is always good." If Smith said the words "A is always good," then that by itself guarantees that we speak truly if we report what he asserted by saying the words "Smith asserted that A is always good."

It might be wondered why I offered you the complex "A is always good" rather than the simpler "A is good". That was because I wanted to give you a tenseless sample sentence. It may well be thought plausible to say:

> If Smith says the words "A is always good," then we speak truly if we at any later time report what he asserted by saying the words "Smith asserted that A is always good."

Not so:

> If Smith says the words "A is good," then we speak truly if we at any later time report what he asserted by saying the words "Smith asserted that A is good."

---

[3] Despite the resulting artificiality, I think it makes for clarity in discussing this issue to reserve "say" for words ("said the words") and "assert" for propositions ("asserted the proposition").

However the trouble here does not show that "good" is context sensitive; rather, it is due to the fact that "is" is.

Still, C&L would say, we can say:

> If Smith says the words "A is good," then we speak truly if we at any later time report what he asserted by saying the words "Smith asserted that A was good"—

good, that is, at the time at which Smith spoke. And as for Smith, so of course also for anyone.

C&L would therefore invite us to agree that everyone who says the words "A is good" at a given time asserts one and the same proposition, namely the proposition that A is then good. What proposition is that? The proposition that is true just in case A then has the property goodness.

And I was therefore mistaken in saying that there is no such property as goodness.

C&L would invite us to accept two further claims. First, although everyone who says the words "A is good" at a given time asserts the proposition that A is then good, people who say those words typically (perhaps always) assert other propositions as well. On their view, there is at least typically no such thing as *the* proposition a person asserts by saying a declarative sentence. If Smith says the words "A is good," he may be asserting not only the proposition that A is then good, but also the proposition that A is then a good tennis player. C&L allow that in order to know what other propositions Smith is asserting—in addition to the proposition that A is then good—you do have to know something about the context in which Smith speaks. But given just that he says "A is good," you already know that he asserts the proposition that A is then good, whatever the context in which he speaks.

C&L would invite us to conclude from that fact, second, that the proposition that A is at the relevant time good is the 'semantic content' of the sentence "A is good". Very roughly, that proposition is the proposition such that the meaning of the sentence by itself fixes that a person who says the sentence asserts it. The concept 'semantic content' is a technical concept, important to linguists. Our purposes do not require that we form a view about what the semantic content of the sentence "A is good" is, and so I will say nothing further about this second claim of C&L's. It is enough for our purposes that if C&L are right, then whatever else a person may be asserting in saying the words "A is good," he is asserting the proposition that is true just in case A then has the property goodness.

<h1 style="text-align:center">3.</h1>

People who find this argument attractive should be forewarned that it may take them further than they are likely to want to go. For C&L argue that "ready" and "tall" also fail the test—as follows.

If Smith says the words "A is ready," then we speak truly if we at any later time report what he asserted by saying the words "Smith asserted that A was ready"—ready, that is, at the time at which Smith spoke. It doesn't matter in what context Smith said, "A is ready." It also doesn't matter in what context we are when we say the words "Smith asserted that A was ready." If Smith said the words "A is ready," then that by itself guarantees that we speak truly if we report what he asserted by saying the words "Smith asserted that A was ready." So everyone who says the words "A is ready" at a given time asserts one and the same proposition, namely the proposition that A is then ready. What proposition is that? The proposition that is true just in case A then has the property being ready.

Similarly for "tall". If Smith says the words "A is tall," then we speak truly if we at any later time report what he asserted by saying the words "Smith asserted that A was tall"—tall, that is, at the time at which Smith spoke. So everyone who says the words "A is tall" at a given time asserts one and the same proposition, namely the proposition that A is then tall. What proposition is that? The proposition that is true just in case A then has the property being tall.

But are there such properties as being (simply) ready and being (simply) tall? A person might be ready for breakfast. Or ready to go to the airport. Or ready to be anointed Queen. Can one be (simply) *ready*? A person might be a tall teenager. Or a tall basketball player. But (simply) *tall*? (Compare being [simply] big of chapter I.) What could these properties *be*?

C&L say it isn't their job to tell us what being (simply) ready and being (simply) tall are. They say that they have shown us that there are such properties, and that it is the metaphysicians' job to tell us what they are.

4.

In fact, however, they don't leave the job entirely to the metaphysicians. They engage in a bit of metaphysics themselves.

They say: "imagine A's being ready to commit a bank robbery, B's being ready to eat dinner, and C's being ready to take an exam" (166). And they ask: what have A, B, and C got in common? They answer:

> Well, they have a common relation they stand in to their respective projects: There's something in common between A's relation to the bank robbery, B's relation to the dinner, and C's relation to the exam. What they have in common is that they are all *ready*. (167)

The first of those two sentences tells us that for A to be ready to commit a bank robbery is for A to stand in a certain relation R to the bank robbery, for B to be ready to eat dinner is for B to stand in that same relation R to the dinner, and for C to be ready to take an exam is for C to stand in that same relation R to the exam. Call that relation R the ready-for relation.

It is not obvious that the propositions that A is ready to commit a bank robbery, that B is ready to eat dinner, and that C is ready to take an exam, are of the logical form 'R(x,y)', but let us go along with C&L and assume that they are.

Given what the first sentence tells us, namely that A, B, and C have a common relation, namely the ready-for relation, to their respective projects, the second sentence goes on to tell us that A, B, and C have a common property, namely being ready. What is that property?

The projects we were told that A, B, and C stand in the ready-for relation to differ. There may also be a project that they share, but if so, we anyway haven't been told that there is. However, we *can* conclude from what we *have* been told that the following is true of each of A, B, and C: each has the property being for some project P, ready for P. But then if what we have been told about them is to guarantee that each has the property being ready, we had better be able to say:

> Necessarily (if X has the property being for some project P, ready for P, then X has the property being ready).

On any view, it can't be the case that X has the property being ready without its also being the case that X has the property being for some project P, ready for P. Thus:

> Necessarily (if X has the property being ready, then X has the property being for some project P, ready for P).

And in sum,

> (Equivalence Thesis) Necessarily (X has the property being ready if and only if X has the property being for some project P, ready for P).

Now many metaphysicians would say that if that is true, then so also is

> (Identity Thesis) Being ready = being for some project P, ready for P.

And that anyway supplies an answer to our question what the property being ready is.

It is therefore surprising to find that C&L reject the Identity Thesis. They say "our view is not that all utterances of 'John is ready' express the proposition *that John is ready for something or other*, but rather that they all express the proposition *that John is ready*", thereby plainly implying that the property being ready is not identical with the property being ready for something or other (97).

While many metaphysicians would say that if being F is a property, and being G is a property, and Necessarily (X has being F if and only if X has being G), then being F = being G, many others would reject that claim. But when they reject it for a pair of properties being F and being G, they typically give a reason for doing so. C&L do give a reason for rejecting the Identity Thesis, but with remarkable brevity. They say that the proposition *that John is ready for something or other* is "very abstract", and that they "don't want to characterize [the proposition *that John is ready*] as abstract" (97). Period. It is hard to see what exactly they can have had in mind.

No matter: they are entitled to their view. While I am sure they would grant that the Equivalence Thesis is true, they reject the Identity Thesis.

In sum, the property being (simply) ready is equivalent to, but not identical with, the property being for some project P, ready for P.[4]

5.

I said earlier that people who find this argument attractive should be forewarned that it will take them further than they are likely to want to go. In particular, it will take them to the conclusion that "ready" is also not context sensitive. But perhaps you will now not mind quite so much having been taken to that conclusion?

C&L want us to agree that everyone who says "A is ready" at a given time asserts one and the same proposition, namely the proposition that A is then ready. What proposition is that? The proposition that is true just in case A then has the property being (simply) ready.

------

[4] C&L take a different line on the property being tall. (See p. 171.) They imagine someone to say: "For something to instantiate tallness there must be some comparison class or other with respect to which it's tall. If that's all it takes to instantiate tallness, it's very easy to do so." The view proposed here is can be expressed as follows:

being tall = being, for some comparison class C, a tall C.

C&L then say: "We take this to be an exceedingly unpromising account of tallness." And they go on to indicate that they take a dim view of even the analogous equivalence thesis:

Necessarily (X has the property being tall if and only if X has the property being, for some comparison class C, a tall C).

They take a third line in respect of yet another of their examples. They say that there is such a property as having had enough. (For they say "enough" also fails their test. If Smith said the words "A has had enough," then we may later report what he asserted by saying the words "Smith asserted that A had, by then, had enough.") What is that property? C&L say that they have no special expertise in metaphysics, but that

here's a possible start of a solution: Every person who has had enough has had enough of something that's contextually salient to him. What all people who have had enough have in common is that for each there's something contextually salient that he has had enough of. (fn 6, p. 167)

Thus in the case of this example, they think the following identity thesis might well turn out to be true:

having had enough = having had, for something contextually salient, enough of it.

As I said earlier, C&L wish to give accounts of the semantic contents of the sentences they are concerned with, including "A is ready," "B is tall," and "C has had enough". That is, theses about which propositions are their semantic contents. It is surprising to find people with that concern regarding it as not up to them to tell us what the truth-conditions of those propositions are.

That sounds *weird*! What on earth could that property be? We now learn that the property C&L were referring to by "the property being (simply) ready" is anyway equivalent to the property being for some project P, ready for P. That may be an odd use of the referring expression "the property being (simply) ready", but given that what C&L were referring to by that expression is a property that is anyway equivalent to the property being for some project P, ready for P, it isn't weird to suppose that there is such a property.

Some things might well still concern you. (i) You might wonder if "ready" does really fail C&L's test for context sensitivity. I will return to this idea in section 7 below.

(ii) You might still wonder what the property being ready *is*. We can express this source of concern as follows. If there is a property (being ready) that is equivalent to, but not identical with, the property being for some project P, ready for P, then what assures us that there aren't several properties, each of which is equivalent to, but not identical with, the property being for some project P, ready for P? And if so, which one of them is the property being ready?

(iii) It is very easy to instantiate the property being for some project P, ready for P. Most of us instantiate it most of the time. At 7 AM, Alice may be ready to get out of bed, ready for breakfast, and ready for her 9 AM class. It may be true to say of Alice at midnight, even though she is asleep, that she is ready for her 9 AM class tomorrow. It follows that she has at those times being for some project P, ready for P. And it might strike you to think that nobody ever ascribes that boring property to a person: hence that nobody ever asserts the proposition that is true just in case the person has it.[5]

C&L have a reply to concern (iii). As I said earlier, they say that there is at least typically no such thing as *the* proposition a person asserts by saying a declarative sentence: people at least typically assert more than one proposition by saying a declarative sentence. And their view, therefore, is not that the only proposition a person asserts by saying the words "A is ready" is the proposition that A is (simply) ready, but only that that is among the propositions he asserts by saying those words.

---

[5] I add that if you are a linguist then you may also be in doubt, (iv), about whether C&L are entitled to their conclusions about the semantic contents of the sentences they discuss. I am bypassing this issue, however.

You might not be mollified by that reply. Suppose we are discussing the question whether Alice is ready for her 9 AM class. Smith says, "Yes, she is ready," thereby asserting (perhaps among other propositions) the proposition that she is ready for her 9 AM class. You might insist that although he therefore asserts a proposition that entails the proposition that she is, for some project P, ready for P, he doesn't *assert* the proposition that she is, for some project P, ready for P. We may certainly suppose that that isn't a proposition he meant to assert. He may insist on that himself.

Again C&L have a reply. They would point to what might be called the looseness of "asserts that". And a debate might ensue about what are and aren't the limits on what a person can properly be said to assert. I will bypass that debate. We must anyway grant that we aren't any longer in the realm of the weird, we are in the realm of the debatable.

So as I say, perhaps you don't now mind *quite* so much having been taken to the conclusion that there is such a property as being (simply) ready—and the idea that it is that property that everyone who says "A is ready" ascribes to A.

6.

Let us now look at the property being (simply) good that, as I said, I take it that C&L would have us suppose is the property that everyone who says "A is good" ascribes to A. What is it? I take it that they would invite us to opt for an answer analogous to their answer to the question what the property being (simply) ready is.

Thus I take it they would address us as follows. Imagine A's being a good tennis player, B's being a good toaster, and C's being good at doing crossword puzzles. Then they have something in common, namely that they are all *good*.

How so? Well, each of them has the property being, for some respect R, being good in respect R. And that is what guarantees that each has the property being good. On any view, it can't be the case that X has the property being good without its also being the case that X has the property being for some respect R, good in respect R. In sum, you should opt for:

> (Equivalence Thesis) Necessarily (X has the property being good if and only if X has the property being for some respect R, good in respect R).

But you shouldn't opt for:

> (Identity Thesis) Being good = being for some respect R, good
> in respect R.

That is because the proposition *that John is good in some respect* is very abstract, and we don't want to characterize the proposition *that John is good* as abstract.

The property being (simply) good is therefore equivalent to, but not identical with, the property being for some respect R, good in respect R.

I mentioned three things that might bother you about C&L's account of the property being ready (a fourth in a footnote), and similar things might bother you about this account of the property being good. What we should notice, however, is that *so understood*, the claim that there is such a property as being good is not in conflict with the claim I made when I said that there is no such property as goodness.

The property being for some respect R, good in respect R, is an even more boring property than the property being for some project P, ready for P. Only animate creatures have the latter property. Many things of inanimate kinds have the former. Good toasters have it, as well as people who are good at doing crossword puzzles. Indeed, I suggested in chapter I that everything has it—that everything is, for *some* respect R, good in respect R. It follows that every property equivalent to that property is in the same way and degree boring. So therefore is the property that I take it that C&L would refer to by "the property being good".

But it was not that property that I denied the existence of. As I say, I suggested in chapter I that everything has it.

What I meant was, rather, that there is no such property as Moore said there is when he said that there is such a property as goodness. And what many other philosophers have also said there is. They did not have in mind a property that is possessed by all good toasters and all people who are good at doing crossword puzzles, a property that if not all things, then anyway just about all things, have in common. They didn't think it was that *easy* for a thing to be good.

What property did they have in mind? Well may you ask. I said in chapter I—following Peter Geach—that there is no property that they had in mind.

In any case, anyone who was attracted by the argument I attributed to C&L in section 2 above, thinking that it could be used in defense of Moore and his fellows, was sadly mistaken.

7.

We should not leave this topic without a brief comment on C&L's test for context sensitivity. (According to their test, an expression is context sensitive only if its presence in a sentence 'typically blocks disquotational indirect reports'.) I said earlier that it is very plausible to think that if an expression fails the test, then the expression is not context sensitive. What I think is questionable is whether they are right about the examples they discuss.

Consider "ready", for example. They say that that fails the test. They say that if Smith said the words "A is ready," then we speak truly if we at any later time report what he asserted by saying the words "Smith asserted that A was ready". It doesn't matter in what context Smith said, "A is ready." It also doesn't matter in what context we are when we say, "Smith asserted that A was ready." If Smith said, "A is ready," then that by itself guarantees that we speak truly if we report what he asserted by saying, "Smith asserted that A was ready."

Can that really be right? Suppose we are discussing the question whether our student Alice is ready to go on the job market. An important question!—going on too early is a bad business. Smith unfortunately could not make it to our meeting today, but you have heard that he has views on the matter. You know that I talked with Smith yesterday, and you ask me whether Smith said anything to me about Alice then.

My talk with Smith yesterday was in fact about the proposal Alice plans to make to the faculty that we change the brand of coffee we buy for the lounge. I asked Smith whether Alice was ready to present her proposal. "Alice is ready," he said.

So when you ask me, today, whether Smith said anything to me about Alice yesterday, I say the words "Smith asserted that Alice was ready." Do I speak truly? Given the topic of *our* discussion, you will very naturally think I am asserting that Smith asserted that Alice was ready to go on the job market. Which he didn't. What should be concluded?

I think that I speak falsely. For *our* topic being what it is, I think that when I say to you, "Smith asserted that Alice was ready," I do not speak truly unless Smith asserted that Alice was ready to go on the job market. Which he didn't. In short, I take it that the context in which a person, say JJT, says the words "Smith asserted that Alice was ready" matters to what JJT herself asserts.[6]

C&L can, and no doubt would, say that I mislead you about what Smith asserted: in saying the words I say, I give you reason to believe Smith asserted that Alice was ready to go on the job market, which he didn't. But C&L are committed to the view that when I say the words I say, I all the same speak truly—for on their view, Smith did assert (among other propositions) the proposition that is true just in case for some project P, Alice was then ready for P.

I find that idea utterly unconvincing. As I said, I think I speak falsely. Thus not merely misleadingly.

A similar case can arise for "tall". I think it pays to mention that a similar case can also arise for "good". Alice has now decided to go on the job market, and has asked you for a recommendation. You are in some doubt about her ability as a philosopher, and you ask me what I think. I say I think she is a good philosopher. To reassure you further, I say that I spoke to Jones yesterday, and that he asserted that Alice was good.

In fact, Jones did indeed say the words "Alice is good" yesterday, and on C&L's view, that guarantees that I now speak truly when I say to you, "Jones asserted that Alice was good." But also in fact, Jones's saying "Alice is good" was in response to my question whether she is a good tennis player. I therefore think that I speak falsely, and not merely misleadingly, when I say to you "Jones asserted that Alice was good".

I leave open that C&L may be right about some of the other expressions they say fail their test. I say here only that they are not obviously right about "ready", "tall", and "good"—for I take it that others would share my intuitions about them.

---

[6] The objection I make here is a first cousin of the objection Keith Derose made to a similar 'anti-contextualist' argument against his view that the verb "to know" is context sensitive. See his "'Bamboozled by Our Own Words': Semantic Blindness and Some Arguments Against Contextualism," *Philosophy and Phenomenological Research* 73, no. 2 (September 2006).

I add, however, that, as I said earlier, C&L offer us three tests for context sensitivity, and I have discussed only one of them. I am sure that they would say that these expressions fail their other two tests as well. I believe that doubts similar to those I raise here could be raised about those other tests, but I do not take space to discuss them.

ADDENDUM 2

Correctness

1.

In chapter VI, section 8, we looked at the conditions under which assertings/answerings/describings/reportings/explainings are internal-correct and external-correct. I then asked: what about assertions/answers/ descriptions/reports/explanations? I said: since these are propositions, there is no such thing as their being internal-correct or internal-incorrect. Correctness in these is entirely external—and it obviously consists in truth. Thus we can say: Smith's assertion/answer/description/report/ explanation is a correct assertion/answer/description/report/explanation just in case it is true.

The very careful reader may have noticed that there is a difficulty here. I do not think it a theoretically interesting difficulty, and that is why I reserved it for discussion in an addendum. Nevertheless it does call for brief attention.

Let us begin with assertions. All assertions are propositions. Are all propositions assertions? Consider the proposition that $7 + 5 = 12$. I am sure that many people have asserted that proposition over the course of history. Is it—that is, is that proposition—an assertion? I said, serenely, that all assertions are propositions, but with what justification? For what *are* assertions? Moreover, if we don't know what the kind 'assertion' is, then we don't know what being a correct assertion is. And if so, then my claim "Smith's assertion is a correct assertion just in case it is true" is not as clear as it looked. (Or anyway, as I hope it looked to everyone who is not a very careful reader.)

What I suggest we say is that there is no such kind as 'assertion'. (No wonder you were pulled up short when I asked whether the proposition that 7 + 5 = 12 is an assertion!) There are such kinds as the kind 'Smith's assertions': a thing is a member of that kind in particular just in case it is a proposition asserted at some time by Smith. Alternatively put: a thing is a member of it just in case it is the propositional content of an asserting by Smith. So if Smith ever asserts that 7 + 5 = 12, then that proposition is among Smith's assertions. (But it does not follow that it is an assertion. Smith's assertions are not like Smith's hats.[1]) So we should not say "Smith's assertion is a correct assertion just in case it is true". We should say: if P is a member of the kind 'Smith's assertions', then it is a correct member of that kind just in case it is true.

We can generalize if we like. Let us say that a proposition is an ASSERTION just in case it is for some X one of X's assertions. (Then the proposition that 7 + 5 = 12, though not an assertion, for there is no such kind, is nevertheless an ASSERTION.) Then we can say: Smith's assertion is a correct ASSERTION just in case it is true. So also for your assertions and mine. And we can say, quite generally: an ASSERTION is a correct ASSERTION just in case it is true.

The same holds of beliefs. Consider the proposition that 7 + 5 = 12. I am sure that many people have believed that proposition over the course of history. Is it—that is, is that proposition—a belief? What I suggest we say is that there is no such kind as 'belief'. However there are such kinds as the kind 'Smith's beliefs': a thing is a member of that kind in particular just in case it is a proposition believed at some time by Smith. Alternatively put: a thing is a member of it just in case it is the propositional content of a believing by Smith. So we should not say "Smith's belief is a correct belief just in case it is true". We should say: if P is a member of the kind 'Smith's beliefs', then it is a correct member of that kind just in case it is true.

And here too we can generalize. Let us say that a proposition is a BELIEF just in case it is for some X one of X's beliefs. (Then the proposition that 7 + 5 = 12, though not a belief, for there is no such kind, is nevertheless a BELIEF.) Then we can say: Smith's belief is a correct BELIEF just in case it is true. So also for your beliefs and mine. And while we should not say (as I did in chapter VII, section 1), "A belief is a correct belief just in case it is true," we can say: a

---

[1] Contrast the imperfect nominal "asserting". There is such a kind as 'assertings', and if an act is among Smith's assertings, then it follows that it is a member of the kind 'assertings'. Smith's assertings, then, *are* like Smith's hats.

BELIEF is a correct BELIEF just in case it is true. Similarly for expectations, assumptions, and conjectures.

To return to speech acts. "Answer" is in some ways like "assertion" and "belief". Is the proposition that 7 + 5 = 12 an answer? The idea that it is is no happier than the idea that it is an assertion or a belief.

What a proposition can be is Smith's answer-to-such-and-such-question. And Smith's answers to question Q are the propositional contents of his answerings of Q, just as Smith's assertions/beliefs are the propositional contents of his assertings/believings.

But here a difference emerges. A proposition can also be *an* answer to Q, indeed it can be *the* answer to Q, even if nobody ever answers Q—even if nobody ever asks Q. Perhaps nobody ever asks whether Alice likes chocolate better than Bert does. Still, I am sure that that question has an answer, and that the answer to it may be that she does. Note that the proposition that she does is *the* answer to the question only if it is true that she does.

Something similar holds of explanations. A proposition can be an, indeed the, explanation of why E kicked his cat even if nobody ever explains why E kicked his cat by asserting it.[2] A variant holds of descriptions. A proposition can be a description of Bert even if nobody ever describes Bert by asserting it; but no proposition is *the* description of Bert.

However nothing similar holds of reports. A proposition can be Smith's report-of-what-C-did-to-D; no proposition is the, or even a, report of what C did to D. As we might put it, "report" is wholly tied to acts—like "assertion" but unlike "answer", "explanation", and "description".

I think that the differences I point to here are interesting, but I doubt that they are theoretically important, and I therefore leave open what their sources are.

And I don't revise the text to accommodate the points that appear in this addendum since it is a mistake to introduce complications that don't pay their way. What matters is really only that the text *can* be revised to accommodate them.

---

[2] I add, though, that "the answer" and "the explanation" only pragmatically imply uniqueness—they are like "the cause" in that respect.

ADDENDUM 3

Reasons

1.

In chapter IX, I suggested that we should reject:

(Reasons Internalism)

| X is a reason for A to V_{act} (objectively interpreted) | only if | X lends weight to the proposition that A's V_{act}-ing would satisfy a want of A's. |

An article by Bernard Williams is widely cited in support of an even stronger thesis, namely:

(Strong Reasons Internalism)

| X is a reason for A to V_{act} (objectively interpreted) | only if | A has a want that his V_{act}-ing would satisfy.[1] |

Williams's article is dense, and it is not clear what exactly his argument for the thesis is. My impression is that its skeleton is as follows. Let X be some fact. Then

(1) X is a reason for A to V_{act}

---

[1] "Williams, "Internal and External Reasons."

is true only if it is possible that A V_{act}s, and that X is his reason for V_{act}-ing on that occasion. (So far, so good.)

Assume that A is now V_{act}-ing, and that X is his reason for doing so. Then

(2) A is V_{act}-ing because he believes (1)

had better be true. (Again, so far so good.)

Williams now says: we explain a person's doing a thing only if what we supply by way of explanation is what motivates him to do the thing. But A's believing (1) can be what motivates him to V_{act} only if his believing (1) *is*: his having a want and believing that since there is such a fact as X, he will satisfy it if he V_{act}s.[2] So (2) can be true only if A's believing (1) is his having a want and believing that since there is such a fact as X, he will satisfy it if he V_{act}s.

Since (2) had better be true, the following had better be true: A's believing (1) is his having a want and believing that since there is such a fact as X, he will satisfy it if he V_{act}s.

Given that A's believing (1) is his having a want and believing that since there is such a fact as X, he will satisfy it if he V_{act}s, *what* A believes, namely (1) itself, is true only if he has a want and, since there is such a fact as X, he really will satisfy it if he V_{act}s. A fortiori, (1) is true only if A has a want that his V_{act}-ing would satisfy. Hence: Strong Reasons Internalism. QED.

Two ideas I attributed to Williams in displaying the argument are entirely unwarranted.

The first is: (2) can be true only if A's believing (1) *is* his having a want and believing that since there is such a fact as X, he will satisfy it if he V_{act}s. Not so. (2) can be true even if it is not the case that A's believing (1) *is* his having a want and believing that since there is such a fact as X, he will satisfy it if he V_{act}s. If A believes (1) *because* he *believes* he has a want such that, since there is such a fact as X, he will satisfy it if he V_{act}s, then that would suffice for the truth of (2).[3]

---

[2] Williams invites us to imagine that someone ask us why A is V_{act}-ing, and that we reply by saying (2). He says: "Does believing that a particular consideration is a reason to act in a particular way provide, or indeed constitute, a motivation to act? If it does not, then we are no further on." ("Internal and External Reasons," 107). That is, no further on in our project of explaining why A is V_{act}-ing.

[3] As I said in chapter IX, section 8, some beliefs are beliefs about wants, and beliefs of this kind about wants should be enough to meet any requirement that Hume's followers are entitled to impose on us.

The second is the idea that if we attend to the conditions under which it is true that A believes (1), we will be entitled to draw Williams's conclusion about the conditions under which (1) is true. I drew attention in chapter IX to the fact that

(Reasons-Belief Internalism)

A believes that: X is a reason for for him to V_{act} (objectively interpreted)	only if	A believes that: X lends weight to the proposition that his V_{act}-ing would satisfy a want of his

does not entail

(Reasons Internalism)

X is a reason for A to V_{act} (objectively interpreted)	only if	X lends weight to the proposition that A's V_{act}-ing would satisfy a want of A's.

Similarly,

(Strong Reasons-Belief Internalism)

A believes that: X is a reason for for him to V_{act} (objectively interpreted)	only if	A has a want and believes that since there is such a fact as X, his V_{act}-ing would satisfy it

does not entail

(Strong Reasons Internalism)

X is a reason for A to V_{act} (objectively interpreted)	only if	A has a want that his V_{act}-ing would satisfy.

For suppose we accept Strong Reasons-Belief Internalism. (It is surely over strong, but let that pass.) We can—and I suggest should—nevertheless reject Strong Reasons Internalism. Consider the fact I called ROPE in chapter IX:

> ROPE = the fact that Bert will drown unless Alfred throws him the rope that he has in hand.

I said there that ROPE is a reason for Alfred to throw Bert the rope he has in hand. If Alfred doesn't care about Bert's fate, then he may have no want that would be satisfied by throwing Bert the rope. And he may therefore believe that ROPE is not a reason for him to throw Bert the rope. But he is mistaken. For it is a failing in him that he has no want that would be satisfied by throwing Bert the rope, and what is true is not that ROPE isn't a reason for him to throw Bert the rope, but only that it is a failing in him that he doesn't believe it is.

ADDENDUM 4

Reasoning

1.

Many moral philosophers who have taken the turn to reasons for action also make a claim about reason*ing*. You might have thought of all reasoning as consisting in passing from a set of propositions (the premises) to a proposition (the conclusion). That, they say, is only one species of reasoning, and they call it theoretical reasoning. They say that there is another species of reasoning, which they call practical reasoning. We should be clear. On their view, the fact that a bit of reasoning is reasoning about practical matters does not suffice to mark it as practical reasoning. They say that there is theoretical reasoning about practical matters. For example, a person who passes from a set of propositions (the premises) to a proposition (the conclusion) to the effect that doing such and such would be good in this or that way engages in theoretical reasoning about a practical matter.[1] To engage in what they call practical reasoning is to pass from a set of propositions (the premises), not to a proposition, but to *an act*.

Let us call this the Difference Idea. What exactly does it come to? There are two understandings of it in the literature.

---

[1] G. E. M. Anscombe said that it is a mistake to think that practical reasoning is theoretical reasoning about practical matters, as mince-pie syllogisms are syllogisms about mince-pies. See her *Intention* (Oxford: Blackwell, 1957).

2.

According to the first understanding of the Difference Idea, instances of theoretical reasoning and instances of practical reasoning are the '*contents*' of episodes of reasoning.[2]

Suppose it occurred to Alfred that all men are mortal. It then occurred to him that Socrates is a man. He therefore believed that Socrates is mortal. Thus he did some reasoning, and the content of his reasoning was the following series of propositions:

> (1) All men are mortal
>   Socrates is a man
>   (Conclusion) Socrates is mortal.

Since the content of his reasoning is a series whose conclusion is a proposition, the series is an instance of theoretical reasoning.

Suppose it occurred to Alan that most men are mortal. It then occurred to him that Socrates is a man. He therefore believed that Socrates is mortal. Thus he did some reasoning, and the content of his reasoning was the following series of propositions:

> (2) Most men are mortal
>   Socrates is a man
>   (Conclusion) Socrates is mortal.

Since the content of his reasoning is a series whose conclusion is a proposition, the series is an instance of theoretical reasoning. (I provided this second instance of theoretical reasoning—in which the premises do not entail the conclusion—in order to stress that friends of this first understanding do not restrict theoretical reasoning to valid reasoning.)

Suppose it occurred to Arthur that drinking milk would be good for him. It then occurred to him that there is milk in glass G. He

---

[2] This interpretation is suggested by Anscombe in *Intention*, §33: she says there that an instance—a case, an example—of practical reasoning is a "practical syllogism". ("'Practical reasoning', or 'practical syllogism', which means the same thing, was one of Aristotle's best discoveries . . ." (57–58), and Aristotle "had found a completely different form of reasoning from theoretical reasoning, or proof-syllogism. . . ." [59].) Moreover, her examples themselves suggest this interpretation.

therefore drank the milk in glass G. He too did some reasoning, and the content of his reasoning was the following series:

> (3) Drinking milk would be good for Arthur
> There is milk in glass G
> (Conclusion) Arthur's drinking the milk in glass G.[3]

Since the content of his reasoning is a series whose conclusion is an act, the series is an instance of practical reasoning.

In sum, the conclusion of an instance of theoretical reasoning is a proposition; the conclusion of an instance of practical reasoning is an act.

What should we think of this? It is clear enough in what sense (1) is the content of Alfred's episode of reasoning. Alfred's episode of reasoning was a series of three events, each of which was a starting-to-believe a proposition, and the three propositions listed in (1) are the propositional contents of those believings. Similarly for Alan.

In what sense is (3) the content of Arthur's episode of reasoning? Arthur's episode of reasoning was also a series of three events. Each of the first two events was a starting-to-believe a proposition, and the two propositions listed first and second in (3) are the propositional contents of those believings. The third entity listed in (3) is not in any sense the *content* of the third event in the series of three events: it *is* the third event in the series of three events.

That difference is the source of the following very striking difference between (1) and (2) on the one hand, and (3) on the other. You or I might reason exactly as Alfred did. Then (1) would be the content of your or my episode of reasoning, just as it was of Alfred's. Might you or I reason exactly as Arthur did? Perhaps as follows? It occurs to me that drinking milk would be good for Arthur. It then occurs to me that there is milk in glass G. Do I therefore—therefore *what*? Draw a conclusion whose content is Arthur's drinking the milk in glass G? That is a nonsense.

I don't deny here that Arthur (like Alfred and Alan) underwent an episode of reasoning, an episode that issued in his drinking the milk in glass G. What I deny here is that (3) is the content of his reasoning. Friends of the Difference Idea have to do better than this.

---

[3] I adapt this example from one of Anscombe's; see *Intention*, 60.

3.

According to the second understanding of the Difference Idea, instances of theoretical reasoning and instances of practical reasoning are themselves *episodes* of reasoning.[4] On this second understanding, instances of theoretical reasoning and instances of practical reasoning are mental processes, though mental processes of different kinds.

Consider the following temporally ordered sequence of mental events:

> (TR) My starting to believe that p
>   My starting to believe that q
>   My starting to believe that r,

in which "p", "q", and "r" are abbreviations of particular propositions. What would mark (TR) as having been an instance of reasoning? It is obviously not sufficient that the first two events caused the third. I suggest that we should say the following. Let "REASON-BELIEF" be an abbreviation of the following proposition:

> If p and q, then the facts that p and that q are jointly a reason for me to believe that r.

Then (TR) was an instance of reasoning if I believed that REASON-BELIEF, and my having the compound belief that p & q & REASON-BELIEF was the reason *why* I started to believe that r.[5]

Consider now the following series of mental events:

> (PR) My starting to believe that p*
>   My starting to believe that q*
>   My forming the intention to V_{act}

---

[4] This second understanding is suggested by passages in Anscombe, *Intention*, e.g., "Now a man who goes through such considerations as those about Vitamin X and ends up by taking some of the dish that he sees, saying e.g. 'So I suppose I'd better have some', can certainly be said to be *reasoning*. . . ." (61). And she adds: "on the other hand, it is clear that this is another type of reasoning than reasoning from premises to a conclusion which they prove."

[5] Note that if it is also the case that p and q, then we can conclude that my reason *for* believing that r was the fact that p and q. See (5_{Vmind}-analysis) of chapter VIII.

in which "p*" and "q*" are abbreviations of propositions, and V_{act}-ing is acting in a certain way. Can *this* have been an instance of reasoning? Let "REASON-ACT" be an abbreviation of the following proposition:

> If p* and q*, then the facts that p* and that q* are jointly a reason for me to V_{act}.

Then it is intuitively plausible to think that (PR) was an instance of reasoning if I believed that REASON-ACT, and my having the compound belief that p* & q* & REASON-ACT was the reason why I formed the intention to V_{act}.[6]

Note that the third event in the series (PR) is a mental event, and not an act—in particular, it is not my act of V_{act}-ing. I have here followed John Broome, who says that reasoning that concludes in an intention "is as practical as reasoning can get. When reasoning concludes in a forming of an intention to act, the intention is in turn likely to cause the intended act. But that last bit of causation is not part of the reasoning process."[7] Indeed, if something gets in the way of my V_{act}-ing—as, for example, if unbeknownst to me I am locked in a closet—then I will all the same have reasoned in undergoing the sequence (PR).

And then we are to say: if (TR) and (PR) are instances of reasoning, then (TR) was an instance of theoretical reasoning in that it issued in a starting to believe, whereas (PR) was an instance of practical reasoning in that it issued in the forming of an intention.

What should we think of this? I think it is, as I said, intuitively plausible that (PR) might be marked as an instance of reasoning by appeal to a consideration analogous to that which would mark (TR) as an instance of reasoning; and therefore it is intuitively plausible that all is well with the idea that practical reasoning and theoretical reasoning are two distinct species of reasoning.

---

[6] Note that if it is also the case that p* and q*, then we can conclude that my reason *for* forming the intention of V_{act}-ing was the fact that p* and q*. See (5_{Vact}-analysis) of chapter IX.

[7] John Broome, "Normative Practical Reasoning," *Proceedings of the Aristotelian Society*, supplementary vol. 75 (2001). I should mention that he does not attribute to the Difference Idea the significance for moral philosophy that many other philosophers attribute to it, and that I discuss later.

If you like that idea, then shouldn't you agree that there are still other species of reasoning?—species that I think have not surfaced in the literature. Consider the following series of events:

> (4) My starting to believe that Alfred kept his word to Bert. My starting to trust Alfred.

Let "REASON-TRUST" be an abbreviation of the following proposition:

> If Alfred kept his word to Bert, then the fact that he did is a reason for me to trust Alfred.

Then it is as plausible to think that (4) was an instance of reasoning if I believed that REASON-TRUST, and my having the compound belief that Alfred kept his word to Bert & REASON-TRUST was the reason why I started to trust Alfred. Since (4) did not issue in a starting to-believe, it is not an instance of theoretical reasoning. Since it did not issue in a forming of an intention, it is not an instance of practical reasoning. So (4) and its ilk are members of a third species of reasoning, reasonings that issue in a starting to trust.

Again, consider the following series of events:

> (5) My starting to believe that Alice is a great mathematician. My starting to admire Alice.

Similar considerations will yield that this too may have been an instance of reasoning. If so, it and its ilk are members of a fourth species of reasoning, reasonings that issue in a starting to admire.

Indeed, consider all V_{mind}-ings for which there is such a thing as a V_{mind}-ing's being a correct V_{mind}-ing. Each of them will supply us with a species of reasoning. So there are *lots* of species of reasoning.

Or should we say there are just two species of reasonings?—one, the theoretical, namely those that issue in a starting to believe, the other, the practical, namely those that issue in a starting to V_{mind}, for any starting to V_{mind} which is not a starting to believe, but for which there is such a thing as a V_{mind}-ing's being a correct V_{mind}-ing.

What I think these questions raise is the deeper question: why do many moral philosophers think that the Difference Idea is both interesting and important?

4.

I take the answer to lie in their also accepting what I will call the Similarity Idea.[8]

Suppose that the following sequence of events took place—

(6) Alice's starting to believe that all men are mortal
Alice's starting to believe that Socrates is a man
Alice's starting to believe that Socrates is mortal

—and that it was an instance of reasoning. Then it was on any view an instance of theoretical reasoning, since it issued in a starting to believe.

Sequence (6) was not merely an instance of theoretical reasoning, (6) was *tight* in the following sense: it would be irrational in a person to believe Alice's premises and disbelieve her conclusion.

Sequence (6) was not tight in that sense just because Alice's premises entail her conclusion. There are entailments that it takes a sophisticated mathematician to recognize. Sequence (6) was tight in that sense because Alice's premises *obviously* entail her conclusion.

Suppose now that the following sequence of events took place—

(7) Alice's starting to believe that if today is Tuesday, then she ought to telephone Bert
Alice's starting to believe that today is Tuesday
Alice's forming the intention of telephoning Bert—

and that it too was an instance of reasoning. It was not an instance of theoretical reasoning, since it did not issue in a starting to believe. Whether a friend of the Difference Idea thinks that there are only two species of reasoning or a lot of them, he would say that (7) was an instance of practical reasoning, since it issued in a forming of an intention. The Similarity Idea is the idea that many instances of practical reasoning are tight in a sense similar to that in which (6) was tight. In particular, (7) was tight in the sense that it would be irrational in a person to believe Alice's premises and form the intention

---

[8] Anscombe is not among the philosophers I have in mind here. She seems to find the Difference Idea interesting and important simply as a discovery in moral psychology.

obverse to that which Alice formed—thus form the intention to not telephone Bert.

Here is a simpler example. Suppose that the following sequence of events took place—

> (8) Anne's starting to believe that she ought to telephone Bert
>   Anne's forming the intention of telephoning Bert—

and that it was an instance of reasoning. It too was an instance of practical reasoning.[9] A friend of the Difference Idea who also accepts the Similarity Idea says that (8) was also tight. He says: it would be irrational in a person to believe Anne's premise and form the intention obverse to Anne's—thus form the intention to not telephone Bert.

He says, more generally, that every instance of reasoning of the form

> A's starting to believe that he ought to V_{act}
> A's forming the intention to V_{act}

is tight in that sense.

We will return to the question whether we should accept these ideas. Let us first ask why many moral philosophers think that they are both interesting and important.

Let us step back for a moment. We should distinguish between two places at which moral philosophers have traditionally wanted to locate a rationality requirement. The first place is within the theoretical. Thus they have wanted, first, to be able to say about certain factual claims on the one hand, and moral claims on the other, that rationality requires that if you believe the former, then you believe the latter. The second place is between the theoretical and the practical. Thus they have wanted, second, to be able to say about cer-

---

[9] Anscombe would reject the claim that (8) was an instance of practical reasoning: "'I ought to do this, so I'll do it,' is not a piece of practical reaoning any more than 'This is nice, so I'll have some' is. The mark of practical reasoning is that the thing wanted is *at a distance* from the immediate action . . ." (*Intention*, 78). Thus there has to be something that could count as calculation, as there is in (7). But it is arguable that the calculation she has in mind is all theoretical reasoning, and thus that the only instances of pure practical reasoning are precisely (8) and its ilk.

tain directives that rationality requires that if you believe the directive, then you act in accord with it. It is their second want that is satisfied if the Difference and Similarity Ideas are both true.

But what do they gain if their second want is satisfied? That is a good question, and the answer isn't clear.[10] But I think there are two outcomes they find attractive.

Consider the question, "Why ought I do what I ought to do?" It has a long history in moral philosophy. On one interpretation, it is a nonsense. But many philosophers have seen a sense in it, and thought it called for an answer. There is a tradition—coming down from Plato—according to which the answer it calls for is an account of why it is to a person's advantage to do what he ought to do. But many philosophers are leery of the prospects for finding such an answer. After all, it certainly at least *seems* to be the case that on at least some occasions, it isn't to a person's advantage to do what he ought to do. But lo, if you accept the Difference and Similarity Ideas, then you do have an answer: a person ought to do what he ought to do because rationality itself requires him to!

We might wonder why that outcome is found attractive. Suppose a person plans to do something he knows he ought not do, and plans to do it because doing it will greatly profit him. By hypothesis, his knowing that he ought not do it does not motivate him to refrain. Is it thought that if we convince him that his doing it is not merely immoral, it is irrational, then *that* will motivate him to refrain? Is it thought that while it makes sense for a person to ask "Why ought I do what I ought to do?" it doesn't make sense for a person to ask "Why ought I do what rationality requires me to do?" (If a person can sensibly ask what's so special about morality, why can't he sensibly ask what's so special about rationality?—where, keep in mind, we do not take it, and he is not to take it, that what's special about rationality is that it tracks advantage.)

Moreover, the question would remain to be answered just how we are to convince him that rationality does require him to refrain, given the great profit to him of proceeding.

Still, that seems to me to be one outcome that the philosophers I have in mind find attractive.

---

[10] It is also a good question, to which the answer isn't clear, what they gain if their first want is satisfied. But I bypass this one.

A second outcome is that a different tradition is comfortably accommodated—this one also comes down from Plato—a tradition according to which the rational person is never moved by greed, cowardice, resentment, jealousy, malice, or laziness to do what he believes he ought not do. He is always in control of himself: come what may, either he doesn't need an iron hand, or he has one. According to this second tradition, reason is not merely the faculty by which we acquire information and draw conclusions from it, it is also the faculty by which we arrange that we act in accord with the conclusions we have drawn. No wonder that is so!—if it is true that if you believe you ought to do a thing, then rationality itself requires that you form the intention of doing it.

I said that the two traditions I mentioned were different. They are surely connected. But let us turn from them to the question whether we should accept the ideas that led here.

5.

Consider (6) again:

> (6) Alice's starting to believe that all men are mortal
> Alice's starting to believe that Socrates is a man
> Alice's starting to believe that Socrates is mortal.

We were told that (6) was tight in the following sense: it would be irrational in a person to believe Alice's premises and disbelieve her conclusion. That is very plausible.

Suppose Alfred says to us: "All men are mortal, and Socrates is a man, but Socrates isn't mortal." Well, perhaps Alfred isn't really irrational: perhaps he's just *slow*. So we say to him: "Look. Imagine that this basket [we point to a basket] contains all the men, and that Socrates is in among them. Etc. etc. etc." If Arthur is minimally rational, then he will in the end say: "Oh, I see now! How stupid of me! Of course!"—now believing that Socrates is mortal.

Consider (8) again:

> (8) Anne's starting to believe that she ought to telephone Bert
> Anne's forming the intention of telephoning Bert.

We were told that (8) was tight in the following sense: it would be irrational in a person to believe Anne's premise and form the intention obverse to Anne's. Is that really plausible?

Suppose Alan says to us: "I ought to telephone Bert, but I intend not to." Should we think that perhaps Alan is also slow? We might try saying to him: "Look. You believe you ought to. So you believe it would be wrong for you not to. Etc. etc. etc." Is it to be expected that if Alan is minimally rational, then he will in the end say: "Oh, I see now! How stupid of me! Of course!"—now intending to telephone Bert? That would be utterly astonishing.

Why does Alan intend not to telephone Bert? Suppose he tells us he just doesn't feel like bothering. We might get him to form the intention of telephoning Bert. (Perhaps we expand on how disappointed Bert will be if he doesn't, and get him to feel ashamed of his laziness.) He still isn't going to say, "Oh I see now! How stupid of me! Of course!" That is the confession of a person who now sees that he failed to carry out a simple bit of reasoning, and nothing remotely like it is going to issue from Alan.

Would a friend of the Difference and Similarity Ideas say that if nothing remotely like that issues from Alan, then that shows that he is too deeply irrational to see that he has failed to carry out a simple bit of reasoning? That *cannot* be right.

And no sensible friend of the Difference and Similarity Ideas would say it. What he can be expected to say is that irrationality is not limited to failing to carry out bits of reasoning. Nor is it limited to *either* failing to carry out bits of reasoning, *or* carrying them out incorrectly.

I am sure he will say that Hume was mistaken in saying:

'Tis not contrary to reason to prefer the destruction of the whole world to the scratching of my finger. 'Tis not contrary to reason for me to chuse my total ruin, to prevent the least uneasiness of an *Indian* or person wholly unknown to me. 'Tis as little contrary to reason to prefer even my own acknowledg'd lesser good to my greater, and have a more ardent affection for the former than the latter.[11]

---

[11] *A Treatise of Human Nature*, Book II, part III, section III.

And he will say not only that that too is irrationality, but that so also is preferring one's own comfort to doing what one believes one ought to do—and that it is irrationality of this second kind that Alan displays if he continues to prefer his own comfort to telephoning Bert.

But now he has two problems. First, he needs to tell us how to square this claim about irrationality with the Similarity Idea.

According to the Similarity Idea, (8) was tight just as (6) was. Thus it would be irrational in a person to believe that he ought to telephone Bert and form the intention of not telephoning Bert just as it would be irrational in a person to believe that all men are mortal, and Socrates is a man, and believe that Socrates is not mortal. But it has turned out that that "just as" is profoundly misleading, for the irrationality in the one person is of a very different kind from the irrationality in the other person.

Second, he needs to tell us how, on his view, irrationality of the first kind is related to irrationality of the second kind. Failing to carry out a simple bit of reasoning is an instance of irrationality of the first kind; preferring one's own comfort to doing what one believes one ought to do is an instance of irrationality of the second kind. Then he has two options.

(i) He can say that there is a property F that is shared by instances of the first and second kinds, and such that it is in virtue of their possessing F that instances of the first and second kinds are instances of *irrationality*. To the best of my knowledge, no friend of the Difference and Similarity Ideas has succeeded in finding a property F that can plausibly be regarded as meeting that condition. And I suggest that there being a serious difficulty here shouldn't surprise us.

(ii) He can say that the only relevant property shared by instances of the first and second kinds is the property 'being an instance of the first or second kind'. (Compare the property I'll call "being a carroll": it is the property 'being a shoe or ship or bit of sealing wax or cabbage or king'.) It can be seen, however, that his choosing this option is going to make trouble for his prospects of obtaining the two outcomes that I drew attention to in the preceding section. First, suppose he says to Alan "Rationality requires you to telephone Bert!—it's irrational in you not to." What new information has he given Alan in saying this if Alan's irrationality just consists in his *either* reasoning faultily *or* preferring his own comfort to doing what he believes he ought to do? Alan is not reasoning faultily, and he already knows that he has that preference. Second, it was to emerge from the Difference and Similarity Ideas that the rational person is never moved by greed, cowardice, resentment, jealousy, malice, or laziness to fail to do what he believes he ought to do. This outcome is trivialized if the rational person just is the person who both never reasons faultily and never prefers his own profit to doing what he believes he ought to do.

I invite the conclusion that we should not accept the ideas that led here.

But I should add that my comments here leave it entirely open to us to say that a person ought not be moved by greed, cowardice, resentment, jealousy, malice, or laziness to fail to do what he believes he ought to do, and that one ought not have the preferences that Hume says are not contrary to reason. The fact that these claims are not warranted by the Difference and Similarity Ideas leaves it open that they are true.

Index of Names

271